D0385171

*There's No Place Like Home*

# GORDON MacDONALD

# THERE'S NO PLACE LIKE HOME

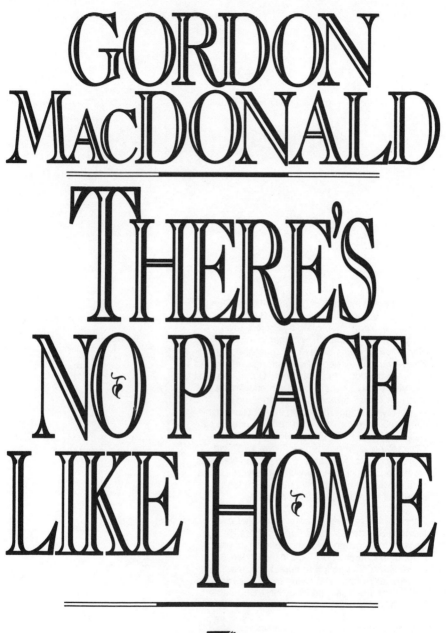

Tyndale House Publishers, Inc.

WHEATON, ILLINOIS

I would like to express my appreciation to Don Posterski, author of *Friendship: A Window on Ministry to Youth* (published by Project Teen Canada), and Maurice E. Wagner, author of *The Sensation Of Being Somebody* (published by Zondervan). Their books have strongly influenced some of my thoughts in this book. During the past few years I have become acquainted with the study on human temperament pioneered by Isabel Myers-Briggs. The best introduction to this remarkable system for understanding people can be found in the book *Please Understand Me: Character and Temperament Types* by David Kiersey and Marilyn Bates (Prometheus/Nemesis Book Co., Inc.). Those familiar with Myers-Briggs studies will see hints of my enthusiasm for it inbedded in certain passages of this book.

Scripture references are from *The Holy Bible: Revised Standard Version* copyright © 1952 by Division of Christian Education of the National Council of Churches of Christ in the United States of America. Other scripture quotations, marked TLB, are taken from *The Living Bible,* copyright © 1971 owned by assignment by KNT Charitable Trust. All rights reserved.

Library of Congress Catalog Card Number 90-70896
ISBN 0-8423-1114-9
Copyright © 1990 by Gordon MacDonald
All rights reserved
Printed in the United States of America

96   95   94   93   92   91   90
8    7    6    5    4    3    2    1

*Dedicated to*
*Mark Gordon and Kristen Cherie*
*who grew up on Grant Street*
*to Tom and Patty*
*who came along to be our children's life partners.*
*and to Gail*
*who more than anyone else*
*made the home on Grant Street a home*
*in which to build people*

# CONTENTS

## PART VI  *The Family Bathroom*

## PART VII  *The Garage*

## PART VIII  *The Basement*

## PART IX  *The Patio*

## PART X  *The Living Room*

## PART XI  *Our Bedroom: the Command Center*

## PART XII  *The Empty House on Grant Street*

# FOREWORD

## From Two Who Lived on Grant Street

### ❧ *Kristen*

IF PEOPLE were to view my life over the past twenty-three years, they couldn't miss the deep influence my mother and father have had on my personal development. Shared physical characteristics and common mannerisms would likely appear more prevalent. I'm sure it would not take much to notice temperament and personality similarities. But if they took the time, they would also see that many of the philosophies and values that motivate me everyday have come from my home life, growing up on Grant Street.

When Dad asked Mark and me to write the foreword for his new book, it didn't take me long to pinpoint the most profound thread I felt in my relationship to him and my mother. Almost immediately the word "peace" came to mind.

*Peace as a child:* Mom and Dad were there and able to care for any need I might find necessary to meet, and then some.

*Peace as a young teen:* No matter what my performance, and even though the world might measure me based on physical appearance or quantitative success, at home I was judged solely on my effort and ideas.

*Peace as an adolescent:* Amid the whirlwind of emotions produced by my insecurity—self-doubt, inner turmoil, and silencing pain—my hurt was all legitimate, each perception worthy of their acknowledgment.

*Peace as a released adult:* Support from the home base would be constant and enthusiastic whether in the form of daily prayer, a phone call, or advice given or held back (until requested).

Peace came to me from our family life in many forms. As I said good-bye to Grant Street, and as I was released from the "fold," I began to evaluate what made our home such a safe place for me. I remember three types of peace that were communicated: relational peace, internal peace, and spiritual peace.

I was taught very early about relational peace. From the womb, it seems, Mom was quoting Ephesians 4:32 to Mark and me:"Be ye kind one to another, tenderhearted, forgiving one another, even as God for Christ's sake hath forgiven you"(KJV). We even sang that verse to a simple melody, and the tune has stuck with me until this day. The need to communicate to one another that we were sorry was stressed almost hourly sometimes as Mark and I battled each other to see our own needs met first. Admitting that I was wrong is a lesson that has gotten harder to maintain as I've gotten older, and if the foundation of the spirit of repentance had not been laid back then, teaching me its necessity for relational peace, I'm sure my relationships today would more often feel the strain of one unable to maintain such a simple, yet difficult, ideal to practice.

I have also learned a lot about internal peace. Struggling with ourselves and who we are is part of growing. I'd like to say such struggles have subsided since I became an adult, but I know they haven't. Mom and Dad were quick to share that life is a process. Few inner struggles actually come to an end, they said. Countless talks (they were called "level-fives" in our home) about this that took place by the side of my bed or on walks around the neighborhood helped me to learn that inner peace pivots on the way our inner eyes view the world around us. The chair across from the desk in Dad's study was a place that I frequented through my teenaged years. There I learned that, though answers to our probing questions are sometimes not easily available, internal peace still is. Many themes that now mark my motivation in life's process were taught in those talks.

Last, but most important, I have learned about spiritual peace. From the beginning, I remember Mom playing songs about Jesus' love on my record player as she lifted the shades to allow the morning sun into my room. But beyond that, I watched my parents as they tried very hard to model Jesus in our home. Though not apparently conscious of what I was observing, I was taking "notes." I have watched with big eyes as they have walked holding the hand of grace in their success, and clinging desperately to grace in their failures. Lessons I cannot yet see have been taught to me by their model of humility before a God of powerful love.

I remember seeing both my parents reading the Bible in the early morning hours, enjoying the quiet of a soon-to-be-bustling house. They would pray on bended knees. Later, I'd hear them from my room discussing together what they had read that day, or what person or thought was on their mind. It was the first routine of every day: getting right with God. How could I help but catch the message? Well, very often I haven't, but Mom and Dad have still remained my cheerleaders. They have loved me with a love modeled by God, but only after first immersing themselves in the mercy found in such love.

As you read through the pages of this book, I hope you sense the same peace Mom and Dad worked to weave into my world of frequently relational, internal, and spiritual chaos. It is there, fighting to find its home in me, because they loved me enough to teach it. Thanks, Mom and Dad. I love you.

Kristen MacDonald McLaughlin
Wilson, North Carolina

## ❧ Mark

NOT LONG ago, my wife, Patty, and I found ourselves watching the television show "America's Funniest Home Videos." Like others, we find it therapeutic to watch people in spontaneous, often comical, moments that force an unrehearsed reaction.

On the program we watched, there were videos of babies being fed foods they disliked intensely or had never eaten before. The camera recorded their reactions to the taste of grapefruit, strained beets, and the delicacy of kosher garlic pickle. You might guess that these indoctrinations to some of the potent tastes of an adult palate were more than difficult for the infants to handle.

Babies responded with distorted faces, looks that seemed to cry out, "Hey, Mom, are you trying to love me or are you trying to kill me?" or, "If I'm going to hate strained beets when I'm an adult, what's the sense of starting to eat them now?"

Was it harsh to subject tiny tots to such strong tastes? Perhaps. But I think it must always be the intention of parents to introduce their children to all kinds of new tastes. This book is about saying good-bye to a home on Grant Street in which a special family relationship existed. Within that house, long before we said those good-byes, lived very strong parents who also felt compelled to introduce my sister, Kristen, and me to many "new tastes." She and I were fortunate to have parents that wanted us to know how those "new tastes" were going to affect us in the world beyond the front door.

I have always been impressed with the environment that my parents tried to establish in our Grant Street home. They were best at what I like to call "household environmental control." They tried to maintain a good understanding of every type of feeling and emotion that Kristen and I were experiencing.

I believe that one of the keys to helping children develop a good sense of who they are is by creating an atmosphere that is "safe." Kristen and I were sure that we could come home knowing that there was going to be someone there who was going to make us feel good about who we were. Our house represented a place of safety from any harshness the world had to offer.

Safety in our home was not only established by the presence of parents but also in the establishment of routines and "memories." My mother has always been the expert in the development of a number of family memories and traditions that we still honor when we get together. Some of them get mentioned along the way in this book.

I appreciated living in a home where parents tried hard to be consistent twenty-four hours a day. When I was young, I had a friend whose father seemed a great man. He appeared to me to be everything that a son would want of a dad. However, what I didn't realize was that my friend's father wasn't the same man in his home that he portrayed to everyone outside of the home. The lack of respect that my friend felt for his dad was the result of this inconsistency.

In our home, my father worked hard to be "even-keeled." As a child it was important for me to know that when I came home my father and mother were not going to take the bumps and bruises of their work day out on me. Rather, they were going to work extra hard to make sure that Kristen and I were the focal point of family life.

All of these ingredients that I've mentioned come out of a home full of love. If that love hadn't been there, we wouldn't have had a chance to grow as whole human beings. Without it, there would have been no hope for our family to exist and for us to grow.

In this book, you'll read about some of the significant themes on which our family life was established. Sure, I was fed my share of strained beets and sour grapefruit. However, it was the introduction of these new tastes and many others in life that prepared me to begin to understand myself and the world around me.

Thank you, Mom and Dad, for saying good-bye to me in such a way that made it possible for me to say "hello" to the world.

Mark MacDonald
Weston, Massachusetts

# INTRODUCTION

## A CLASSY GOOD-BYE

&. *There's no place like home for building young people to be a pleasure, both to God and to their generation.*

I FIND it difficult to say a classy good-bye. It is even more difficult to say good-bye to someone who has been a part of my life for more than two decades and has shared a bond that reaches deep into the heart. It is difficult when there has been a partnership of tears, exhilarating moments, and tender interludes that defy words. It is difficult when you have made certain people a top priority in your thoughts and choices, poured into them every available resource you have, worried, rejoiced, and loved them with a sense that their life was more precious to you than your very own.

I am not speaking of the good-bye that comes at death, but that which comes when a person who has played the role of parent releases a son or a daughter to leave the family and get on with the rest of life.

Four years ago, I said one of those good-byes as I walked down the aisle of a church. On behalf of my wife, Gail, and myself, I released our daughter, Kristy, to Tom, who had asked her to marry him. Three years later, I said a second of those good-byes as our son, Mark, our older child, committed himself to Patty in a similar wedding ceremony.

Officially, our lives of parenting had come to a conclusion.

The good-byes were a kind of "signing off" on twenty-five years of what we like to call *people building* in a home. For better or worse, we had done what we could to build two people who were now making their own choices about how they would live in this world and serve their God. The good-byes on both occasions were bittersweet experiences because, as parents, we were concluding a major segment of our lives that we would never repeat.

It seemed like only yesterday that Gail and I ourselves had met, managed a swift courtship, made a commitment that led to a wedding ceremony, and then fashioned the home into which we would later bring children.

Long before their conception, Gail and I dreamed of what those children would be like. As almost every would-be mother and father do, we had speculated on their physical appearance, the kind of personality characteristics they might inherit from us, and what we hoped they would become. Since we were Christ-followers, we naturally held as our highest hope that they would see God's work in our lives and relationship so that they also would seek the same faith.

Before the children came along, we eagerly watched other parents relating to their children in restaurants, in church, and, when possible, in their homes. We speculated on who was doing the best job and why and what we could learn from what we saw. We grew curious about how our parents had raised us, looking back to the events and relationships that had paved the way for our growth.

Then dreams and preparation gave way to reality and our firstborn came as a gift from God. Three years later, a second followed. A son and a daughter, in the order we had wished, at the times we had hoped and planned for, in places where we felt we could provide the necessary resources.

Conceiving and birthing two children was a relatively simple matter (although Gail will wince at my passing off nine months of pregnancy and twenty-four hours of labor pains as "simple" ). A countless number of people have done that much. No, the real challenge presented itself when the children entered our home and joined something we all call a family. For it was there in the family that we discovered that *raising*, or *developing*, or *building* (the term I prefer) these two children into responsible people would test every bit of willpower and determination we had.

It seems to me that Gail and I had every advantage we needed at the start of our family's life. How unlike two of the most famous parents in the world—Joseph and Mary, the earthly parents of Jesus! Humanly speaking, the timing of his birth could not have been worse, the surroundings more hostile, the pressure greater. Mary and Joseph didn't even have the privilege of choosing their son's name, and they had no say in influencing what he would do with his life. That had already been planned in heaven and subsequently announced to them.

Despite all that dissonance, they did a remarkable job of building a person we know as the Son of God. "And Jesus increased in wisdom and in stature, and in favor with God and man" (Luke 2:52).

One could hardly wish for a better description of a son or daughter than that simple sentence from the pen of Luke, the Gospel writer. Nor could one wish for a better mission statement in the building of children to responsible adulthood.

It was a good enough mission statement for Gail and me. We were committed to the fact that there is no place like home to pursue it. We decided early in the process that for us to build a child was more important than building a career, hers or mine. In fact, building or discipling a child to maturity would be a career of sorts. While there would obviously be other careers in our lives, the order of priority was clear. *Family was first.* Betray that priority? Of course we did it many times, I'm afraid.

But we kept returning to it in our life-planning process. I don't think we strayed from it for too great a time.

Business people might call people building in a family a long-term investment. It takes about twenty years to determine if the priorities and the plan are well-conceived. We're into the payoff period now. Apart from a few things we would like to do over or better, we have no regrets. Our initial choice was the right one. After that, God gave grace and wisdom. We are pleased and grateful for the adults our children have become.

When Gail and I first brought children into our home, the so-called one-income family was still perceived as a high value in our Western way of life. But the number of people content to live in that system was dwindling. Nevertheless, the ideal model of family life was still built on the notion that a man entered the work force and generated income. That would make it possible for his wife to remain at home and be a mother to their children.

Perhaps it needs to be noted that the neighborhood style of life that I've just described is itself a relatively small blip on the history of American family life. For many generations, mother, father, *and* children produced the family income on farms, in small stores, or in businesses. Only in the twentieth century did that prevailing family form change so that children could receive an education, mothers "keep" house, and fathers work in places away from the home. I speak, of course, in large generalities, with a realization of the many exceptions.

Today we are familiar with another model of family life. By choice, or economic necessity, women have rejoined their husbands in the income-producing work force, and this activity, once the responsibility of the men, is now a shared one. As a result, large numbers of children, once spending most of their time in the home and controlled by one or both of the parents, are now influenced by peers, community and school programs, or by professional day-care workers and nannies.

This new condition is acceptable to some, unacceptable to others. For those who consider raising children to be a people-building exercise, done best by those who love them the most, there is a great consternation over what the coming generations will be like. How can a system raise children and give them values, loving attention, and parental grace better than a family can do it? It seems an impossibility.

There are other changes in family life that are even more extensive and more frightening than what I've already mentioned. Today we talk with familiarity about things that were hardly in our vocabulary when Mark and Kristy were born in the sixties. We speak with concern on such matters as child abuse, sexual and physical. We discuss the plight of latchkey kids and the relative merits of various day-care centers, now considered by many to be an entitlement from government and industry.

Twenty-five years ago, drugs were considered to be a problem among the poor of the inner-city. Today, drugs and alcohol consumption are the concern of officials of nearly every school system in the country. The dropout rate from public schools, especially among minorities, is shocking. The consequences of sexual promiscuity and teenage pregnancies weigh heavily upon our society, and the efforts made to provide sexual education for young people seem to have done little to resolve the problem.

We are in a time of tremendous confusion about what is normal for a family's life. Media, education, government, the church, the world of psychology are all weighing in with theories, theologies, statistics, and research. The bewildering number of opinions about what is best in the raising of children leaves a would-be parent gasping for breath.

There is a tidal wave of media efforts aimed at raising consciousness about abusiveness, male chauvinism, and homeless kids, to name just a few. Unfortunately, in the pursuit of good drama, great themes, such as the role of fatherhood, are treated with such disdain that more than few are tempted to label all men or all marriages or all religious homes, for example, unhealthy and destructive.

Two opposite and very strong winds of opinion seem to be blowing as we head toward the turn of the century. There are those who enter into marriage, or living arrangements, with a view of home that does not include children. And there are those who have turned back toward the conviction that the raising of children is an indispensable part of the full life experience. We are regularly hearing now of the so-called house husband, the man who shrinks career ambitions in order to maximize time with his children. An interesting turn of events, if even for just a few, after decades of complaints about the absent father.

We read about women who prefer to raise children without a father in the home, and we can only guess at the long-term consequences of this choice. One gains the impression that there are some who look at the raising of children as something akin to the acquisition of a pet. In this case, the child's presence is for the gratification of the parent. These people don't seem to recognize that the child is a human being who will join the next generation to shape a bit more of history.

Into this mix of diverse and often confusing parental models come the man and woman who would like to raise children about whom the same thing would be said as was said of Christ: "[He] increased in wisdom and in stature, and in favor with God and man."

Gail and I call that people building, the marvelous opportunity to give glory to God by creating an environment in which children can grow to become everything God has designed them to be. This is done not for the gratification of the parent, but as an act of human generosity. One gives oneself for the growth and development of another.

There is no place like a home to do that. What we are speaking of cannot be done in a school, in a laboratory, or on a sports field, or even in a church. Something important can happen in each of those places, but there is no place like a home where it all comes together.

More than a dozen years ago, I wrote a book called *The Effective Father*. I wrote the initial manuscript when our children, Mark and Kristy, were preteens. Now they are adults. Now the world has changed in ways I never thought imaginable then. Now we have said good-bye. They are no longer our children, although Gail and I quietly call them that out of habit. They are our friends. They still call us Mom and Dad, and they seem to confide in us and seek our judgment in ways that both extend and expand the intimacy we had with them when we were at home together.

But it is a time to rework the thinking I did in that original book, to reflect the new times about us, to acknowledge what we learned in the last years Mark and Kristy lived with us as son and daughter. I feel that it is time to throw out a few more ideas, from one older man to younger men and women, about things we learned along the way that might be helpful in the formation of a home in which more young people can be built to fit the Jesus model.

This has been a very difficult book to write. On every page I have seen the possibilities of exceptions and extenuating circumstances that go beyond the generalizations and overarching principles. But looking back, there is one thing I know beyond doubt. Home is the place where people grow best. I'm thinking of a home where live a man and a woman who seek to understand the balanced partnership of mothering and fathering. And where there is a home where a single parent must do the job of both, the principles remain the same; the work is just a bit harder.

Gail has joined me on every page of this book. This has been a team project, and, as we have worked over the many comments in each chapter, we have found ourselves filled with nostalgia, thanksgiving, and occasional regret that we did not try harder or do better in the building of our children.

Treat this book not as a text, not as a research piece, not as a manuscript filled with attributions and quotes, as some of my books have been. Simply read it as a long talk between friends, a reminiscence of a couple of "old folks" who tried to build people in a home and are convinced that there's no place better to do it.

As hard as the two recent good-byes have been in our lives, they have made it possible for us to say a kind of hello. For having said those official good-byes at the altar to our children, we have said hello to four marvelous adults, our two and the two they married. They have become our friends, our cherished cheerleaders, our prayer partners, and the source of our greatest sense of accomplishment when we think about what we've achieved in life.

Most of what we did together as a family before we said good-bye was done in a house on Grant Street in Lexington, Massachusetts. Let me tell you about that place and some strange things we did on the day we moved away from there.

# PART I

## The House on Grant Street

# ONE

## GOOD-BYE, GRANT STREET

❧ *There's no place like home when the people who live there making "building one another" their highest priority.*

IN MOST New England towns there is one point where all main roads converge. People call that spot the center. "I'll see you at the center," they tell someone when planning an engagement. Or, "Go to the center and take a left on Bradford Street," they say when giving directions.

Most of the roads that meet at a town's center were once little more than cow paths or trails from one settlement to another. When first blazed, they wound their way through dense woods. It was said that a squirrel could have traveled for 500 miles or more without ever descending to the ground.

Lexington, Massachusetts, typical of those New England towns, has its center also. Massachusetts Avenue (Paul Revere's famous route from Boston) comes through Lexington center and makes a junction at the village green (or commons) with Bedford Street. Bedford Street then heads north toward New Hampshire and Vermont. "Mass Ave" (as locals call it) swings to the left and continues toward Concord and that famous bridge where, more than two centuries ago, the colonial minutemen halted the forward momentum of the arrogant British regulars and sent them reeling back toward Boston.

Near the center in Lexington, a road called Grant Street

empties into Mass Ave. Today, Grant Street is only about two miles long, but I'm sure old maps would show that it was once just a horse path that followed a creek on the east side of Merrimack Hill and connected Lexington with parts of Burlington, the next town.

About a mile down Grant Street there is an ordinary-looking ranch-type house built in the 1950s. There is really no reason that house would catch anyone's eye. There are far more elegant, more colonial-type homes along the way, and a common ranch-type pales in contrast to them.

But perhaps there was one day a few years ago when some drivers might have slowed and gawked at this house. On that day, a large moving van, orange with black company lettering on the side, sat out in front taking more than its rightful share of the road. It would have been clear to anyone that someone was moving.

Across the front lawn that day were strewn pieces of furniture taken from every room and the basement. Here was a sofa; there a bookcase; behind them a refrigerator. There were wardrobe boxes, mattresses, floor lamps, a piano, a lawn mower, a sewing cabinet, and much, much more.

I feel strange emotions in a scene like that. It is as if suddenly nothing in the life of a particular family is confidential any longer. The curtains on a family's secrets are suddenly drawn back, and privacy is shattered. Look at it! There on the grass for all to see are the relics of intimate home life: furniture, appliances, pictures, and tools normally seen and handled only by a family and its close friends. There are the household secrets of nicks and scratches, spots and blemishes, the worn places, the unrepaired items that someone promised to fix months ago. Look at the things bought at sales, hammered together by an amateur woodworker in the garage. There are the prized family heirlooms, the once-dreamed-for things that had been paid off by installments, the original wedding presents, and Christmas gifts. Properly distributed in the various corners of a cozy room, they help make a house become a home. But scattered and stacked on a front lawn, they seem like pieces in a junkyard. One has this melancholy sense that the sight is a symbol of the personal relationships in that home that are undergoing radical alteration, as child and parents say good-bye to each other and move on to a new phase of life.

You may have guessed it already. That was our house with the cluttered front lawn on the last day we lived on Grant Street. That was our furniture and our clothes that were being boxed up and moved away. After twelve years, our family of four was saying good-bye to Grant Street.

Every few minutes during the anxious packing process another neighbor would stop by for a last embrace and a remembrance. With each we would recall the special memories. The year everyone shoveled out from under a stupendous snowstorm or the year our kids went "trick or treating" together or the time we all worried and prayed over the sickness of someone's child. Farewells like the one we said that day to Grant Street are very, very painful.

But saying good-bye to Grant Street that day was an even more profound matter than just saying so-long to the neighbors. For in a sense, our family itself was saying farewell to a way of life that would never be repeated. Mark, our firstborn son, was well into college. When he would graduate in another year, he would start his own home wherever that might be. And it was the same for Kristen, our daughter. She was entering college and, while remaining in the area, she would move to her own apartment.

Their parents, Gail and I, were heading to a new part of the country and to a new phase of our lives. The twelve years of intimacy and intensity of our family life in the home on Grant Street had reached its end. From this moment forward—like so many other families who reach that point of maturity—we would have to be content with visits and only occasional renewals of our lives together.

Mark was a man now, and Kristen, a woman. Within the embrace of our parentage they had reached a stage of personal development and growth that was as extensive as we could make possible. The next steps, the further choices, would have to be theirs. From now on we, their mother and dad, could only watch, pray, applaud, advise when asked, and cultivate their friendship. Our work—the task of people development as parents, while not perfect by any means—was finished. They and we would have to live with the results.

The movers and their helpers were efficient, and it was not long before the van was packed. Each item that had earlier littered the lawn was now stacked and pieced like elements of a jigsaw puzzle so that nothing would be damaged during the two-thousand-mile journey to a new house where Gail and I would take up life without our children.

When the rear and side doors of the truck were closed and sealed, we said good-bye to the movers. We told them we'd see them at our common destination in four days. The diesel engine roared into motion, and seconds later we waved good-bye as the orange van started up Grant Street toward Massachusetts Avenue and Interstate 95, not far beyond.

Long after the truck turned the bend up the street, we could hear the driver working the gearshift, gaining speed as he headed westward. Soon the diesel sounds were gone, and all was quiet.

Gail and I turned back toward the now empty house and walked hand in hand toward the front door. In the driveway, our station wagon was ready to travel. The back end of it was full of those items we didn't want to entrust to the moving van: my computer, our stereo components, and Gail's plants. Not much else.

Now we had only to lock the doors and get into the car and

drive away. But as I turned the deadbolt, I was suddenly seized with nostalgia. "Let's go through the entire house one more time," I said to Gail. "There's not much to see, but I'd like to have a final look." Gail agreed, and we went back in.

As I said, the house on Grant Street was rather simple, but it was surprisingly sizable. Simple, that is, by American standards; but a mansion, I suppose, to third-world people. It had four bedrooms, one bathroom, a large living room, a dining room, a kitchen, a huge basement, and an attached garage.

The two of us began our final tour. We would start in the glassed-in entranceway that opened to the kitchen, pass through the hallway to each bedroom, down the stairs to the basement with its finished recreation room, up and into the living room, back through the dining room, and back into the kitchen.

We had not gone many steps on this venture when we began to recall images of past events.

"Remember the time you and Kristy were in here and . . . " There was laughter.

"I can still see you and Mark in there doing . . . " There was a tear.

Soon, I began to realize that every room contained deep, moving memories. As I walked down the hallway I was overpowered by the thought of all that had happened in this now-empty house on Grant Street. We hadn't simply lived in this place. Something called people development had happened here. A boy had grown into a man, and a girl, into a woman. A father and mother had learned a lot about themselves in the process and had done some growing of their own. In a good home, everyone develops.

And that is one of the main reasons a house is called a home. No, the structure on Grant Street wasn't just a building, not just a dormitory. It was a home, a place where people—in this case, parents and children—grow in increasing maturity.

So, on this final walk-through, every room became a wellspring of the recollections of people development. And with each recalled incident thoughts streamed in about the principles of people building. Long after we would drive away in pursuit of the orange moving van, those principles would continue to rattle around in my mind.

There in the dining room, for example, Gail and I spoke of the day when our two children, then ages five and eight, started a furious quarrel, a typical, generic sister-brother conflict. From their mouths poured forth names and accusations designed to wound each other. The volume of their exchanges quickly increased to (or degenerated into) high-pitched shouts at one another. In the kitchen, Gail and I listened until we could take it no longer, and then I moved into action.

Assuming the most intimidating posture I could command, I manfully strode into the dining room and placed one of my hands on each of their two small heads. I positioned them within about ten inches of each other so that their eyes were forced to meet. I said, "Listen to me carefully! Read my lips!"

They both tried to look up from their captive positions.

"This is home," I said, making my voice boom with authority. "A home is unlike any other place you will ever be. In this home we build one another. Did you hear what I said? We *build* one another. Did you hear that?"

"Yes, Daddy," Kristy said. She was always the first of the two to respond to brute power.

"Then say it back to me. What do we do in this home?"

"We build one another," both children said.

I went on. "Outside that door (I looked at the front door to enhance the drama) you never know how people are going to treat you. Some of them may criticize you, call you names, find all sorts of ways to make you feel like a nerd (already their favorite word for outsiders). But inside that door, things are different. Here in this home you can expect that people will love each other, care for each other, and help each other to be better persons. That's called *building*. And what you've been doing to each other isn't building; it's called destroying. I find tearing people down unacceptable in this home. Are you hearing me?"

"Yes, Daddy," Kristy said again. Mark nodded his head.

"So what do we do in this home?"

"We build each other." Two voices came back.

"I can't hear you."

"We *build* each other" (louder).

That minicrisis in the dining room that day helped us verbalize what we came to see as the mission, the purpose, of our home on Grant Street.

When there was a harsh word spoken, I would hear Gail ask, "Now, would you call that a building statement?" On other occasions when there was an unkind action, someone might ask, "Do you think you helped build in ———'s life when you did that?" More than once, when someone (including myself) entered Gail's kitchen and made a disparaging remark about what was on the menu for dinner, I heard her say, "Now you head right on out the door and come back in when you can say something that builds." Gail could be tough, and she would not let the offender off the hook until they exited and returned with an edited, improved version of the original comment. Most of the time these replays ended in laughter.

In later years, we knew that the lesson had been learned when Gail or I would say something sharp or unkind to one another. One of the children would say, "Dad, were you building in Mom's life when you said that?"

At the home on Grant Street we decided that parenting children boiled down to people building. And the objective? It was people development that enabled a young person to make responsible choices about his or her values, styles of relationship, direction in life, contributions to the larger world, and God.

9

The dining room was not the only place where memories of family encounters came alive during this last passage through a now empty house. As I said, each room had its own offering. What had begun as a quick look around lasted more than an hour. Gail and I recalled time after time when the four of us had built or unbuilt in each other's life. We came to understand that twelve years can account for an accumulation of many good stories and some unfortunate ones.

Finally, we did lock the door, then got into our station wagon. Engine started, we backed out of the driveway. We took one last look back. "Good-bye, Grant Street," I said. And then we were gone.

Our home turned back into a house. Our lives as people developers to two children in that place had ended, and we had to get on to other things.

# TWO

# THE INEVITABLE SOUR HOURS

*❧ There's no place like home when, in the toughest moments, people "trade" in grace and forgiveness.*

WHEN I caught him doing it as he stood in the kitchen, three specific feelings leaped out of my innermost being, all at once. Each demanded the right to be recognized first.

The first feeling was one of righteous, parental indignation. I was very, very angry, and I wanted to explode.

But, crazy as it might seem, there was this second feeling: a strange rush of amusement. What had happened (or at least *how* it happened) struck me as very, very funny. I wanted to bellow with laughter.

Now, the third feeling was fear. I perceived defiance, a revolution of sorts, and what I saw seemed to suggest that I might be losing control and influence as a father. That left me feeling very, very defensive.

I remember wondering, as I jumped to conclusions, if this was the beginning of that downhill family experience so many mothers and fathers describe. Was this the moment when things in a home seem to turn sour between family members; when love, communication, and mutual support suddenly disintegrate?

All of these wild feelings had arisen as the result of a sharp, adverse encounter I had with Mark, our firstborn. The two of us stood in the doorway from the hallway to the kitchen of our home on Grant Street. We had stood toe to toe while I forcefully commented on something he was doing that I found objectionable. I made no effort to mask my outrage at his behavior and his attitude about it. Of course, the look on his face made it clear that he wasn't altogether pleased with me. But I was his father, I was older, and I was in charge; so I had the last word. Then, after delivering that word, I turned my back and started up the hall.

But after I took just a few steps, something told me to turn about suddenly. And there, where I'd left him, stood my ten-year-old boy in the process of stiffening his arm at a rigid right angle, closing his fist, and extending his middle finger. Just as I turned, he had thrust that arm and its protruding finger in a vertical arc in my direction. Because he was doing it so energetically, there was no way for him to stop. He couldn't alter the motion to make it seem as if he were only scratching his chin or picking his nose. No, what he intended to say, in sign language behind my back, came through loud and clear to my face.

Now it is possible that particular gesture means something nicer in other lands and cultures. But, at least in North America, it can imply only one thing, and the meaning is not good.

As I said, when this happened, I was inflamed . . . and amused . . . and afraid, instantly, and all at once.

The righteous indignation was there because I believed that no child should ever treat his father (or mother) with such disrespect. No child, under any circumstances, should use such earthy signals to express any kind of feelings. Also, I was wondering where this son of mine had learned this gesture, anyway? Strange that I should be confused about this since I had employed the same signal behind my father's back when I was the same age. Where had I learned it?

At the same time, something inside me was also terribly amused at this age-old message of animosity. Almost every boy, sooner or later, has sent it in a father's direction. It was so funny, seeing him standing there, frozen, paralyzed, surprised that I had caught him! In fact, he was so amazed that he forgot to drop his arm and put away the finger. He just stood there—arm and finger at attention. A look of horror spread across his face. I would pay any amount for a video of that moment. I needed to laugh so badly.

But there in the hallway I felt also a sense of fear. It was the same kind of crippling feeling I'd had on other occasions when I honestly didn't know the next appropriate step to take as a father. I thought these were times when I was expected to say something smart, or when the family looked to me for a wise decision, or when I knew I had to assign needful discipline. They were times when I would be more prudent to ignore some piece of foolishness, letting matters take their own course.

There was sometimes fear when I sensed that my growing children and I were becoming different people, with different temperaments, tastes, and talents. I was afraid that they just might choose to see life and its various possibilities from another perspective. I'd read somewhere that such expressions of emerging individuality were supposed to be good news. But may I be frank? A part of me was hard to convince that those other ways were superior to mine.

Then, there was also a fear that I might somehow lose my sense of intimacy with my children if I did the wrong thing, if I misused my power or my influence. The worst fear, of course, was that one or both of my children might someday decide on a policy of interfamily defiance. I'd seen so many other children do it, especially in their teen years. I was scared that my children might decide one day that they didn't like me, that they didn't like my ways, that they didn't like my God.

And maybe it was that last version of fear that most powerfully gripped me as Mark and I faced each other in the hallway, he knowing he had been caught, and I wondering what to do next. Right or wrong, I perceived that Mark was saying that he didn't like his dad, and while that was OK for a short time, I was apprehensive, and irrationally so, that he might never change his mind.

So this moment in the hallway was not the first nor the last time I'd known or would know fear as a parent.

I would know fear years later the night one of our teenagers stayed out far beyond the curfew we had settled upon as a reasonable time to come home.

In the past, I had known a similar fear when one of them had come home with a note from the school principal saying that there had been a discipline problem at school.

There would be another day of fear when I overheard a boy in the neighborhood wondering out loud to a friend whether or not my daughter would "put out" on a date. With my assistance and hers, he would discover to his disappointment and my satisfaction that she wouldn't. But that didn't stop me from being frightened at the time.

I remember being fearful when that same daughter at the age of two almost died in a hospital from a self-induced overdose of turpentine.

And I recall fear when I sensed one or both of our children were going through stages in which there seemed (on the surface anyway) to be little or no interest in our family's way of faith.

Those were just some of the tough moments when all the glamour and happiness symbolized in the happy family disappeared from the photograph on the wall. Those were the anxious moments when parents face the fact that the development of children to adulthood can be a consuming responsibility. It requires an amount of knowledge and wisdom—not to speak of time—that none of us have in abundance.

Usually, when I reminisce about family events on Grant

Street, my romantically inclined mind tends to remember only the moments of family success. I can remember when one of the children played on a championship team, when another was a leading character in the school play, when a neighbor praised our children's behavior, and when the kids decided to cook dinner for their parents. I remember exciting vacations, unusually intimate discussions, successful disciplinary encounters, and the landmark moments: first menstruation, driver's licenses, first dates, and graduations.

The historian might call that filtered kind of thinking revisionism: the rewriting of the events of the years to prove a present point or to make oneself look good.

That's the temptation when one writes about parenthood and looks back upon the years when it all happened. I am tempted to revise the history of events on Grant Street: to cull out all but those moments when I (or my wife, Gail) made good decisions and did wise things or when our children's performances made their parents looked good.

But that's not the history of Grant Street. Because what happened in that home was a checkerboard of experiences. I made some terrible decisions; Gail did not always say the right things; and Mark and Kristen did not live up to our expectations—or their own. The fact is—does it even need to be said?—in that home on Grant Street, we were four human beings trying to grow and develop one another. Sometimes we were all on our best behavior, but on a few other occasions we were a relational disaster area.

A negative case in point: No doubt, there were more momentous events in our twenty-year parenting process, but a particular night in the early years comes to mind. Both Gail and I felt that we were total failures, that we were plain, pure, poor parents.

We were in the dining room on the night of my thirty-fifth birthday. The children, then preteens, had been informed that there was to be a major family celebration. Dad would be the man of the hour.

Earlier, I had told Gail that I would prefer to spend that special evening at home with the family. We would not go out, I said, and we would not invite friends in. Gail heeded my wishes and planned a menu of my favorite foods. So when I came home on birthday night everything was prepared: the table was set, candles lit, and the birthday dinner cooked to perfection. But it soon became clear that, while everything else was ready, our children were not. If I was indeed the man of the hour, apparently not everyone in the house on Grant Street absorbed the message.

The first indications came when I called Mark and Kristy to the table and they did not appear promptly. A favorite TV show rerun was on, and they were so engrossed in it that they ignored my call. It took four more announcements—each progressively firmer—to convince them to come upstairs from the basement recreation room. With good humor befitting a birthday person, I ignored the tardiness and stifled my usual conviction about instant obedience. This is no evening for confrontation, I'd thought.

A second indication that things might turn sour came when Mark and Kristen entered the dining room and immediately began to complain about the food they saw on the table. One decided that she wasn't hungry; the other said he "hated" lima beans. With undisguised disgust, both flopped down at the table, planting their elbows on the table to symbolize overwhelming disappointment. They began to argue about why one had a larger glass of ice water than the other.

I sat silent. Gail reminded them that this was my birthday meal and that we intended the occasion to be a happy one. That brought peace long enough for a brief prayer of thanksgiving.

But the peace was soon shattered. Few things went right during the meal. The fiercely debated glass of water was tipped over; there was reaction to the "large portion" of limas (actually one tablespoonful); the conversation was studded with tattling, protest, ridicule, and sarcasm. Two children I dearly loved were out of control. Gail grew progressively more hurt as she saw her carefully planned birthday party slipping from intended joy to actual misery.

We tried guilt. But a reminder that I had chosen to be with the family on my birthday rather than older friends had no effect. Other comments to the effect that this was supposed to be a party got no where. Nothing worked to dissolve the surly mood at the table in the dining room. Neither Gail nor I could find anything that would alter the momentum of what was turning out to be a bad evening: no gentle words of correction, no threat of punishment, no appeal to reason.

I had this compulsion to tell the children that they were not pleasant company on my birthday evening and that they should immediately adjourn to their rooms. But I kept on believing that some bright action could rescue this dinner Gail had worked so hard to produce and I had looked forward to experiencing with my family. (Where are the books on successful parenting when you need them?) I was wrong! Does any other family have evenings like this?

The apex of the disaster was reached when both kids finally cleaned their plates and abruptly announced that they would like to go back downstairs to the television until we parents were finished. "Why don't you call us when it's time for dessert?" they said. "Maybe we can catch the last part of 'The Brady Bunch' " (a popular TV program at the time).

"No," Gail said. "You're not going to leave the table on your father's birthday to watch television. He wanted to spend this evening with you, and . . . "

"Let them go," I said. "Just let them go and do what they want."

Normally I would not have permitted them to leave the table

either. But in this case I was just happy to see a disaster suspended. The children had failed; we parents had failed; the family had failed. On their part immaturity, selfishness, and loss of self-control had won. On our part, we had not found a way to bring events to order and to see the intention of a special experience through to its completion. As for the family: there was no love in all of this, no growth, no celebration, no enjoyment of a tradition. It was just a terribly sour hour. *What else could any of us have done?* I wondered. So just let them go, I concluded, until we could think of something else. Good decision or bad? I don't know.

When they were gone, Gail and I sat and stared at each other, almost in shock. What had gone wrong? Why were our children performing so selfishly, so insensitively that they hadn't even cared that it was their father's birthday? Why had we been so inept at handling the situation?

If you are as reflective as we are, such thoughts usually turn into larger, more frightening, questions. Where were our children heading in life if they could not be more thoughtful than they had been this evening? Were we raising calloused and uncaring human beings? Had we inadvertently taught our kids so poorly about generosity and celebration that they were interested only in those things that centered upon them? When a parent is scared, there can be a lot of doomsday projections about the future. And that's what we were doing in the dining room on my thirty-fifth birthday.

Finally, Gail rose to clear the table. "I'll get the cake and the presents," she said.

*No way!* I thought. Ice cream and presents after a family scene like this?

"Wait," I suggested. "Let's clear the table, clean the kitchen, sit back and watch what happens. I'm in no mood for festivities after what's just gone on. Maybe this could be an evening from which we can all learn something."

Gail agreed to my suggestion, and later we went to the living room to relax and talk. A couple of evening hours passed. Not a word from the children downstairs. *Surely*, I thought, *they'll come upstairs at eight to get the party going again.* But they didn't! *Perhaps at nine?* Nine came and went and we could still hear the TV grinding out one program after another. Normally, we never permitted that much television in one evening, but something in me said to let this thing play out to its final consequence without any interference.

At 9:05 P.M. Gail asked, "We can't let them get away with this, can we?" I admitted that I had no idea about what should be done. But one thing was sure. There was no way that there could be a conclusion to the party tonight. We would all have to learn that selfishness causes sadness for everyone. The lesson would cost a father something, but if the lesson was learned, it would be worth it.

At 9:30 I called downstairs to the children to come up to bed. They came. "What about the party?" one asked. "Isn't Dad going to open our presents? Aren't we going to eat some cake?"

"No," Gail replied. "A party happens when people want to show love to one another. A party happens when people are all working together to please the person for whom the party is held. That hasn't happened tonight. So we've decided that there will be no party. Perhaps we can have it on another evening when our family shows that it's possible to get along with one another and control ugly feelings."

Suddenly there was shock. Then protest. Finally, tears. Later I sat at the edge of Kristy's bed while she sobbed out every word that she could think of to express her newfound sorrow and remorse. "Daddy, when my birthday comes, let's not have a party so I can know exactly how you feel tonight. I'm so sorry."

As I rubbed her little back, I could almost feel the rebellion, the mood, the feelings of selfishness draining out of her. And when she fell asleep, I could see little trails where tears had streamed down her cheeks.

A few minutes later I talked quietly with Mark as he slowly drifted into drowsiness. Most boys do not cry easily, of course; Mark was no exception. He was silent for many minutes, and I wondered what he was thinking. Was there any regret in his mind. I had to know.

"Son," I said, "naturally, I'm disappointed about the party this evening. But far more disappointing to me is that it seems as if you really don't care about what happened. Am I reading you correctly? Are you telling me that it doesn't matter to you that your father's birthday party never got off the ground?"

At first, silence! Unnerving silence.

Then slowly, painfully, the response came. "Dad, all evening I sat down in the basement wanting to tell you I was sorry. But I couldn't find the right words. I just couldn't bring myself to do it. I don't know what happened tonight. At the table the nasty words just kept coming out of my mouth. I couldn't help myself. I'm sorry, Dad."

A few minutes later, Mark was asleep.

I returned to the living room where Gail sat. The disappointment and frustration of the evening had left us drained. Once again we rehearsed what had happened and how it had reached a tender conclusion in each of the bedrooms. But even that could not stop us from wondering if there would be many more evenings like this one with issues of greater magnitude and discouragement? Would the misery of those three hours be lengthened into days, months, or even years? As I said, we knew many parents who had had that kind of experience. Were we next in line?

Foolish thoughts, perhaps? But what parent is there, single or married, who hasn't taken one event in the home and lost his or her perspective? Who hasn't at that time felt that he was coming eyeball to eyeball with a bleak family future? It is a doleful moment when a parent begins to lose courage and confidence in his or her ability to develop children.

In times like those one does not think of the children as having failed. Rather, the temptation is to think the parents are the losers. The self-accusing questions are relentless. That night we were asking: What had we failed to anticipate? What did we do wrong? Should we have been more forceful or more compliant? Did we do or say anything that was harmful to the children? Were we losing the challenge to gain their love? Their respect? Their desire to please us?

Later I wrote these words in my journal.

> *How could it be, God,*
> *That at one moment*
> *I could confidently express*
> *What I believe to be the principles of genius*
> *In raising children,*
> *Of being an effective father?*
> *But at another time*
> *Fall so utterly impotent*
> *So as to suspect*
> *That I know nothing*
> *That I've done nothing*
> *That it all amounts to nothing?*
> *After having poured*
> *The treasures of heaven*
> *Into this life of mine,*
> *Are you often hurt like this?*
> *Are there strange divine moments*
> *When you also feel this futility,*
> *This "powerlessness"*
> *When those called by your*
> *Family name are out of control*
> *And ruin your celebration?*
>
> *Do you ever share this feeling*
> *That cuts tonight so deeply into my spirit?*

*If you do,*
*I, too, am sorry.*

It has been many years since my son accorded me what is commonly called "the obscene gesture." Today he and I laugh heartily about that encounter in the hallway. It has been just as many years since that ill-fated birthday party in the dining room. When our now "grown up" family looks back and remembers, we shake our heads in wonderment that things like that could ever have happened. But they did: those tough moments, those sour hours.

We were learning in those days that a family is an environment of growth. In such an environment, people need to be developed into whole human beings after the original intentions of the Creator. Development and growth sometimes means pain and failure.

No one—parents or children—contributes correctly to the growth environment every time. No one can account for the amazing and infinite mixture of circumstances, hormones, moods, personality and temperament conflicts, not to speak of the energy called evil that seethes in every one of us, that tempts us to incomprehensible behavior. Failure and defeat? Sometimes unavoidable.

But if every sour hour is drained of its lessons, then growth and development has occurred. "We learn almost nothing of value from our victories, but we usually gain our greatest insights in our defeats," a football coach once said. He could have spoken for the family also.

Mark's gesture in the hallway taught me that kids have feelings too. He had to find ways to manage the anger that arose in him just as I had to learn how to control the anger in myself. The great birthday caper in the dining room taught me that sometimes children learn the most when the discipline comes from the natural consequences and not the punishment that fathers and mothers are tempted to give out.

We all grew in that sour hour. I don't ever recall that we had another family celebration that wasn't marked with great hilarity and an outpouring of affection for the person of the hour.

There in the dining room and the hallway in the house on Grant Street, we were building people: ourselves and two children. That house was a garden of sorts. It was a workshop. It was a playground. It was a nursing station. It was a fortress. It was a cathedral. We loved it there. And that's part of the reason it was so hard to say good-bye.

# THREE

## WELCOME TO GRANT STREET

☙ *There's no place like home if the environment within is marked with calmness, safety, and nourishment for the mind and spirit.*

MANY years before, we had come to Grant Street from the Midwest with a young family. In a move of a thousand miles, there had been excitement, of course. But there had also been great anxiety—powerful, indescribable feelings. We worried about the pressures we might face in parenting our children in the New England culture.

Frankly (don't laugh, New England), we had entertained feelings of intimidation when we read in the media about the seemingly ultra-smart people of the northeast. We perceived them always to be seeking ways to debunk matters of faith and life that we thought important. We knew we weren't afraid of modernity. But the move to Grant Street came at a time when certain intellectuals were enjoying world attention. They thought it was cute to challenge young people to experiment with drugs, engage in unbridled sex, and to tell any parent over thirty to get out of their lives except to send money. As parents in our early thirties, we took that personally.

Perhaps our concerns on that moving day to New England are a bit overly exaggerated. On the other hand, we know today, twenty years later, that families are living with the devastating effects of cocaine and its harsher derivative, crack. We see them living with the tragedy of AIDS and the increase in teenage pregnancies. We see the results of the alienation that developed between the older and younger generations. No one I know seems to think these results are cute.

It seems a long time ago that we agonized over these things, but in coming to Grant Street, Gail and I were preoccupied with concern that this new (or old) culture would be hostile to the life principles we believed in so strongly. We worried that our children would absorb tastes and behavior patterns that would be adverse to our faith. We were anxious that our children's playmates might have a detrimental influence upon them. It seemed never to have occurred to us that other parents might worry about *our* children having a negative influence upon theirs.

Since we were moving to an area of the country where intellect, achievement, and success were high values to almost everyone, we pondered the possibility that our children might get snatched up into a nonstop life on the so-called fast track, a world in which opportunities seemed limitless, demands were relentless, competition was ruthless, and weak people were considered valueless.

In this sea of fearful questions, I guess we were wondering if life on Grant Street would be too threatening to our family. Would it starve out the intimacy we'd already worked so hard to build with our preschoolers? Would the ways of Grant Street tempt our children to dislike our God, the church, the things we felt we stood for? Would we all face those insidious seductions that erode the spirit and leave us heartless inside?

If you grimace at the description of such troublesome thoughts, remember that Gail and I were like any set of young parents or single parents who took seriously the building of people in a home. Sure, we were in danger of being overprotective, oversensitive, overreactionary; and sure, we could have worried ourselves into morbid paralysis. No doubt about it, we could have become so defensive that we built a fortress about our family. But that would have given our children few opportunities to engage in the realities of life. They would never have gained the necessary experience in making their own choices about such questions as: who is a genuine friend? what is right and wrong? where does one find models of real character? and how shall I walk before God?

We could have constructed a fortress through a negative attitude about life on Grant Street, through the imposition of endless nonnegotiable rules, through a suffocating permission system that recognized church activities as the only safe thing to do. By doing so, we might have achieved a short-term success in keeping the family together. But we would have probably faced a long-term failure in our objective to build a young man and woman who would know how to make responsible choices.

It was probably good to be vigilant about these concerns. But what we should have most concerned ourselves with was not how threatening life might be beyond Grant Street, but whether or not our *home* on Grant Street was the sort of place it needed to be. We should have been making sure it would be a growing place, where developing children could be sure that they would find maximum love and parental mentoring so that they might be equipped to make those responsible choices. We should have been making it a safe place to which one could retreat in the wake of failure and find mercy and restoration. A calm place, where the relative disorder of life on the street might be escaped for a while. A nourishing place, where one could gather strength for tomorrow's experiences. And a predictable place, where a family member might know for sure when they came home they would be hugged, heard, and valued.

I should have been reminding myself that most children are

not as adversely affected by the hostilities of a nonfaith culture as they are by the inconsistencies and the superficialities of a home where parents say one thing and do another, where affection is withheld, and where relationships often stew in a cauldron of unresolved conflict. The greatest single cause of bad young people is not a bad world but bad parenting.

I was helped to that conclusion in the early Grant Street days by an article in a news magazine that spelled out just how wrong things can get in a family. The reporter noted the death of a renowned German businessman and the resulting terrible chaos in his family.

> *When West German industrialist Friedrich Flick died, he left a personal fortune estimated at $1.5 billion, a business empire that embraced all or part of some 300 firms and a reputation as perhaps the crustiest, craftiest magnate ever to operate on the German business scene. Flick was dedicated wholly to his work (he buried his wife at 3 P.M. one day in 1966 and was back at his desk two hours later), but unlike such German industrialists as Alfred Krupp, Robert Bosch, and Ernst von Siemens, he never really made anything; he simply put companies together. "He always made the right moves" summed up one awed observer.*
>
> *At his death, the Flick empire generated annual sales in excess of $3 billion. But for all his enormous power and wealth, the old man had one very human shortcoming: he could not control his family. By last week, a Flick family fight over der alter Herr's empire had employees, bankers, and politicians alike shuddering over the eventual impact it might have on the West German economy. (Newsweek, Sept. 25, 1972)*

I've read horror stories that described bad parenting before, but *Newsweek*'s brief picture of Flick's performance and the devastating results on a national economy left me awed.

I have rarely read a more poignant description of what happens when achievement in work eclipses achievement in relationships. All the money in the world and all the power there is to make humankind quiver will not substitute for what it takes to create a growth environment for children. Sons and daughters cannot develop without love and parental mentoring.

Flick's faults as a family man underscore that success in one area of life does not guarantee effectiveness as a parent in the home. The man was hitting impressive home runs in the office where the bottom line was power; but he was striking out pitifully at home where the bottom line was people development.

Herr Flick is not unique, of course. His failure is simply a bit more noteworthy because it affected so many other people in his generation.

The Flick story is a single worst-case anecdote. There are a thousand other variations of the same theme. And to be fair, every generation in history has produced its examples of what we now call dysfunctional families. But who teaches us to be good parents? It is assumed that our parents did. Bad assumption. Is it possible that Herr Flick's errors of parental judgment stem from a bad childhood experience of his own?

The truth is that we often repeat what we have experienced, thinking it to be right. Only later do we discover it was far from normal or healthy. The vicious cycle may continue until someone decides this must stop and chooses to become a student of how healthy families come to be.

But in the past decade or two, the collapse of the family as we have known it has seemed to accelerate at an alarming rate. From a relatively stable North American society, where the extended family was the core unit upon which all relationships were built, we are moving toward a fragmented society where single-parent families appear to be the rule. From a time when three generations often shared the same homestead, we are moving toward a time where the generations rarely mix. How has this happened?

For centuries, families lived together and worked together. One cannot assume that in every family of the previous centuries there was great love, tenderness, or even parental sacrifice. Children were often little more than beasts of burden. They were seen as an economic asset (an unpaid employment in the family's business). It was assumed that they would provide for their parents in their old age. This was a primitive form of social security, and the system still exists in the poverty-ridden areas of our world. Affluent people often wonder why people in overpopulated, famine-torn countries continue to have large numbers of children. They do not understand the high percentage of deaths among children. Nor do they appreciate the fact that parents see children as part of their few economic assets.

In nineteenth-century America, children were treated with greater dignity and value, not just because they were income sources for the home and farm, but because a civilization, from a higher moral sense, was coming to appreciate the dignity and value of the human being. Laws regulated the amount of work children could do inside and outside the home. Education became available to more than just the offspring of the rich. Advances in health and hygiene cut the death rate dramatically.

In this context, children grew in a relational environment where there were scores of male and female adults who provided models of mature (and usually healthy) maleness and femaleness. They worked and learned alongside their parents as well as others, and they acquired a system of values and performance patterns that spelled out for them what responsible living was all about.

But this stable mentoring system began to change in the twentieth century, when increasing numbers of men left the home and began to pursue income from jobs away from the home or farm. Few changes in community life, I suspect, have had as great an impact upon the nature of the family than the one that separated income-producing work from the place where the family lived. Farmers left the farm; the owner of the family store went to factories, offices, and larger stores. Children stayed at home and entered the world of compulsory education. Work and normal adult relationships became increasingly scarce. Learning passed from the control of the parent to the control of a professional teacher. A kind of segmentation in life began to appear. Home was for sleeping and eating; school was for learning; and income was produced in the factory or the office. The three rarely coincided.

There was usually an extended family of grandparents, uncles, aunts, cousins, and others. There was a stable neighborhood, which included men and women a child might know throughout his or her preadult years.

I am in what may have been the last generation that enjoyed the luxury of such community stability. My neighborhood and extended family was quite consistent for the first eight years of my life. During those years the Johnsons lived next door; beyond them were the Kimpels, the Ewings, and the Snyders.

Mr. Johnson was the neighborhood grump, the man who yelled every time a kid strayed onto his front lawn (and stray we did). I first learned how to cope with cranky people, thanks to Mr. Johnson. Mr. Kimpel was my childhood friend's father. He was kind and smoked a pleasant-smelling pipe. I think he was the first man I ever knew up close who smoked.

The Ewings were crude; they drank lots of beer, and Mr. Ewing walked around a lot in his undershirt. His son and daughter were the neighborhood bullies. Mrs. O'Connel was the epitome of the gentle senior lady whose kitchen always smelled of freshly baked cookies.

This was my childhood society, my first world, and there was continuity and culture there. These people knew me, and I knew them. I dared not step out of line, for they were not afraid to crack the whip and inform me that my behavior was unacceptable.

The people who owned the local stores and shops also took an interest in my friends and me. If I acted smart in the drugstore, Mr. Wagner, the owner, told my mother about it the next time she came in to shop. If Mr. Fastbinder, the butcher, thought I was reckless when I crossed a busy street, the word reached home quickly. As a boy, I was held in the constraints of a community that took joint responsibility for the development of children, whether they knew it or not. As a result, I learned from men and women of all sorts and types. And together—the grumps and the gentle—they provided me a composite picture of what a man or a woman was and what was expected of a child becoming a grownup. I knew what I was to become, and I knew what I should not be. They were quick to let me know.

The next generation of children didn't have it quite the same way. They were the generation of movers after the war. Stable neighborhoods began to break up as the nasty "Mr. Johnsons" migrated to Florida in retirement, as fathers and mothers heard the call of the West or wherever the company said to relocate. Soon children were separated from their extended families, their stable neighborhoods, and the shopkeepers who taught them how to make change and fill grocery sacks.

Now, in most homes, the burden of people development lies solely upon a father and a mother. A child has one significant model of each gender from which to learn about maleness and femaleness. Other contacts and other models are catch-as-catch-can: dedicated schoolteachers, athletic coaches, Sunday school teachers at church. Almost all significant work (apart from house chores) happens out of sight. The only productivity most children see coming from their fathers—this is not a novel observation—is a piece of paper called a check, if they even see that. Apart from cutting the lawn and fixing the car on a Saturday, the activities of men have become a mystery to many children.

My earliest years as a pastor were taken up preaching to

families like the ones I've just described. I grimace now as I think of some of my challenges to fathers to be the kinds of men their children needed. And on Mother's Day, I put a similar burden on mothers. Like many others, I elevated fatherhood and motherhood to a kind of sainthood, and I inadvertently produced more than a little guilt as I and other preachers warned men and women not to shirk the priority of being everything their children needed: always available, never unwise, consistently affectionate, flawless in character, "Solomonic" in discipline. It was a lovely idea, but the expectations were probably raised to an intolerable level. So we usually ended up not a little discouraged because there was always something that could have been done a bit better.

But few of us foresaw that there would be another wave in restructuring twentieth-century families. We had not foreseen the value shift in the thinking of many parents in the seventies. Once it was common for a young man to say, "Someday I want to have a family, and I will get a job to support them," and for a young woman to say, "Someday I want to have a home where I can make a place for my husband and my children." It became more common for a new generation of men and women to say, "Someday I want to have a career, and if time permits I'll consider marriage and . . . maybe . . . a kid or two. But it will be a long time before I am ready for that kind of thing."

Not only did a new generation begin to debate the conflict of children and career, they also began to ask whether or not children weren't an intrusion on their expectations of endlessly traveling the world, competing in marathons, and driving BMWs.

At almost the same time, Western society became aware of the proliferation of the single-parent family and the second-marriage family. In the former, one of the parents is absent. The other parent, who is usually employed full-time, has almost full responsibility for the development or the raising of the children. These people talk about visitation rights. The latter family model includes stepfathers and mothers and children from second and third marriages, which merge and unmerge, depending upon the time of the year and school arrangements.

Some romantics still like to think that the so-called nuclear family—a father who produces income, a mother who keeps the home, and children who grow in this context—still prevails. But the fact is that this traditional family model is rapidly vanishing. The single-parent home, the home with a history of second and third marriages is becoming more the rule than the exception. I feel sad about this, but one has to deal with what is.

Unlike my childhood neighborhood, with its neighbors and shopkeepers, it is now possible—quite probable—for a child to grow to upper teens and never enjoy one substantial relationship of intimacy with a father or a mother. No neighborhood, no extended family, no dual-parent experience. Perhaps a rare encounter with an adult in the school system who feels capable of providing those extracurricular relationships that develop children to maturity.

This picture is not a pleasant one. It confronts the one who cares deeply about the nurture and development of children with a major series of choices: priority choices, spiritual choices, fiscal choices, time choices.

A new vocabulary of family life has quickly invaded our common conversations, and it got there without most of us being conscious of it. Words like *latchkey kids* (those children who come home from school to empty houses and wait for their parents to arrive from work), *day-care centers* (places where preschool children are cared for during work hours), and *child abuse* are well entrenched in our conversations. We cluck our tongues at the first, show concern about the second, and are sadly amazed and perplexed at the third.

All of these are the result of a way of life in which the family as a place for people building has been downsized in favor of economic pursuits and maximum pleasure. Lost in the shuffle is an understanding of what it takes to sustain healthy, nourishing human relationships.

When marriages break up, there will usually be an instant single-parent reality. The mother, who is the one who is usually expected to assume responsibility for the children, will be pressured to juggle the pursuit of a career or job and the maintenance of a home. Where marriages remain intact, the standard of living in our country now makes a two-income family more and more a necessity. Of course, the key is often the choice (but not always so) a family makes about its standard of living. But the family in which the decision is made to forgo certain luxuries in favor of only one income-producing parent outside the home is rare indeed.

What this costs the home is its capacity to engage in serious people building. We are talking about something that is a labor-intensive, time-consuming, routine-observing activity. Quality people development cannot be done by surrogates such as day-care personnel, nannies (although good ones do make a difference), and afterschool programs. People building is done best by parents, and it is done best in a place called home: a safe place where there is room to grow without paying the heavy price society exacts when someone fails to meet a standard. "Home," as Robert Frost once observed in one of his poems, "is the place where they have to take you in."

Herr Flick seems to have cared very little about people building. I never knew him of course, and I wish to be charitable in my ignorance. He may have tried to delegate the development of his children; perhaps he hoped that their mother and the servants in the home and the teachers at a private school could do the job. Apparently, they couldn't—or didn't. The result? Angry, greedy offspring who fell upon their father's estate like sharks upon blood.

We saw all these changes to the North American family happening as we came eastward to Grant Street. Perhaps it was our wild, young imaginations. Every time we read or heard of someone who was demeaning the role of a father and mother, or who was proclaiming the sanctity of career over people building, the voice seemed to come from New England. And here we were, headed straight toward Grant Street, to the center of that kind of new world thinking. Is it any wonder we were scared?

These things so concerned us that they came close to influencing our decision to move to New England. There were other options that I'm almost embarrassed now to admit I considered: such as life in a small midwestern community where we could raise our children on a small farmlike piece of property (horses, fields, and quiet evenings). But Gail and I have always enjoyed the tougher challenges, and we felt compelled to believe that no place in the world is a bad place to raise children *if* you believe and observe the principles of people building within the home.

And so we said no to the Midwest (nothing wrong with the Midwest; it just wasn't for us at this time) and yes to New England. Three days after we arrived on Grant Street, the phone rang, and the caller informed me that he was principal of the local school where our children would be attending. "Why don't you bring your children over to the school this afternoon, and we'll get them registered, show them their homerooms, and generally make them feel real comfortable about the new experience."

I couldn't believe it! This high-strung, fast-paced, secularized, and antifamily community has a school principal who makes personal phone calls and invites you to come down and get acquainted?

We went: Mark, a third-grader, Kristy, ready to start kindergarten, and me. I watched this man relate to our children, treating them like important human beings, and I was fascinated to see their anxieties dissolve. This was *some* educator, I thought. "You're a Christian, aren't you?" I finally asked, after I'd observed his demeanor for almost an hour. "Yes," he answered. "And I knew you'd be concerned about the place you were coming to and how your children would fit in here. I am committed to making every child feel free to grow in my school."

It was a gift from God. It was God saying to me, If you will put your priorities straight, if you will trust me when I give you a dream to pursue, I'll make sure that the right things happen that will give your children a chance to develop.

Suddenly I saw a new side to Grant Street. This wasn't such a bad place after all. Maybe, just maybe, our two would find a life here that was full of chances to grow and engage the world at its best. I felt sheepish about my fears, embarrassed that I had been guilty of such unfounded generalizations. Perhaps one could raise a family in this place. So, taking a deep breath, we said hello to Grant Street.

# PART II

## The Door to the House on Grant Street

# FOUR

## KEEPER OF THE DOOR

*There's no place like home if those in charge care passionately for the moral and spiritual "messages" that are allowed in the door.*

OUR home on Grant Street had two front doors: a main entrance, more formal in appearance, that led visitors straight to the living room for "serious" visits, and a second entrance off to one side that admitted family and "everyday" friends to the kitchen where life was real and lively. The formal entrance was rarely used. The second seemed like a revolving door, people coming and going at all times.

The well-used side entrance was faced with a white aluminum storm door, which had a unique metal-popping sound when opened or shut. It was a sound just loud enough for me to hear when anyone came home during the quiet hours of the night. No matter how hard certain members of our family (guess who?) might try to sneak in quietly after Gail and I had gone to bed, I was instantly awake, thanks to the noisy storm door and a "mother's ear." I often resolved to eliminate this irritating pop, but I never quite got around to it. Each time I reasoned that it provided a perfectly sensible (and cheap) alert system to announce our children's homecoming. Was it unreasonable to ask why one should spoil a good thing?

It was toward this side door that Gail and I turned when we decided to make our final tour of the now-empty rooms.

Opening the outer storm door and hearing the familiar pop once more, I slid the key into the well-worn lock of the inner wooden door which Gail, years ago, had painted in New England blue. Unlocked, the door handle turned easily. Years of daily entering and exiting had taught me just how far it had to be turned before the bolt released. That simple little twist of the door handle was just one of the familiar "feels" of a home we had occupied for so long.

You can "romanticize" about a simple door just so much, but this just wasn't any old door. Memories had been made at that entrance. There was the replacement windowpane and glazing in the door that reflected the craftsmanship of an amateur handyman. (His young son had once kicked a soccer ball with too much vigor and too little accuracy.) There were the gouges in the door jam, evidence of the unsuccessful efforts of a would-be burglar. And there were the scratches at the base of the door where Holly, our dearly loved toy poodle, now dead, had often signaled her impatience to come in out of the cold.

More than once, Gail and I had waited by that door for a son or a daughter to come home to give us a report on an exam, a new job, a first date, or a game. We had seen the faces of our children come through that door stained with tears, soiled with dirt, or splashed with smiles. We had hugged one another at that door when our children left on overseas summer projects; we had prayed for one another at that door when one of us left to face a particularly unique challenge in the day; and we had shouted through that door (not too shrilly, I hope) for people to come home for dinner, for baths, or for discipline.

It had been through that door that the family came and went each day. Early in the morning we all trooped out of that door into the world of school and work. Then in the afternoon we returned and entered that safe place we called home. One rarely went out of the door and reentered through it later in the day in the same mood or with the same energy level. There were morning farewells, when one or more of us left with either heavy hearts or light ones. And there were evening entrances with the same contrasts, depending upon what had happened during the intervening hours. Yes, it was more than just a door. It had been *our* door: the door through which we passed as we went to and from our obligations and responsibilities.

But a door can also be a dangerous place. Not only is it a point of admittance for loved ones and friends. It can be a place where enemies might seek access. In the New York apartment where we now live, one would be foolish if the door was left open or unlocked and no one watched to see who might try to get in.

Down in the lobby of our apartment, miles and years away from when we said good-bye to Grant Street, there is a man we call the concierge. His main responsibility is to guard the door of our building and decide who should be admitted and who should be turned away. Now, we love New York, but we also know that the city includes people who would like to enter our apartment intent on robbing us and even causing bodily harm if that were necessary to achieve their objective.

The task of the concierge is to monitor the door downstairs and to make sure that doesn't happen. He is the keeper of the door, and he is carefully trained. He is held accountable by the apartment manager to make sure that no one ever gets in who could be harmful to anyone who lives here. In a sense, any man or woman who has accepted the responsibility of building children in a home is similarly a concierge, a keeper of the door. And I'm not talking about replacing windowpanes and painting doors blue. I'm suggesting that parenting, at the very base, means standing vigilantly at the door of the home. It means determining what people and which ideas will have influential access to our sons and daughters during their earliest, most vulnerable years.

Each evening when we lived on Grant Street, I assumed the responsibility of being the literal keeper of the doors when at bedtime I walked about and checked to make sure that they were properly shut and locked. A few times I neglected this important tour of the house. As a result, I had awakened in the middle of the night feeling anxious until I left the bed and assured myself that the doors were secure. I don't think I ever resigned this task, even when the children were much older and came home after Gail and I had gone to bed. It was too much of a nocturnal habit. The doors were my responsibility. And it was no simple decision to permit anyone freely to enter or leave our home.

When Mark and Kristy were newborn babies, the issue of doorkeeping was a relatively simple one. They certainly weren't going anywhere unless they were in our arms. It was an easy matter to make sure the doors were locked to keep out intruders of any kind.

But time changed that simple responsibility. Almost before we could see it coming, intruders began to enter our home through other kinds of doors. And we were not always pre-pared. I'm not speaking of the intrusions of would-be thieves or kidnappers. I'm thinking of the invasion of ideas and influ-ences that sought access to the children's mind and hearts.

I'd never thought about the telephone, the television and radio, the recording industry, and the printed page as intruders. But they were, nevertheless. The people who promoted them and the people whose faces and voices were featured on them sought entrance into our home. They came seeking our young children's loyalty, their money, their belief systems, and their worship. They came saying they wanted only to inform, amuse, or stimulate, and sometimes they did, for good or for ill. But the fact is that they came, and they came forcefully. Who was the concierge? Who was the keeper of the door to determine which of these "visitors" should be admitted?

There would come a day when our children could keep the door and decide for themselves. But how would they know how if a doorkeeper had not been there in the earlier days to identify who was an intruder with hostile intent and who was a visitor with beneficial design? This lesson is not learned on one's own.

Here and there some mothers and fathers have kept the door (and I mix my metaphors) by stopping the clock. Or, to put it another way, they have built walls around their families, made cloisters of their communities. Progress is seen as evil, and new styles of dress, transportation, education, and leisure are labeled "privately unlawful." Outsiders may see this as a rather romantic life-style, even make trips of hundreds of miles to see how these people live "the simple life-style." Who is to criticize what appears on the surface to be a throwback to a beautiful age, which we all think of as stress-free and humanizing?

But it is obviously an impossible way for most of us to raise our children, even if we might see some benefit in it. A more common pattern of doorkeeping is the creation of unbending rules and rigid disciplines. This is a life-style often driven by suspicion. Nearly everything in the outside world is pictured as hostile and conspiratorial and something to be guarded against. When I see people with rule books as thick as the phone book for their children, I am reminded of the days of my childhood when my mother would take me into the children's department at Macy's. Just as I was set to embark on my lustful promenade among the toys, my mother would sternly remind me: "Don't touch anything!" For children who live in a family where everything is oriented around rules, where everything is treated with a "don't touch," living in the world is a lot like my experience in the toy store. Just look and yearn, but don't touch, never enjoy!

It was a special day when we decided that our children were responsible enough to have their own keys to the doors of the house on Grant Street. Perhaps the entrusting of a house key to a child is one of the earliest rites of passage on the road to maturity and development. The presentation is almost always accompanied with a similar charge:

> *Your mother (or father) and I have decided that it's time for you to have your own key. We want you to realize how important it is that you take very good care of it. You should never let anyone else use it, and you should never let anyone in the house when we are not here.*

Why did we finally give those keys to our children? Because we concluded at some point in their development that they were mature enough to open and shut the doors themselves. We determined that they could be trusted to handle a certain amount of responsibility and discretion. When we gave them the key to the house, we were inviting them to join us in being keepers of the door.

In recent years, we have become aware of a whole generation of latchkey kids, children who, at a very young age, are provided keys to their home because no one will be there when they arrive home. For whatever reason (serious economic stress, the reality of a single-parent home, or just two parents who wish income-producing careers), the latchkey child becomes responsible to be the keeper of his own door.

Those who keep the door of their homes by building walls or creating endless rules to guard against the outside world can be dangerously excessive. But the opposite extreme is just as injurious. I'm thinking of the permissive parents who have little or no concern or awareness for the intruders at the door. These may simply be too busy, too preoccupied with the issues of their own adult lives to understand the importance of being concierge for their children's home. Or they entrust this function to a nanny or a constant stream of babysitters or day-care workers.

When I open the Bible I hear the apostle Paul strongly advocating doorkeeping. He warned the Ephesian Christians that life in the world could be spiritually dangerous. He believed the most dangerous intruders into one's life or home were the invisible ones whose first entrances seemed harmless. When he wrote the Corinthians he encouraged great alertness. The battle was spiritual, he said, and the enemy was smart. The apostle Peter thought of the intruder as a roaring lion, "seeking whom he may devour." Theirs, Paul's and Peter's, was no paranoiac fantasy. They feared for people who did not take seriously enough what was outside the door trying to get in.

If parenting begins with love, this then may be the first form that love takes: a commitment by parents to stand by the doors to discriminate between those things that will build and those that will threaten or snatch the lives of our children.

Here are some samples of what I think about when I talk about doorways to a home and to the lives of children.

It's no secret that television is probably the most prominent doorway into the modern home, offering a round-the-clock stimulus to the childlike mind and heart. The Saturday cartoons feature a family in which there is constant bickering and infighting, fantasy plots that delve deeply into spiritualist characterizations, and high-tech violence in which there is little implication of consequence when people are killed in the constant series of interplanetary wars.

All week long children, behind unguarded doors, are bombarded with the values of various situation comedies where all forms of morality are displayed as alternative life-styles and with no comment on possible negative consequences. Humor is skillfully employed so that all but the most discerning find themselves laughing repeatedly at scenarios that—if viewed in reality—would offer us great pain and disturbance.

Violence on nighttime television provides an endless series of car chases and crashes (most without serious injury), murder, and creative mayhem. Daytime talk shows often feature subjects and personalities that stretch credulity. The soaps tell an endless story of a form of life that most of us would never tolerate in the reality of our homes. But there it is to be viewed, digested, and perceived as normality by children sitting at the unguarded doorway of the television screen.

Recent research has noted that more than 80 percent of the actual or implied sexual encounters on daytime soaps involve people who are not married to one another. One commentator said of this conclusion, "It suggests to children that normal mothers and fathers do not have sex with each other; only with other people."

In recent years the videotape has become a door of its own, as it brings into the home everything from the best of the arts to the worst of smut. We should be pleased with the positive possibilities that videos present for healthy entertainment and instruction. But an unguarded door now provides opportunity for children to gain access to pornography or the so-called soft porn films that so many adults are reported to be watching.

*Children are excellent observers but poor interpreters.* To the extent that this is true (and my experience is that it is), the concierge in the home has to remind himself or herself constantly that our children will never be able to make the discriminations. They can't do the mental and moral editings that we adults think we are so good at doing when we open the "door" of the television and invite the world of entertainment into our home.

The printed media—the newspaper, for example—joins television as a doorway to important information about the world or, alternatively, a doorway to distortions about truth and human values. Small children may not read the content of the news. Yet, they are drawn to the pictures and they accumulate impressions of a world that is far beyond the home. And one cannot forget that they are impressed with what interests parents as they read and comment on what is printed. Like it or not, people building of one kind or another is happening.

While I've been concerned that our older children become well acquainted with the newspapers, I've also been aware (who wouldn't be?) that the press cannot be trusted to pursue a high standard of moral quality when it features certain people as community celebrities. An interview feature might take note of a woman successful in entertainment who lives with a man and boasts of the freedom they both feel to date and play house with others. A spotlight article might center in on a businessman who makes no apology for his greed in massing a fortune for his own benefit. The press exists to make money; it prints what sells. One is not overwhelmed with examples of newswriters' concerns with what might fill the minds and shape the values of children.

Keeping the door does not mean censorship. It means taking the time to talk with children about the strange (or common?) values that spring off the page from such items. If one is not standing by this door, an accumulation of these stories may begin to convince some youthful minds that such celebrities may have something to offer and should be taken seriously.

The answer to the problems presented by the electronic and printed media does not lie in banning them or canceling our subscriptions. That's been tried, and in most homes, it doesn't work. The only answer is awareness and active participation in the selection of those who come through the door. And that takes time, demands the setting of priorities, and tests patience.

In a broader sense, standing by the door means being aware of the effects of public education upon the lives of our children. As I have already made plain, Gail and I have an enormous appreciation for the work of public educators in the lives of our children in their early years. As a result, we have grown uncomfortable when we have heard the generalizations of many well-meaning (but sometimes misdirected) Christians who criticize the efforts of educators in the public school system without the balance of well-deserved praise.

But there are issues that doorkeepers in the home need to monitor carefully. A father describes for me the total communications blackout between himself and his daughter. As we retrace the steps of their relationship, he says, "I suddenly realized that school activities had taken over her life. It was band practice at seven in the morning until class time, it was play practice until supper time, and then it was heavy-duty homework until midnight. I found it easy to allow her schedule to be occupied with everything else but time with us. In the meantime, I pursued my own interests."

If anyone accuses the educational world of overextending its proper influence, educators could rightfully snap back and blame the family, which has been all too willing to abandon the doors because life is too fast and too busy. The more the family surrenders its responsibility for standing by the door, the more the state will be found willing to step in and assume responsibility (until it runs out of money).

It is not only people and systems that claw for the attention of our children; it is also the prevailing life-styles and philosophies. The most all-pervading of these is materialism and its mentality of affluence.

The doorkeeper soon discovers a tidal wave of persuasions that begin early in a child's life. The pressure for a stereo and television in every bedroom; the desire for telephones (and even answering machines for each separate line); the acquisition of video games and associated hardware; a fleet of radio-controlled model cars. These and much more.

The dress codes (or fads), the parties, the recreational afternoons at the mall come soon after and can quickly soar out of control. They can create a level of dissatisfaction and boredom for the children in a family where standards have not been set at the very beginning.

Doorkeepers will suddenly become aware that the air waves respect no physical door and that radios, Walkman cassette and compact disk players offer a style of music and verbal content in the home that is potentially destructive and abusive. Music encouraging virtually every form of violence, racism, sexual aberration, and destructive temptation is available. Those who believe that some forms of recorded entertainment ought to be labeled as dangerous to one's health are on the right track.

What I've tried to highlight here are merely samples. Many other potential would-be intruders standing at the door could have been listed, such as the overwhelming influence of the peer culture (about which much more will be said later), religious cults, and the invasion of drugs.

Doorkeepers who are single, therefore having to do this alone, will need and appreciate assistance and encouragement from others. The time, energy, and perspective needed comes with difficulty for one person, who has to make all the choices on what should come through the door and what should not.

Recently a single woman in her early thirties came to visit with me because she was pregnant. The man in her life wished to marry her, and his income made the financial factor insignificant in the matter. Her chief concern was the effect that the newborn child would have upon her own career. For that reason she was considering abortion, raising the child without a marriage, or the more traditional marital arrangement as her list of options. As we dealt with each of the alternatives and came to the final one, I heard her say, "I would be glad to take time off, have the baby, spend two months at home before going back to work."

"Who's going to keep the door?" I wondered aloud.

"Who's going to what?" she asked.

"The door," I said again. "Who is going to love this child enough to stand by the door during the first ten years of its life and make sure that it doesn't get abused, exploited, misled, or misshapen? I'm talking about things like character, faith, values, and the ability to sustain healthy relationships."

"Well, isn't the issue really quality time rather than quantity time? I'll just have to make sure that when I get home from work I can have quality time with my child so that those things will result."

I adopted my most personal yet most firm tone of voice and said, "A——, listen to me carefully. It's my hope that you will conclude that abortion is not even an option. So let's go on from there and think about other alternatives. No matter the rightness or wrongness of your conception, you have a human being growing inside of you. If you are not willing to raise the child you're going to birth, then put it in the hands of someone who will. But, if you think that all you have to do is to stand by the door for two months and then let someone else get paid to do it for you, you have lots of heartbreak ahead. Someone has to be by that door all the time. Figure out which one of the two of you it's going to be. But don't leave the door in the hands of anyone else."

There is probably no more effective way to keep the door than by the way mothers or fathers choose to live themselves. The choices they make on a daily basis, to permit or exclude intruders or visitors to enter their lives, are the choices that will most impress their children.

When we finally gave over the keys to the real door of the house on Grant Street, the instructions we gave at that moment were not half as valuable as the lessons learned over the years as Mark and Kristy had seen us handle our own keys. If we had been good models of our own instruction, then there was reasonable certainty that the house would remain secure, even though others in the family now had keys just like ours.

The door is open now, and we enter this house of ours for the last time. The storm door pops, the doorknob turns, the blue inner door swings open, and one more time we enter that safe place called home where children were built.

# PART III

# *The Kitchen*

# FIVE

## THE KITCHEN PROCLAMATION

ॐ *There's no place like a home where people do a lot of talking and work even harder at listening.*

THE ORIGINAL owners of the house on Grant Street must have been the do-it-yourself kind. The placement and dimensions of the rooms hint at a floor plan that was probably first drawn on butcher paper by a husband and wife. Their objective was to build as inexpensively as possible, accumulating what we sometimes call "sweat-equity."

These amateur architect/builders handed on to our family one large living room, four tiny closets, one sizable and three small bedrooms and a one-car garage with a narrow entrance. As I've already noted, it was, by American suburban values, a simple home. By the standards of how most of the world lives, however, it was undeniably a mansion.

One of the most desirable spaces in this Massachusetts home was the large kitchen. The planning and design team must have included a woman who wanted lots of space when she cooked there for her family. And it's clear that it was important to her that everyone in the home congregate there as often as possible. Unless you came into the house through the rarely used front entrance, you had to come through that blue side door and walk straight through the kitchen. Like a busy street corner, it was a natural place for people to meet and carry on family business.

The day we first saw the kitchen, Gail and I were impressed with its size. But we anguished over its decor. A glossy ceramic tile halfway up the wall was pink with black borders; the wallpaper rising up the rest of the way to the ceiling was gold, black, and aqua. The metal cabinets were white; the countertops were gray, speckled with a plethora of designs and colors I'd rather not describe. The curtains introduced four other colors and the linoleum flooring was beyond reclamation. We quickly realized that what was beauty to one family might be unsightly and disquieting to another.

In the weeks that followed our moving to Grant Street, Gail and I made the kitchen our first redecorating priority. I covered the pink tile with paneling; Gail replaced the original wallpaper with a delightful blue and white waverly print. I built shelves to hold Gail's knickknacks; she discovered a process that permitted her to paint the white metal cabinets with a second shade of blue that complemented the wallpaper. Crisp white eyelet curtains framed the windows and the floor got carpeted. When we finished, the once loudly decorated kitchen assumed a tranquil, warm, inviting appearance. At least, that was our opinion.

At one end of the refinished room we placed a table and chairs that had been rescued from someone's basement where they had been abandoned because of a broken leg and peeling paint. Gail had stripped the table and restained it; I had repaired the broken leg and reglued the chairs. When we finished, we felt we had a beautiful dining table set for almost no investment of money. It served us well for the twelve years we lived on Grant Street.

It was into this kitchen, now empty, that Gail and I walked as we began our final trip about the house. The table was gone and the shelves were bare, but the paneling, the carpeting, the wallpaper, and the painted cabinets remained. Now the room seemed stark and bare. That didn't seem right, because this room had been the focal point of much of our family life and people building.

"There's no question in my mind about what was the most important thing that happened in this room," Gail said to me as we stood in the kitchen.

"The great meals you served us?" I asked.

"No, I'm thinking of the talks we had around the table. As long as I live, I'll never forget the talks. I'll miss them about as much as anything."

The talks. They almost didn't happen! That they did happen was largely due to an announcement Gail made one day while the family stood in the kitchen, waiting to leave for school and work. The way she spoke that morning made all of us realize we had better listen up.

"I have something to say to you," she had started. "I've noticed that it's becoming very easy for one or more of us to miss supper. We find it difficult to have breakfast together; we almost never have lunch together; and now we're beginning to lose out on dinner too. So listen carefully. We're not going to be like lots of other families who just go to the refrigerator and fix themselves something to eat whenever they want. We're going to eat dinner together on as many nights of the week as possible.

"Now, I don't care what time we eat together each evening; I just care that we do it. So before you all leave in the morning, I want you to agree on a dinner time for that evening. I'll have everything ready, whether we're talking five o'clock or seven o'clock. And I expect that you'll be there. I don't want anyone calling and saying that they'll be late or that they can't make it. Dinner is mandatory. And, by the way, dinner is not over when we're through eating. We're going to stay at the table until we've had enough time to find out what everyone has done with their day. So plan accordingly. Do you hear what I'm saying?"

We all heard what Mother was saying. Gail could be tough.

And that's how the kitchen talks started. Whether she realized it or not on the day of that great announcement in the kitchen, Gail had enunciated one of the most important functional values there is in the life of a family. A family has got to learn how to talk and to create the routine spaces when talking can take place. People development cannot happen if talking does not regularly happen.

As with all young families, there had been a time when total control over the family calendar had been relatively simple. The children, as infants, ate when we ate. They sat in special high chairs in the first years, then in a regular seat propped up by a pillow, phone book, or special sitting device. They spilt their milk, choked on food they didn't like, occasionally cried for one reason or another. What talking we did in those days was done in fits and starts; we rarely finished a conversation. But you could still say that we were together.

Many meals began with great enthusiasm and ended in general frustration, with food splattered on the floor, a parent playing "airplane" or any other game that would entice a child to eat. Nearly all conversations were in baby talk. We learned the value of reverse psychology: "Now I want you to eat five bites of this, *but* you may not eat six." It worked . . . until the kids turned fifteen.

In those days neither a mother nor a father was terribly disappointed when the children left the table after some tumultuous meal, resulting in a moment of peace and quiet. Family meals did not often rate high in the category of favorite leisure time activities.

But the school years changed all that. Now there was at least the potential for us to converse with each other, eat a full meal, and even leave the table liking one another. But no one warned us that this might not last for long.

We hardly recognized what was happening, but, soon new

calendar realities began to enter the life of our family. The children began to linger after school for sports, music, and dramatic events. They began to "eat over" at someone else's house. They engaged in frequent church and community activities that included some version of dinner.

As Gail and I became increasingly involved with a busy schedule, I too began to miss more than a few dinners at home. And if we were together at the table, it was not unusual that, halfway through a dinner, the telephone would ring, and someone—a church attender or a friend of one of the children— would want to discuss something that involved fifteen or twenty minutes of conversation time. The result? Another meal ruined; a very disappointed mother; an unhappy evening.

Then, of course, we began to face the occasional claims of television. "Mom, could we eat down in the TV room tonight? We don't want to miss . . ." It was an easy thing to allow a tray to be taken to the basement. And what happened? Mother and Dad ate upstairs; a son and a daughter ate downstairs. That was not destined to happen too many times.

We came to realize that well-meaning people outside of our home were not particularly committed to our family's time to communicate either. "Have you noticed," I said to Gail one day, "that almost every person that has something to do with our children's world is either single or married without children?"

"What are you getting at?"

"Well, it occurs to me that when people like that plan functions and retreats at church and activities at school, they are not likely to ask themselves what the impact will be on family life. They don't feel the same loss we feel when the kids are constantly gone. The point is that we, not they, are going to have to determine when family activity comes before school or church functions.

"We're not being threatened by bad opportunities," I went

on, "time with our kids is being threatened by too many good things to choose from. For example, we haven't had a normal weekend around here for five straight weeks. One of us has been gone on some wonderful opportunity. The wonderful opportunities are killing us."

"But maybe," Gail said, "these people are creating such events because there are so many kids whose families don't care whether they're home or not."

"You're probably right. But that doesn't mean that we have to let others control our family calendar because other families might not care."

I forget where the discussion went from there, but it was clear that we were both feeling a growing anxiety that we were in danger of losing touch with our children. If we were to be the primary builders of their young lives, we would have to reclaim a prime piece of their time. No one had to tell us that people building depends upon talking, learning from one another, knowing instantly when someone is struggling, sharing life experiences, and developing a common spiritual growth experience. The kind of talk-time that makes all that possible was being threatened by our personal schedules that were almost out of control.

It was this concern that led us to make a decision about family dinners. Searching the normal schedule and seeking those spots when family time could be accelerated, we agreed that dinner had to become, in principle, an inviolable, mandatory commitment for all of us. We would catch-up with each other there.

"You'll pay the biggest price," Gail had said when we reached our conclusion. "You're going to have to be tough in planning your time around those dinners."

"I'll do my best," I'd responded and agreed that we would try to reach our goal an average of five times per week.

It was in the wake of those thoughts that Gail made her

announcement that I have immortalized as her famous *Kitchen Proclamation:* Dinner is more than eating; families that do not talk together do not develop; and if the dining/talking hour is not planned and managed, it will probably not happen.

There were other provisions in Gail's Kitchen Proclamation. The television would not be permitted to intrude on family dinner (that brought a groan from the children). Because we were living in the era before the telephone answering machine, the phone would be taken off the hook, leaving it unanswerable (this brought a groan from me). Friends were welcomed to dinner, *but* they had to participate in all dinnertime activities. And *no one* was to be excused from the table until after dinner talks had been completed and, we hoped, with a prayer and possibly a Bible reading.

This was a revolution in the making. If Gail and I could make this proclamation and its provisions stick, our lives were going to change.

"What will I do about church dinners?" I asked when I got past the euphoria of the decision and faced reality.

"Simple," Gail responded. "You and I eat here with the kids at five; then we eat lightly at the church at 6:30."

"But what about soccer season, when I'll be coming home late from practice?" Mark asked.

"No problem; you tell me what time you'll be getting out, and we'll pick you up and plan dinner accordingly."

Gail had all the bases covered.

And that's when the kitchen became the most important room in our home for people building. True to her word, Gail served dinner for our family at the time we all agreed upon each day. And though we struggled at first, we all learned that when the eating was finished, there would be an extended time of talking.

If it was difficult for a family like ours to pursue this discipline, single parents will find it considerably harder. An unmarried parent must not be surprised when it seems as if everything militates against carrying out the kitchen proclamation. But that should not discourage anyone from trying, and when failing, trying again . . . and again.

Family worship? Don't all good religious families have family reading and prayers? We'd tried many times and failed. I was often unprepared. Bible reading became much more interesting for the children when they did the reading. A prayer might be interrupted by someone's burp or other unsociable sounds followed by a quick deterioration into uncontrollable giggling.

"We need to be more faithful to devotions," Gail said as she and I talked one day about our progress at the table.

"What do you think should be happening?" I asked.

"We need to be praying more; giving the children more Bible study. I don't think you realize the seriousness of this thing. You really need to be better prepared. Don't you think that family worship is as important as anything you're doing at church with other people?"

How do you answer that? She was correct, of course.

"I'll tell you what," I said. "If you're saying that I'm accountable for this—and I probably am—then I'm going to delegate a chunk of it. You plan the family devotion for each night, and I'll be ready to fit into that plan in whatever way you say. All day long I'm praying with people, pushing them to grow; I admit that I'm tired of it by the time I get home. How about helping me?"

Gail leaped to the opportunity.

"There's only one thing I want to make clear. I am more interested in the family having an intimate experience with God and with one another at the kitchen table than whether or not we have a totally correct worship activity every night."

Gail agreed.

Agreed, that is, until the first night the family began to talk about how the children should relate to a student in their school who was making life miserable for everyone. The conversation grew intense as we all pushed ideas back and forth across the table, ranging from vindictiveness to mercy. Suddenly I heard Gail say, "Well, let's get on with our Bible study."

"I think we should finish this conversation," I suggested, and we did.

An hour passed, and then it was time for the children to leave the table for an evening engagement.

As they rushed from the house, Gail's shoulders sagged, and she sighed.

"What's the matter?" I asked.

"We never got to the prayer and Bible study," she said.

"But we talked," I responded. "We got into each other's heads and hearts. God was here, and I have to believe that he was pleased by our time."

And we began to learn a lesson that evening in the kitchen. The objective was growth, fellowship, communication. Sometimes it happened over the Bible; sometimes in simple prayers; sometimes with laughter and tears; sometimes with sharp disagreements. But we talked. We took the time. We told the world (through a busy signal) that we wouldn't answer the phone. We determined that, within reason, we wouldn't fit into other people's schedules when theirs violated ours. And we stopped letting the media dictate the content of the hour with its reruns and quiz shows. Through sheer willpower, it happened.

The talking did not happen merely because of the Kitchen Proclamation, although that opened the door. It happened because we took some steps beyond the simple logistical ones of planning.

Gail and I began to have our own personal talks before dinner began. We kidded one another, calling the predinner moments our marital quiet time. I would phone her just before I headed home from work so that she could arrange her tasks at the house accordingly. We would go to the living room when I arrived and talk about what each of our days had been like. We both strongly believed that no event in any day was outside of God's attention, so we tried to talk in terms of what God had taught us during the day. Who had we seen? What decisions had been made? What problems were each of us facing? What concerns did we have about the children? Things like that.

Gail and I were trying to address the immediate business of marriage and adult talk so that we could guarantee that the later table talk would be centered upon matters of interest to the children. Looking back, we believe it worked well.

At the table, we learned to ask our children questions that could not be answered with yes or no. "How was your day?" was generally answered with a simple "Good!" or "Wicked!" But a question like, "What was the most interesting part of your day?" was handled first with a groan ( "Aw, Dad!" ) and then with an answer if it was pressed.

"What teacher got to you the most today and why?" "What are you learning in . . .(subject)?" "What are your friends thinking about when they listen to S—— sing?" "Why do you think more boys are wearing these . . . ?" "I'd love to hear why you think kids are doing . . . " "I have a decision to make, and I'm wondering how you kids would handle it if you were me."

We came to realize the importance of giving our children the chance to teach or to inform their parents. Why, I came to wonder, do parents think that teaching in a family is only a one-way street? Why do parents feel the obligation to know everything? Why can't we permit our children to lead us through certain experiences or areas of knowledge?

"I'd be fascinated to hear more about what you're learning in that computer class."

"What are the things that are impressing you in your reading about Stonewall Jackson?"

"What sort of a game plan do you formulate against a team like that?"

"How do you go about learning a song with tricky rhythms like that?"

Now, this same kitchen, the site of so many family conferences, was bare. Gail and I stand in the middle of the empty room and look toward the place where the table had been.

"You know what I'll always remember?" I say to Gail. "How at the end of our dinners Kristy would always get up from her seat and come over to sit on my lap. She'd put her arms around my neck and squeeze. Sometimes she'd sit there for thirty seconds; sometimes for several minutes. I always had this feeling that there was something very important happening in those seconds."

"I think there was something happening. While she sat at the table talking with you, her mind was being stretched. But she also needed to make sure that her daddy really loved her and had affection for her. If she got enough affection from you, she didn't need to go out in later years and find it with some boy."

Gail sees a spot on the kitchen sink that she had not seen when she was preparing the kitchen for the next family that was coming to occupy the house on Grant Street. And as she rubs at it with a piece of paper towel, she says, "And I remember the day Mark sat at the table and felt perfectly free to show us his tears as he talked about how hurt he was that a girl he liked had lied to him. I think about the times the kids really needed to say things like that, you know, talk about fears, disappointments, dreams, and hopes. Who would they have said those things to if we'd not been there at the table?"

Some years have passed since we stood that day in the kitchen saying good-bye to the house on Grant Street. It's hard to remember the topics of many of the conversations that passed across the old rehabilitated kitchen table. But I know that they all mounted up to something when Gail and I go today to the homes of our children and their spouses. There's something that hasn't changed. We love to eat together. And we do more than eat. We stay at the table no matter whose kitchen we're in. And we talk. We talk about the same things we used to talk about, except that the subject matter is more adult oriented now. We talk like friends; we teach each other; we laugh and cry; we often pray without any sense of awkwardness. And no one rushes away from the table. We like being there.

It's not unusual when the eating and the talking is over that my lovely, grown-up, married daughter comes over to where I'm sitting and plants herself on my lap and puts her arms around my neck. "I still love you, Dad," she says.

And I am glad. Glad that we took that phone off the hook, unplugged the TV, planned our schedule around the evening hour, said no to the frenzy of other people's demands on our time, and didn't fight Gail's Kitchen Proclamation.

Lots of great meals were prepared and eaten in the kitchen of the house on Grant Street. But long after they were forgotten, the talk went on. And that, far more than the food, helps build people in a family.

# PART IV

# A Little Girl's Bedroom

# SIX

# WELL DONE!

*  There's no place like a home if a rigorous effort is made to discover and applaud the gifts and capabilities of each family member.*

AS I'VE ALREADY noted, the house on Grant Street had three bedrooms. Since we were only a family of four, our two children enjoyed a privilege denied most of the world's population: the luxury and the privacy of their own room. That meant, of course, that each could be decorated according to individual tastes in colors, furniture, and posters or pictures on the wall.

Though the house was now empty on moving day, no one would have had difficulty figuring out which of the bedrooms had belonged to whom. The colors of one were pink and white; those of the other were earth tones.

It was into the first, the room where Kristy had spent most of her girlhood life, that Gail and I now entered. When we got there, I spoke first. "The two of you really had this room fixed up beautifully."

I was recalling the placement of wicker furniture that mother and daughter had found at a sale and painted a brilliant white. I visualized the bed that Kristy, when a high school student, had decided to give to an organization whose mission it was to care for the homeless. She chose after that to sleep on the floor.

I also took note of the slightly lighter spot on the wall where for years a floor-length mirror had been attached. I could still see our young blonde standing in front of it, with dreams of girlhood stardom, holding a pretend microphone as she lip-synched the voice and music of a favorite female vocalist coming from the stereo. To the right of the door a desk had stood where she had done her schoolwork in more serious moments.

Gail and I learned a great deal about a specific cluster of people-building gifts in this room. I'm referring to the exchange of a kind of human energy that is possible in personal relationships: a flow of empowering love, if you please, that can move back and forth, almost like electricity, from one person to another. When this current of energy flows—from a parent to a child, from a mentor to a learner, from a coach to an athlete—three remarkable things are likely to result: a reinforced assurance of belonging, an increasing sense of personal value, and a growing confidence that one is competent to make a contribution to his or her world.

The Gospels mention occasions when Jesus and others heard a voice from his Father in heaven saying: "This is my beloved Son. I am pleased with him. Listen to him." There could hardly be a better example of the transfer of loving energy moving from the Father to the Son. In those phrases there is belonging (this is my Son); there is value (I am pleased with him); and there is competence (listen to him; he is trustworthy).

I ask myself if there is any theme more wondrous, more mysterious, and maybe more underestimated in human experience than the story of what happens when one person chooses to impart his or her life-forming love upon another. It seems to me that to build a person through the gift of one's loving energy far surpasses the accomplishments of building a business or producing a work of art.

I often hear people degrade the functions of parenting or mentoring. It is my reverence for people development that causes me to be perplexed whenever I hear them try to build their case that the pursuit of a career or achievement is a superior function. How, I wonder, could anyone conclude that there is a greater task than providing one's generation with a son, a daughter, or a disciple/protege who has chosen to live life as a giver and not a taker!

Neither Gail nor I were quite this philosophical, nor would we have used the phrase "a transfer of human energy" in the days when we knocked on the doors of our children's rooms and engaged in frequent personal conversations, those encounters that parents need to have with their children. But, we were always acutely aware that, as parents, we possessed a heritage of spirit that had to be given to our children, gifts best provided by a mother or a father, gifts offered at the right times, for the right reasons, and in the right places.

We were also aware that if those gifts were denied because the givers were too busy, or too tired, or too insensitive, or too enmeshed in other priorities, we ran a risk. The chances of a child growing into the adult years with serious deficits in areas of personhood were greatly increased. The deficits generally occur in their self-confidence, decisiveness, or their ability to make lasting commitments.

The father or mother whose time is severely limited and the single parent who must play both the role of mother and father on so many occasions face a major challenge here. Their time must be seriously allocated. What it takes to give loving energy to children is time—significant quantities of it. People building is a time-consuming function. It takes time that cannot always be planned or scheduled.

In our home on Grant Street we came to submit to a harsh and demanding reality: there was going to be a period in the lives of our children where great amounts of "on-site presence" in the home would have to be provided by at least one parent. The gifts of loving energy that were so often given in a room like Kristy's could not have been given by a nanny or a day-care worker while both of us were gone, developing careers instead of people.

I stood with Gail in this pink and white bedroom, brooding over the energy transfers that had taken place here. I found myself retrieving memories of the many tender talks Kristy and I had when she was a small, tomboyish girl, trying to figure out what was expected of her in the world outside our home. I recalled some of our frank discussions later on as she wrestled with the implications of her passage through puberty. I remembered the plans and dreams we'd evaluated as she headed through high school and toward college. We called such talks "level-fives," our family code for very, very serious conversations (in contrast to "level-ones," our code for trivia).

"Kristy," I'd say as I stood at the door of her room, "we've got to have a level-five about . . ." Or, "It's been a long time since you and I have level-fived about . . ." She'd laugh at me when I'd say, "I'm in the mood for a level-five; how about you?"

A good level-five engagement could transfer plenty of loving energy if it was mixed generously with several ingredients: affirmation, approval, appreciation, acceptance, and affection. The objective? To provide the necessary assurance from a trustworthy source so that a child feels lovable enough to belong, valuable as a person, and competent in what he or she does.

Some of the saddest people I have known were never given these gifts of human energy. I get the impression in watching them that they feel they must spend their entire lives proving to themselves (and perhaps to others) that they do indeed belong, that they are valuable, and competent. These are things one ought never have to prove.

The adult who slips into the habit of name-dropping and trying to impress others with the extent of his "connections" may likely be telling us that he or she was never given the gift of belonging. Always feeling a bit on the outside, they reveal a need to impress people that they are really on the inside . . . of something, anything.

Some people go to extremes in trying to impress others with their physical appearance or "cool" behavior as determined by society's latest celebrities. By doing so, they may be signaling that they never have been made to feel that they are valuable or special as persons.

The ones who need to boast of personal accomplishments, such as impressive talk about academic degrees, about their latest achievements, trying to get recognition and appreciation in public, may really be telling us that they never felt that their competence was acknowledged as a child. They are hoping now to hear from someone that they are recognized for what they can do.

The equally dismal alternative to these quests is seen in the person who turns his or her back upon the generation and shows disdain for everyone's opinions. They do this by "dropping out," by refusing to make any sort of peace with the "system," by dressing in costume and acting in ways that mock the prevailing styles and codes.

I've been guilty of generalizations, of course, but I believe it is helpful to remind ourselves of these extremes to which some go when the gifts of loving human energy have not been given at the right time, by the right people, in the right places.

The effective transfer of loving human energy that begins with *affirmation* should make either of these extreme behaviors—passionate conformity and achievement or angry rejection and rebellion—unnecessary.

Affirmation, an extremely powerful form of human energy, was most likely to happen in Kristy's room when she and I sat across from one another at a homemade desk we had put together when she was eight or nine. It was the site of some of our most important talks, which often had to do with the issue of competence: the feeling of adequacy and capability.

At least once a school year, for example, I would pick up signals that there was a course (or a teacher) that had created feelings of anxiety or intimidation for our daughter. More than likely, the message would come when I'd see her sitting at that desk staring into space, discouragement written all over her face. In such cases the issue boiled down to a struggle with competence.

I'd shift down into my level-five tone of voice and ask about how things were going.

"Daddy," she would start, "there is no way I'm going to pass this course. I don't understand a thing that Mr. T—— is saying. Everyone else in the class is so far ahead of me. You know what the kids are like in Lexington. They've all got this class knocked [meaning licked]. I've got a test coming up in two weeks, and I don't think I'm going to get one answer right. I think that you should write a note and get me out of this class."

On each of those occasions the response of a parent who wishes to be a people builder is highly significant. There are those key moments when what one says or does next may go a long way to determine a child's reaction in the future. If a child is tempted to perceive herself as inadequate or incapable in the face of an enormous challenge, will that become a mental habit? Is that how she will respond each time things turn rough in the future? Not if in key moments like the one I'm describing, she can hear from someone she trusts that she is indeed competent in her achievements and her potential. That's affirmation.

"Honey," I would usually say, "I've seen you in these situations before. Last year it was that science project that almost whipped you. And one other time it was writing that story for Ms. T——. Remember?"

"I remember."

"And how did you do on the science project?"

"I got an *A*."

"What about the story you wrote?"

"I don't remember."

"Well, I remember, and you do too. You got an *A* on that too."

"OK . . . but . . . this is really different."

"Maybe this time it is, and I'm not going to be hard-nosed about it. But I do have this strong conviction that God has given you a very sharp mind, and so far I haven't seen you tackle anything you can't handle. I'm not pushing you for *A*'s; I'm just interested in your stretching yourself to do the best that you can. I don't want to see you limit yourself or that mind of yours because it's clear to me that you can do just about anything you're committed to doing."

I doubt that there was ever a year during Kristy's schooling days that we did not have that same conversation, almost word for word. Only the course description or the teacher's name changed. Two or three weeks after these encounters I would stroll into her room when she was again at her desk, sit down off to one side, and ask how things were progressing in the course we'd previously discussed.

"OK, I guess. We had a test yesterday."

"How do you think you did?"

"Probably a *B* or a *C*. It wasn't that hard after all."

A week later I'd usually see an *A* or *A*- paper sitting on that same desk if I stopped in again.

With a feigned sense of shock I would exclaim with some degree of dramatic inflection, "Did you once say that this course was beating you? Are you the person who once told me that this was the course to end all courses, that there was absolutely, positively, no way you could ever manage this?" I'd ask.

"Stop it! You don't know how hard I've had to work on this stuff."

"I know, and I'm awfully proud," I'd say. "I told you that you had a good mind; I've told you that there was nothing you couldn't do if you wanted it bad enough, and I've told you that . . ."

"Oh, Dad, not that again . . . " But she loved it!

When one speaks about affirmation, the issue is not a matter of offering some cheaply given applause to build up another's ego. It is to acknowledge the adequacy and capability that God, the Creator, built into each of us.

Jesus spoke of a time when servants would stand before their Master and hear a word of commendation concerning their service. "Well done, good and faithful servant" would be the message to those who had been reliable. It was not an affirmation concerning perfection but faithfulness.

It seems to me that we have all been created with the hope of hearing that "well done" some day. We hunger for that divine affirmation. But it would appear that the Creator has also made us with a desire for lesser—but still significant— voices of approval from the principal people in our circles of relationship: our parents, our spouses, our close friends, even to some extent the general community.

We all need the "well done." If we don't get it, we die inside a little bit each day. In short, we flourish or shrivel in life depending largely on a sense of God's approval, the approval of others, and finally our approval of ourselves.

Some years ago I visited with a physician who specializes in the research and treatment of migraine headaches. He shared with me his frustration that there was little known about the causes of one of the most painful conditions people can experience. What had further caught his interest was that the overwhelming number of patients he treated shared two things in common: they were presently striving for unusual success and they felt greatly deprived of affirmation from a father. There was often an expression of bitterness and rancor from patients about parents who had never adequately communicated the "well done."

"Do you know what I think they are all trying to do when they push themselves so hard?" he said. "They're dying to please their daddy! They're demanding that their fathers approve of them. I'm telling you, these are people in every age bracket. Even people in their sixties. They've never gotten over not having made it with their fathers when they were kids. They never heard that they were good enough. Now, how that relates to headaches, I'm not yet sure. But I can tell you this: the relationship between people with the pain and people who have never forgiven their fathers for these things is uncanny."

He went on. "The saddest part of it all is when you talk with someone whose father is dead. Even that doesn't stop them; they're unconsciously trying to figure out a way to gain approval from him. I don't know how they're going to make it happen, but they keep on trying. They've fallen into a habit they can't break: seeking approval like a drunk looks for booze."

What I heard this physician saying was that the frantic, driven life-style of the overachiever is frequently the result of a childhood where there was an absence of the transfer of the human energy of affirmation. I am not speaking of high achievement, the commitment to pursue a quality of excellence in one's career and relationship, but of overachievement: that insatiable drive to do more, accumulate more, and experience more with the hope that one will finally coerce a "well done" from a parent who has refused to give it in the past. If this habit of overachievement goes unchecked long enough, it becomes a way of life, a circuitry of the mind that will likely endure for a lifetime. It leaves a person exhausted, unsatisfied, and angry. After years of feverish activity, there is no "well done" from any source that can bring rest and satisfaction to the inner person.

An alternative reaction to the failure to have heard the "well done" in younger years is withdrawal and retreat. We are seeing this pattern in more than a few of the new generation of men. They are entering adulthood struggling to learn how to make decisions, commitments, and or have healthy relationships with women. Not having heard those timely "well dones," they have developed grave personal doubts about their capacity to love, to excel, to make sound choices. It often makes early manhood a confusing and unsettling experience.

I sat one day at lunch in midtown New York City with a middle-aged executive whom I greatly admire. We talked about our memories of our fathers.

"My dad," he said, "never saw the good in anything I dreamed about or accomplished. If he saw anything it was the one thing I'd not thought about or done, or he had a way of immediately bringing up the next thing there was to do. He was always raising the bar."

"Raising the bar?" I said quizzically.

"Yeah, you know like at a track meet. Ever watch the high jumping event?"

"Sure, many times," I answered.

"What happens each time someone jumps over the bar without knocking if off?"

"Oh, I see what you're saying. They raise the bar another inch or so."

"Exactly. That's what my father did. He always raised the bar. He never stopped for a moment and said, 'You've done a great job; you're good at that; I'm proud of you.' No, it was always on to the next notch. If I got a 97; his first reaction was that next time it should be a 99. Crazy thing about the high jumper, you know: even after he wins, they raise the bar one more time and tell him to go for a record. In effect, he can't go into the locker room until he fails. Whether or not he was aware of it, that was the way my father thought."

Did I ever think like that when Kristy and I had those level-five talks in her room? Answer: I probably did. Yes, there were probably times when I pushed her too hard, *not* because I wanted her best, but because—like all parents—I wanted *me*, her father, to look good. Need I say that on such occasions I revealed an astonishing lack of wisdom?

Did I ever withhold affirmation that was deserved? Probably: maybe because I was too wrapped up in my own selfish need for affirmation, or maybe because I was insensitive and blind to something that was important in her personal world. Perhaps there were times when I, like a lot of other fathers, just didn't know how to say the "well done" so it was effectively heard. More than one father has commented, "I never received it myself; I don't know how to give it."

It's a delicate matter: the gift of this important love-energy called affirmation. Given too freely, it loses its value; given too little, it loses its potential to enable another to grow. The challenge to plot a course right down the middle everytime I went into that pink and white room and engaged in a "level-five" was enormous. But I've never regretted that I took on those challenges.

# SEVEN

# WHO ARE YOU, MY CHILD?

*❧ There's no place like a home if each family member is released to be the unique person God meant for him or her to be.*

THE SIXTH grade's spring play had just ended to the tumultuous applause of proud parents. No one seemed to mind that the air in the crowded gymnasium was oppressive, the seats hard, and the hour late. Who cares about such incidentals when you think your kid has just been part of an academy-award-level performance? When the principal dismissed the audience, we parents broke up into small groups for the usual friendly chatter.

It was then that I witnessed a tiny after-the-show drama that had absolutely no significance for anyone except a young girl and her father. The child had played a minor role in the program, and now she came from backstage to find her parents, obviously anticipating their response to her performance. When she spied her father talking to another man, she cried, "Daddy, Daddy" and rushed to grab his hand.

She was still jumping up and down in the expectancy of his reaction to her part in the play when he jerked his hand away and said sharply, "Barbie, don't interrupt me! Can't you see that I'm talking? Wait until I'm through!"

I may have been the only one who saw it, but it was clear to me that the light in a small girl's eyes was immediately extinguished. The message received had been blunt and—under the circumstances—quite cruel: "Your performance is not as important to me as talking to my grown-up friend."

I am a very sensitive man. This is not necessarily a virtue—only a fact of my temperament. I do tend to feel and identify with other people's wounds. In that moment I felt the hurt in that child as if her father's words had been directed at me personally.

Though I did not know either the girl or her father, my own reaction to this exchange was one of indignation. I sensed that the father's response had been destabilizing to his daughter's self-esteem. It's probable that as she backed off sheepishly from the aborted encounter, she felt demeaned, unliked, and convinced that she had failed to please a most significant person in her personal world.

Just as a referee with a whistle interrupts play in a basketball game, I wanted to run over, stop that adult conversation between two boorish men and cry "Foul!" I wanted to call a violation of the rules and principles of people building. Since I'm not that courageous, I didn't.

But what if I had? As the apostle Paul once said, in describing a hypothetical situation, "I write as a fool." What if I had been nervy enough to approach this father and say, "Can we talk?" Assuming he would not have told me to "bug off" and mind my own business, and assuming that he would have submitted to the scrutiny of a slow-motion instant replay, where would our conversation have gone from there?

Would he have protested my "call" with the old cliche, "Children are to be seen and not heard"? Or would he have defended his reaction by noting that a polite and courteous child would have waited until there was an appropriate time to enter an adult conversation?

Let's get really hypothetical. What if the two of us could have become friends, poured coffee, and talked about people-development matters in one of our homes. What would have our agenda included?

After what I'd just seen, I certainly would have wanted to put affirmation and affection high on the list. I would have wanted to talk about the transfer of loving human energy, the significance of the "well done" (which his daughter had definitely not heard), and something else: what had been said when he refused the physical connection she'd sought by grabbing his hand?

I want to be very clear about one thing as I talk about this hypothetical conversation. I would not participate as the "preacher," the expert who had all of these themes mastered. No, I would want to talk as a man who, more than once, had acted just as insensitively toward my son and my daughter. I would want him to know that I'd also missed the signals my children were sending, and hurt them, by neglect or by impulsive action. Yes, there are some past moments, many past moments, I would say to him, that I would dearly love to redeem.

As we would drink our coffee and talk about our kids and our roles as people-building parents, I think I would want to ask him if he'd ever thought about the possibility that he and his daughter were strong contrasts in personalities. It seems possible to me that what happened that night in the school gymnasium was not just a matter of a breech of parental politeness.

Perhaps I was seeing the clash between a girl who needed instant feedback from key relationships (in this case her father) and a man who had a resistance to expressions of feeling that were too overt or enthusiastic. Maybe this man found it very hard to express his approval and chose to disguise his reluctance by claiming that he was involved in a more important conversation. He would not be the first parent with such a problem.

If that is the case, I would like him to know what I've had to learn the hard way. The parents committed to building people in the home must work to *discover and value* who their children are, not who they would like them to be.

Gail and I talked about the importance of this as we stood in Kristy's pink and white bedroom on moving day. Gail was alluding to it when she pointed to the baseboard under the window and said, "I'll never forget how Kristy used to have her stuffed animals so carefully lined up on the floor against that wall. Remember how important it was to her that their places in line never be changed?"

"Yes." I remembered it very well.

We had raised a daughter who found security in the order and systemization of things in her life. Nowhere did that show itself more than in the way she kept her room. Her desk was always carefully organized both on its table top and in the drawers. Inside there would be a box for pencils, another for paper clips, a third for rulers. Each was labeled according to its purpose. Years later after Kristy had gone to college, we finally broke up her old desk and burned the wood. I had a tear or two in the process when, in one of the sections, I even found a space labeled, "This place for things too big to fit in other places."

Kristy's closet, her dresser, and her bookshelves were all marked with the same order. We found this interesting because in the earth-toned bedroom down the hall lived a boy whose living quarters were the epitome of disorder. How had two children with such contrasting views of neatness come from the same womb? Temperament does make a difference.

No where was the order in Kristy's life better illustrated than in the placement of the stuffed animals and dolls that sat against the wall under the window. Each night the animal or doll that was first in the line was awarded the privilege of sleeping with her in her bed. The next morning, it would be returned to the end of the line. In twelve or fifteen days its turn to be with Kristy for a night would come again.

When Gail or I came to Kristy's bedroom each evening to share those last moments with her before sleep, a small ritual ensued. "Daddy (or Mommy), would you hand me S——?" Each doll or animal along the wall had a name.

Sometimes, I would slyly select an alternate one from the middle of the row. But I never succeeded.

"No, Daddy. That's the wrong one. It's S——'s turn. He'll feel terrible if he doesn't get to sleep with me tonight. He's been looking forward to it all day."

"But look at this one," I would say, in a mock serious tone of voice. "Doesn't he look cold?" Or, "He's pleading to get in to the front of the line. I know because we've talked about it, and he's asked me to do a personal favor and arrange for him to be with you tonight."

"No, it's not his turn. He'll be all right with all the others. It's S——'s night."

In her bedroom Kristy attributed personal feelings to virtually every object. As much as possible, she liked to rotate the wearing of her clothes, just as she selected the animals and dolls, lest any of them feel hurt or neglected because of unfair treatment. This tendency to assume that everything has feelings is a trait of many sensitive children, and it should never be ridiculed by someone who does not understand it. I guess I understood it because Kristy had inherited the trait from me.

I had also learned in that bedroom that my daughter was most at peace when she knew where her parents or some responsible person was when she went to sleep. In doing this, she was echoing the words of the Psalmist who had the same thing in mind when he wrote, "I will lift up my eyes to the mountains from whence comes my help. . . ." He was at peace as long as he knew where help was available. And Kristy was at peace when she was sure about the location of help and security.

The ceremony in the pink and white bedroom that led to sleep did not end with the selection of a doll or stuffed animal.

The window shade carefully had to be drawn to a point five inches from the bottom of the window frame. The covers had to be pulled up to Kristy's neck and made tight with no wrinkles. After evening prayers, the door had to be closed to a point approximately six inches short of being shut so that the light in the hall would come indirectly into her room. And after all this was done, there would be one final exchange of conversation. I learned to expect it.

"Where are you going to be, Daddy?"

"In the living room, honey."

"When are you going to bed?"

"Oh, in about an hour, I guess."

"Don't go to sleep until I'm asleep."

"I wouldn't think of it, sweetheart. I love you."

"I love you, Daddy."

Until Kristy entered into her double digit years, there were few evenings that didn't end just the way I've described this one.

Yet just steps away was our son who, as far as we could see, eschewed ritual. A bedtime visit to his room was something like hacking one's way through a jungle of clothes, books, and sports equipment. There in a bed cleared off for the purpose of sleeping one would find Mark and our dog, Holly.

After a prayer, this quick interchange: "Dad, close the door tight, will you?"

"Good-night, son."

"Good-night, Dad."

"Love you, son."

"Love you too, Dad." He was gone. No shades, no dolls, no questions, no concern about the security of the house.

The two children were different in so many ways. Each had to be accepted and valued exactly as they were. Little would have been accomplished by saying to Mark, "Why can't you organize your room as effectively as Kristy has done?" And

Kristy would not have been helped by our saying to her, "Why can't you just sign off and go to sleep as easily as Mark does instead of requiring all these detailed arrangements before you're ready to say good-night?"

I had learned in our daughter's pink and white bedroom that she was a remarkably impressionable child. Her mind was attuned to the possibility of emergencies. She handled these sensitivities and fears by building maximum structure into her life. Routine, sameness, predictability: these things were at the root of tranquility for her.

"Daddy, if we had a fire in the house at night, where would we all meet when we got out of the house?" She'd heard a talk on fire prevention at school and came home to organize the entire family on how we should react in a time of emergency. To set her mind at ease, we had all gone through a drill and practiced meeting at a predetermined spot outside. Since it was a nighttime drill, our neighbors saw us through their window and came out to find out what was going on. I think they were surprised when we told them.

Taped to the four walls of Kristy's bedroom were scores of cards and posters with scripture verses, prayers, and insightful mottoes. They were frequently exchanged, and by reading them one could easily discern what was currently on her mind. Usually the content came from things she was reading or had heard someone say. You could tell what she was trying to learn and struggling to master in her personal life.

A parent who would be a builder of children sets out to discover all of this and takes what he or she finds very seriously. How can I understand and accept this youngster for who and what he or she is? Is there a way to communicate how much I value these characteristics of personhood that I am discovering? And how can I avoid being too critical of those traits of personality that are different from mine? Many of Kristy's bedtime characteristics I did not share or fully understand as an adult. A part of me found them time-consuming and trivial. It would have been so easy to have communicated that to her by my attitude and irritability.

I often wonder, for example, what it would have done to her if her mother or I had scorned her desire that the shade be pulled down just so far; if we had laughed at her serious desire to be fair to all of her dolls and animals; if we had insisted on shutting the door all the way or not at all. What if we had refused her in her desire to give her bed away when she was a teenager, or what if we had ignored her request to make sure the family had drilled for an emergency? What if we had *demanded* that she be just like us instead of being herself?

Long after our children had grown up and left the home on Grant Street, Gail and I came to appreciate the value of determining the psychological type of each person in a family. Only in retrospect did we realize how sensitive a child had lived in the pink and white bedroom and how quickly we could have crushed her spirit. Fortunately, we had accepted her style of personhood early in her infancy and permitted it to flower.

Students of psychological types (such as those following the work of Isabel Myers-Briggs) tell us that just as people have a preferred hand with which to write, they also have other preferences in the way they choose to function in their inner and outer worlds.

For instance, children may prefer to seek for a source of energy by being with people *or* they may prefer solitude within themselves. In their learning experiences, one child may be more apt to observe the big picture and identify emerging patterns while another might prefer to observe details and facts and their practical implications.

There are other preferences also. When making decisions, some lean toward that which makes for harmony and peace between people while others lean toward logic and reason. Finally, children may pursue a life-style that needs decisiveness and structure or one that invites considerable spontaneity and flexibility.

All these preferences are valid and need to be encouraged, not belittled. People-building parents do not attempt to change a child. They work hard to discover who the child is, to distinguish "the natural bent of the twig."

The signs of Kristy's natural bent came in the earliest years—her deep emotional reaction to distressing scenes on television, her deep sense of sorrow when someone in her circle of playmates was hurt or humiliated, her great concern never to disappoint or hurt her parents. These could have been seen as vulnerabilities or weaknesses and could have been exploited or ridiculed. But if they were accepted as strengths, they could become building blocks in her development as a young woman. She could then be a powerful asset as a friend to those around her. That is exactly what happened.

Those were the sorts of things I was learning at about the time Gail and I joined other enthusiastic parents at that sixth grade play. Perhaps you can better understand now why it bothered me so much to see a man who should have known better reject his child in such a way so as to make deep gouges in her spirit. Perhaps what he did that night would be forgotten in fifteen minutes. But perhaps not.

# EIGHT

## SHOW ME YOU LOVE ME

❧ *There's no place like home if each person knows with certainty that he or she belongs and is unconditionally bonded to the family.*

IF THE MAN at the school play had been willing to talk further about some of the people-building tasks in parenting, I would have raised the subject of affection. I would have talked to him about the significance of that painful rejection he showed in pulling his hand so forcefully away from his daughter. I'd call it counter-affection: the physical act of personal repudiation.

At that moment, was he ignorant of the fact that those physical touches or connections symbolize special relationships? They are an indispensable part of the current of loving human energy that flows between people in a family. Put in a formal way:

> *Affection is an act of loving connection expressed in touching, stroking, holding, hugging, or kissing. It is the most important form of affirmation we can give to our children.*

A woman in her late twenties comes to talk with Gail and me about a marriage problem. As the details spill out, we listen to a tragic confession of her unfaithfulness to her husband, which borders on outright promiscuity. In the conversation we scan the past years, trying to uncover the roots of a sexual behavior pattern that seems to border on the addictive. One of us asks her about her relationship to her father.

"Were you two close?"

There is a rueful laugh, and then this: "I honestly can't remember a time when my father so much as touched me, even to punish me," she responds. "In fact, until I was a teenager and started going out with boys, I don't remember a time when I was touched affectionately by any man." When she says this, I think to myself that we have probably reached the root of her present struggle. Her quest for healing and for liberation from a terrible bondage will have to begin by facing up to this "affection deficit" and understanding its negative impact upon her.

Having missed the normal, healthy flow of affection that ought to have prevailed throughout a child's experience, this woman now struggles in the deepest spaces of her inner life to understand and control great unsatisfied yearnings for physical connection. Not everyone who shares a similar experience may choose to react in this manner in their adult years, of course. But her story is not uncommon. Her recollection of the past reminds me that all children have a remarkable need for affection from the day they are born.

Some have suggested that affection is an echo of the experience of the womb when each of us felt the warmth and security of a mother's encompassing body. Each of us then knew the greatest amount of safety one person is able to offer another. Following the birth experience, something deep within us longs to retrieve any part of that feeling of earlier bondedness. As infants, we recall it when we lie peacefully being nourished at our mother's breast. We remember it when we are enclosed in our father's arms. At such times we hear or sense the familiar rhythmic beating of the parental heart; we feel protected; and a kind of energy is transferred within this moment of serenity.

We see a perfect example of affection when we spot a mother or father carrying a child in a special sling designed to hold an infant snugly to the parent's chest. It is certainly not a clinical comment, but I do not think I have ever observed an infant crying in distress when it was being carried in one of those slings. I have seen many babies fast asleep in them, even when the parent is in a chaotic supermarket line or with a mass of people rushing through a shopping mall.

One senses the incredible need for touching when a child takes a fall or is startled by a crash of thunder. While on a walk, Gail and I see a child stumble and bang her head sharply as she hits the ground. We wince at the impact. We watch as she straightens up, feels the pain, instinctively looks about for her mother who is raking leaves across the yard, and runs crying to her. She is quickly absorbed into her mother's arms of affection and consolation. In seconds the crying ceases, and the child soon returns to play, assured by the physical connection that everything is OK. Loving human energy has done its job.

At the age of eight, Kristy played in a town soccer league for girls. One Saturday morning, Gail and I stood on the side lines as she played the fullback position near the front of her team's goal. A ball came rolling toward her, and she prepared to kick it forward. But losing her balance she merely brushed the ball with her foot, changing its direction so that it went past a surprised goalie and into her own team's goal. The other team had scored an easy point because of Kristy's error. Some of her teammates quickly surrounded her saying, "You jerk! You've probably lost us the game!"

It was a moment of maximum humiliation for this daughter of ours, and the coach, too young and immature to realize the importance of the moment for building character in a team or the need to soothe the feelings of a mortified child, chose to pull Kristy out of the game, maximizing her sense of failure.

I watched Kristy begin to walk off the playing field in despair. She was clearly hurt, humiliated, and empty of spirit. Then suddenly her eyes caught those of her mother and me, and instantly she broke and ran toward us. In seconds her face was buried in my stomach as she sobbed out her embarrassment. "I didn't mean to lose the game for everybody." It was a time for connection, a transfer of loving energy.

As both of us stood in solidarity with our daughter, I looked around and noted how few parents had bothered to come to the soccer game that morning. I thought how easy it would have been to have stayed away myself. As I stroked her blonde hair and held her close, I quietly said to Gail, "What if we'd not been here?"

What if we hadn't been there? Would Kristy have gotten past the bad experience? Probably! But maybe not without some scar tissue on the soul that affection and connection were able to mend.

A day would come in the future when Kristy would have to handle humiliations and defeats drawing on her own inner strength. But that day was not here yet, and until it came, she needed those who loved her to provide that special touch so indispensable to a person's development.

As a child grows, affection takes on an enlarged significance. It tends to diminish as a message of protection and increases as a message of *belonging and acceptance*. Touching now emphasizes something about specialness. It says: "I invite you into the intimate circle of my life."

We all ache to hear this invitation to belonging and acceptance. If we cannot receive it from the proper sources, we may seek it in other ways that are not as healthy and life giving. The messages of affection do not even stop there.

There should be a steady progression of affection between parent and child from the earliest days of life. At that age, the issue is protection and nourishment. Later affection will mean loving, belonging, and acceptance. Later, affection—in its maturest form—will ultimately advance to an experience involving healthy sexuality. We have a natural attraction to a person of the opposite gender, a desire to give and receive affection in a way that symbolizes our wish to know that person to the fullest possible extent—to the level of the heart.

A man and woman "become one flesh," the Scripture says of the marriage act. The phrase refers of course to that most dramatic of all affection: sexual intercourse. It also refers to far more than that: for we need to acknowledge emotional, intellectual, and spiritual intercourse, the supreme *koinonia*, or fellowship, between people committed to one another. Physical or sexual affection is simply the sacramental picture of that possibility. But this prospect is seriously jeopardized if it has not been prefaced in earlier years by simpler forms of affection by parents who believe in people development.

It seems axiomatic that most mothers provide an ample amount of affection to their children. Rarely does one talk with women who have difficulty giving their children the cuddling they need. After all, the mysterious order of life has taken mother and child through a remarkable bonding experience: nine months together as one has lived within the other; then the continuing connection at the breast and in the arms; and finally the ongoing cuddling and stroking that most of us take for granted as a primary function in the mothering relationship.

The transference of human energy between a mother and child is a fiercely private and powerful thing. Who can understand it? Who is not amazed at the "pound-for-pound" strength of a mother as she nourishes her child even, if necessary, at her own physical expense. And who is not impressed with the fighting spirit of a mother to protect at her own risk her child from enemies. Normally this mother-driven intimacy continues, changing only in the forms appropriate to each stage of a child's maturity.

But what if, in this new age of the 1990s, a mother chooses another role in life, one that makes this life-giving energy of intimacy and affection unavailable to a child for long periods of time each day? Can the process of transferring human energy by intimacy and affection be delegated to a day-care worker or to a professional nanny? Probably not without some consequences. In a day when many mothers have entered the work force, whether by choice or by economic necessity, this has become a burning question. Unfortunately, a whole generation or two may have to live a full cycle of life before we know if the consequences are entirely negative or if there can be other compensations.

A father's touching and affection is also of enormous importance. More than one modern writer has decried the tendency of some men to pursue a kind of remoteness that denies their sons or daughters the unique kind of intimacy that can come from a father. It is an encouraging thing to sense that this warning has been heard by many younger fathers in recent years.

A *New York Magazine* article featured the stories of a number of young male executives who had modified their work habits in order to spend more time with their infant children. It is by no means a fad. It is heartening to sense that men may be rediscovering that intimacy and affection offered by a man may play a powerful role in the development of a child's sense of belonging.

But not a few men grew up in homes where their fathers were remote. One father says, "I never received affection as a child; I'm not sure I'm comfortable giving it. In fact, I don't know how to give it." Perhaps there are some men who need a primer on how to be intimate with a child.

I found, for example, that my son loved to have his hair tousled and his ears massaged. When he was quite young, I discovered to my delight that I could convince him to sit like a statue in church services simply by doing this. I'm not suggesting that he was getting much out of worship, but he certainly learned that a church service could be a time of warmth and closeness with his dad. I can't help but speculate that what happened there in the intimacy of those moments might have been a good preparation for the jump he made later when he had to establish his own relationship with God. Did the memories of affection with an earthly father make it easier to trust the heavenly Father?

Our daughter, on the other hand, was the back-scratching type. How many memorable evenings one of us spent sitting on the edge of her bed in the pink and white bedroom rubbing her tiny back as she inched toward sleep! I can still recall (and not without some emotion) the evening when, in a moment of reverie between father and daughter, she impulsively took my face in her two small hands, rubbed my day-old whiskers and tenderly—almost in slow motion—kissed the tip of my nose.

Many fathers, perhaps unconsciously, begin to withdraw physically from their daughters when they notice the first overt signs of puberty. The hugging, the lap sitting, and the frequent kisses are liable to decline if a father worries about their effect upon his daughter simply because her body is maturing. What he may not take into account is that this is the season when she needs him most.

In our times the subject of the sexual abuse of children has arisen with frightening force. Movies about incest, television talk shows featuring women who relate in graphic detail their sickening encounters with abusive fathers, and court cases where men have been charged with sexual misconduct have put a scare into many fathers.

This is a subject that most men feel uncomfortable discussing even with other men. Many fathers quietly worry that affection given to their daughters will be somehow misinterpreted. I have had young fathers confide their fears that others might misunderstand their affection so they come to feel unnatural about touching their daughters at all. If there is this sort of anxiety in the heart of a father, the chances are that he will retreat from his daughters. The result? *Everyone loses.*

This problem, of course, is further complicated in homes where there is a stepfather, and parents in a second marriage have to agree carefully about the importance of affection and how it can be given without misunderstanding.

There is no easy answer to these matters. Sexual abuse and incest are serious problems in our age. Still, one observes that there are some in our times who take a militant perspective on these issues. In pressing their warnings, they have tended to smear the role of fatherhood, putting men on the defensive. In an effort to protect children, even the courts have appeared to move closer to a position where a father, when charged with sexual misconduct, is perceived to be guilty until he proves himself innocent.

A small but increasing percentage of tragic cases have affected us all. Those in Christian churches must not be blinded to the fact that some of these cases of abuse and related problems are found in religious homes.

But the people-building father cannot permit these matters to frighten him away from the importance of healthy affection with his children. Fathers must not be frightened into an unnaturalness of relationship, especially with their daughters.

Those who counsel with youth observe that a high percentage of girls who enter into promiscuous sexual relationships at an early age come from homes where fathers have withheld affection. Such fathers failed to meet the need of their young daughters to be properly touched and physically affirmed.

It was this insight that caused Gail and me to ask the woman who had come to talk of her struggle with marital unfaithfulness about her father. "I honestly can't remember a time when my father so much as touched me, even to punish me," she had said. Resolving that intimacy deficit will have to be the starting point of any healing she will find in this awful moment in her marriage.

It is easy to understand how some parents could make the mistakes this woman's parents made. I have heard some fathers say, for example, "I guess I'm not the affectionate type. My parents were from the old country and they never expressed affection openly. I never have either." How do we convince such fathers (or mothers) that times are different now, that this is a day when loving feelings can and should be conveyed through affectionate touching?

It can be easy to miss the signals when our children ask for affection. Impatiently, we may shake off the hand they extend to us when we walk beside them. Or we may feel intruded upon when they suddenly interrupt our concentration, asking for a hug or a seat on our lap.

A father recounts for me a series of such interruptions as he was reading his evening newspaper. He was just about to explode with irritation when a more pleasant alternative crossed his mind. He placed his newspaper on the floor and took his child into his arms. The transference of the human energy of affection lasted for about thirty seconds. Thirty seconds for one "tank" to fill another.

Satisfied, the child wiggled out of his father's arms and returned to play. There also followed twenty minutes of unin-terrupted newspaper reading. "I think he was just testing me," my friend recounted. "Normally, I would have spent a total of five minutes resisting his interruptions. Thirty seconds was all it took to assure him that I loved him and that I was willing to tell him so."

Affection is more than hugs and kisses. As children grow older, their need for affection does not cease. But they may prefer a different way of receiving it. One father tells me that his son passed through a period where he didn't want his dad to kiss him good-night. The father pondered this request and later mentioned it to his son. "I've been thinking about your not wanting me to kiss you good-night. I'm willing to play the game your way, son, but I do need a substitute action. There has got to be some way I can tell you that I love you and that everything is really great between us. If you prefer that I not kiss you, would you accept an occasional squeeze on the shoulder?" The boy saw no problem with that.

From that time on, the father honored his boy's wishes. He didn't kiss him good-night, but he always squeezed the boy's shoulder. But the father never fully comprehended the importance of this transaction until one night when he began to leave the room without extending the usual gesture of affection.

"What's wrong, Dad?" his son called after him.

"Why do you ask?" the father wanted to know.

"You know. You didn't grab my shoulder the way you always do."

"You're right, son. I blew it," the father said. He turned back and performed the small rite of affection that both had come to accept as the important expression of love in that phase of a son's life. A father had learned a valuable lesson. What was relatively inconsequential to him had become a very important matter to a son, who had once frowned upon kissing.

What if this father had misinterpreted his son's desire not to be kissed and had eliminated affection entirely? What if he had heeded the boy's youthful wishes about not kissing but had missed the deeper, unspoken desire of his heart, which was: "Dad, I need your affection as much as ever, but during this time of growing up, please offer it to me in a different way." And his father did! Wise father; satisfied son; an enlarging, people-building relationship.

I also tried to keep this principle in mind when our son used to come off the soccer field and wished only a congratulatory handshake. But I remembered the principle again when, a half hour later, he quickly fell asleep in the car and rested his head on my shoulder. I would put my free arm about him, and I was able to extend all the love, the pride, and the affirmation I felt in those private moments of father/son intimacy. It was an acceptable time and place, and the emerging image of masculinity was not threatened. The "guys" weren't looking. Later when this same son of ours played in the national collegiate championships, our form of affection returned to hugs. When his mother and I were called to join him out on the field for the presentation of awards, affection flowed freely. This young man of ours—now free from peer pressure—no longer required a handshake to insure his masculinity. A father and a mother and their now older son could hug warmly and tightly. Affection never ceased. Its forms may have changed, but its transference of human energy never did.

The Bible informs us that Jesus often lived through days packed with relentless pressure. One person after another sought him out for conversation. There were meetings, confrontations, and training sessions. There were long walks, big decisions, magnificent healings. From the perspective of the men who followed Jesus as disciples, it was a tough life-style.

Perhaps that's one reason they were so protective of him. One can understand why they would try to screen those who might try to get to him. This Jesus was an important person, they thought—certainly far too important to spend much time with mere children. From their shallow vantage point the messianic ministry was more significant than kids. Leave them alone and they will grow up; then they can have time with the Lord. That was the disciples' view.

But Jesus saw it differently. On one occasion when the disciples were fresh from debating who among them was the greatest, Jesus took a child and put him into the midst of them. Wrapping his arms around the little boy or girl, Jesus said, "He who receives this child receives me." We don't know the child's name or family. All we know is that the Son of God, the Prince of heaven, was saying that children are incredibly important—first, because they are human beings. And they are important because that age is the most formative period of their lives. They are important, also, because they need and deserve the kind of treatment that will develop them to be the kind of people God designed them to be. The disciples took a long time to learn that. So do many mothers and fathers. That's a major reason why a large part of the Christian gospel is so frequently misunderstood.

I wonder if the man I've come to know in my fantasy would accept all that from me? I would wish so. I know that it will not take too many humiliating encounters like the one I saw in the school gymnasium that night before an impressionable young girl will assume that the kind of energy she needs to develop toward adulthood will have to come from somewhere else.

The time Gail and I have spent in Kristy's pink and white bedroom is over. We must leave it and head for other parts of the now empty house. But it's very hard to leave. There are too many memories in every corner of this small space.

*We brought a girl to that room twelve years ago*, I think to myself. *And now she's left, a woman.*

# PART V

## A Boy's Bedroom

# NINE

## THE CLOSET COMPROMISE

❧ *There's no place like home if people can make decisions to-*
*gether that continually enlarge the ground of trust.*

NO ONE would have doubted for a minute that a boy once lived
in the room Gail and I now entered, on our final tour of the
house on Grant Street. The earth-tone colors and the wallpaper were distinctly masculine. To the right were shelves on
which a number of championship trophies and medals won in
athletics had formerly been displayed. In a corner was a discol-
oration in the carpet from an old chemistry experiment. By the
window was a hairline crack in the wall, probably only discernible to those who had witnessed the overzealous wrestling
match.

A small hoop and net attached to the back of the door
reminded us of the thousands of "slam dunks" and "three-
pointers" shot by Mark and his friends during indoor bedroom
tournaments, using a small sponge rubber basketball. There
were times when the whole house had reverberated with the
jarring collisions of young male bodies against the walls and the
door as friends competed with the intensity of NBA profes-
sionals.

"They're going to kill themselves in there," I'd say to
Gail when my reading concentration was threatened by the
continuous noises of grunts, groans, cheers, and high-fives.

"They're just being boys," Gail would remind me. "Would you rather have them off on some street corner hanging out?" she would ask.

"How about listening to Mozart and reading the biography of Churchill? I'd prefer those alternatives."

Most boys are not naturally given to the theme of order in the keeping of their rooms. Mark was no exception. More than once I'd seen Gail sigh in frustration over what to do with a place that looked like a disaster area. Clothes piled several layers thick on a chair, on a desk, in the corner, or under the bed. Books scattered, sports equipment radiating a locker room odor, and a bird cage badly in need of cleaning.

We loved that room, and we loved the boy who grew to become a man in it. If walls of that bedroom could remember and talk, they would tell of the conversations Gail and I had with Mark about how he should deal with a friend who'd disappointed him, why world history was more important than gym, where babies come from, when he'd be permitted to date, and who would make the final decision as to what tasks he was responsible for around the house. The walls would talk of stories read to him when he was a child and of the college catalogs we read together when it came time to think of leaving home.

On this final tour, when it came down to identifying one event that might be supremely significant in this bedroom-study hall-gymnasium, we were hard pressed, until . . .

"I've got it," I said suddenly. "Do you remember the time I crawled into the closet with Mark and spent a half hour in the dark?"

Gail remembered. "Yeah, that's it," she said with a smile.

Mark had been a sixth-grader. It was about the time in the lives of most children when peer groups become a serious part of social development. I'm speaking of that moment when the pressure to identify with the tastes and opinions of others begins to become as important (if not more important) as identifying with one's parents and extended family.

In Mark's class a group of about a dozen boys and girls had emerged from the pack. Their athletic ability initially brought them together. Their capacity to socialize at a "cooler" level than the others and their general enjoyment of similar activities drew them closer.

Mark was a part of that group and joined them every afternoon after school or in someone's backyard. They played soccer together, tossed a basketball, or passed a hockey puck back and forth.

Then one spring day, the group unwittingly created a crisis in our Grant Street home.

"Mom, Dad, guess what?" Mark had shouted as he burst through the door after school. We couldn't guess; so he told us.

"The group is going to the Cape [Cape Cod] for the weekend next month, and they're going to stay at the K——'s summer house. We're going to have a ball."

In two sentences we had been given several pieces of information. There was indeed a group. It felt it had decision-making powers. It had built a wonderful plan for an entire future weekend. And Mark was going to be part of it all. The inference beyond the information was that we should be overjoyed about this.

"*We're???*" I asked, stalling for time and drawing the syllable out so that all sorts of messages of caution accompanied it.

"Yeah, they want me to go. All the neat kids are going." He said this as if the sheer weight of the guest list alone would lift this issue far above a parent's usual right to question the wisdom of the venture.

"Who are all the neat kids?" one of us asked, now coming to full alert with the realization that this was no small matter to Mark.

"There's Eddie, and Sandra, and Kelley, and . . . "

"You mean this weekend is for boys *and* girls?" one of us questioned again.

"Yeah, what's wrong with that?"

"Bud, do you remember the times I've mentioned that you should not make any plans for going places with people until you'd come and asked first?"

"Sure, I remember."

"Do you remember that I told you that I would never be influenced to say yes simply because you'd committed yourself to something ahead of time?"

"Yes, Dad, but . . . "

"Son, I'm afraid that when I told you that, we were talking about a time like this. Your mother and I are not prepared to send you off a considerable distance from here on a weekend with a mixed group of kids we don't know very well. We know nothing about the plans for supervision, and, frankly, we're not very confident that Mr. and Mrs. K—— will spend much time with the group while you're down there."

There! It was out. A parental decision. Quick and tough. Quick: I'd applied an overarching principle we believed in for all family planning with the kids. And tough because deep down inside of myself I was proud that Mark was "cool" enough to be asked. I dearly wished that I'd been asked to be part of such a group when I was his age, and the fact was that I hadn't.

Mark was instantly crushed. He was speechless. This prized invitation, the wish of a hundred other kids in the school, was his, but I was snatching it away.

It was clear that Mark had carefully planned this announcement of the upcoming weekend to us and approached us with maximum enthusiasm. He had been smart enough to know that we would be uneasy about such a function. He thought the only way to break through our resistance would be to convince us of its importance to him and his social status. No doubt he reasoned, "How could they let me down when the 'neat' kids have chosen to include me?"

In seconds Mark was gone from the room where I had made the decision. The house returned to stillness, and Gail and I returned to our tasks. But it was clear that we both felt poorly about this quick and tough decision I'd made. I found myself trying to justify what I'd done to get it off of my mind.

*Life is full of disappointments*, I said to myself. My father and mother had said no to me many, many more times than Mark had ever heard noes from his parents. But, most significant of all, our son had violated a standing family rule: committing before permission. Convinced of my position, I muttered to myself that Mark would simply have to learn the hard way that a principle was a principle.

Rules are certainly a convenience in a home. Once a rule is established, one is free from deep and risky thinking. If someone presents a problem, challenges the order of things, needs a decision on an unprecedented matter, all we had to do was find the appropriate rule and apply it. Enough said. No need for judgment. And that's what I had done with a rule when Mark confronted me that day with his first major effort to break away from home and do something significant with people other than his family.

The house on Grant Street was a silent place for the next hour or so. I even managed to distract myself from the painful feelings of the encounter that we'd had with our son. But when it returned to nag my mind, I began to walk about and check on the morale of the rest of the family. Gail was in the kitchen; Kristy was in the back with some friends; but Mark had disappeared.

"Where's Mark?" I asked Gail.

"I have no idea," she answered. "I thought you knew."

I checked his room. Nothing. The basement. It was quiet. The garage. No one there either.

"Did Mark say anything to you about going somewhere?" I asked Gail again.

"He never said a word to me," she said.

And then it hit me. His room! Something was different. I headed down the hall to his doorway and looked in. What was strange? Then I realized what had caught my attention. The closet door was shut. In Mark's room that never happened.

I opened it. At first I saw nothing, but I sensed something. And then I heard a sniffle come from the back of the closet under the hanging clothes. I knelt down. There was our son. His knees against his chest, our dog Holly cuddled against him as if she were trying to identify with his pain. As his eyes blinked in the intrusive light, I could see that he had been crying. In an instant I was fully aware how pulverizing my quick and tough decision had been. I had used a rule in a situation that required judgment.

I thought of times when I had been Mark's age and when I had been hurt deeply by the course of events that had swept over me with seeming insensitivity. I thought of times when I'd hoped for an exception to the rules or sought an appeal to a decision. I was reminded of experiences when I thought that adults had simply consigned my dreams to insignificance and brushed me off with a quick and tough interpretation of their rules.

Then I wondered if there are ever times when a parent who wants to be a builder of people has to say, "Let's think this one through again."

As I knelt there looking at Mark in the closet I had the feeling that what I chose to do in the next seconds might have a lot to say about the relationship he and I would have as father and son for the next several years. One never knows about such things (and it's frightening to contemplate). What was happening here just might be a landmark moment in his development as a young man.

Mark's closet was not large. But there was room enough to

accommodate two people on its floor if they scrunched together. So wordlessly I pulled out a few scattered shoes and
boots, crawled in, shut the door behind me and took the vacant
place beside him. There we sat in the dark together for what
must have been fifteen or twenty minutes. No talk, just contem-
plation as I pondered how we'd gotten to this point and Mark's
quiet weeping as he worked through his disappointment.

Does a people-developing parent ever have a change of
mind? Are the rules you believe in ever bendable? Had this son
of ours ever given us any discernible evidence that he could not
be trusted, even when he was in a situation lacking proper
supervision? Had he ever lied to us? Had he ever shown himself
to be sneaky, or destructive, or irresponsibly frivolous when we
had given him more freedom than usual?

What is he hearing in my impulsive, stick-to-the-rules decision? Do there come times when a father or mother have to
take a risk or two and permit a learning experience? Do rules
alone run a home? Or should there be times when children are
given an extra amount of trust and freedom to see how it will
be handled?

Finally I broke the silence.

"Son, maybe I made too quick a decision out there a little
while ago. I'd like to talk with you about this thing again." The
closet door remained shut, and we sat together in the darkness.
Holly had fallen asleep and was snoring.

"What's there to talk about? I really wanted to go. You've
said no."

"Well, let's talk about my 'no.' Your mom and I feel very
strongly about certain things. For one, we had an agreement
with you that things like this had to be checked out with us
before you said yes. You've violated that and so we're made to
look like the bad guys because we put you in a bad spot with
your friends.

"We're also not very keen on the idea of boys and girls going

111

away for a weekend, not to speak of the lack of adults that will be around."

"But Mr. and Mrs. K—— are going to be there."

"But you've told me several times about the kind of life they lead, how their kids are left alone all the time. You've told me before that you wouldn't care to ever live in a home like that, despite all the nice things they've got. Now how do you think it makes me feel knowing that that's the way they'll probably run things down there at the Cape?"

"But, Dad, we'll be all right. Nothing bad will happen."

"I believe you believe that. And you've given me no reason to question you. But you did break a rule, didn't you? You committed to going somewhere without asking your mother or me first. Do you agree that you didn't play by the rules?"

"All right, I didn't play by the rules."

"So if I were to ignore that fact this time, how can I be sure that you'll not break the rule the next time just because I caved in now?"

"I wouldn't do that."

"Gordie!" Gail's voice sounded from somewhere down the hall. She's the only one in my world permitted to call me by that name. I tried to ignore her call.

"Gordie, where are you?" Gail was clearly insistent about saying something to me.

"In here," I called out as loudly as I could. Holly began to wake up; I could feel her stir between Mark and me. Then she crawled forward and scratched on the closet door. Gail, now at the entrance to Mark's bedroom, heard the scratches and opened the closet door. The look on her face was priceless as she stared down at Mark and me sitting side by side on the floor of the closet.

"We're having a serious talk in here," I said. "You're welcome to join us if you want, but you'll have to shut the door behind you."

"I think I'll leave the two of you alone," she said as she shut the closet door. We were in darkness again.

"Look, son, I feel that I was unfair to you on this decision. I'm prepared to change my mind about this trip to the Cape and let you go. But if I do that, you're going to have to promise me something."

Mark was fully alert now. "What's that?"

"When you get home on Sunday night from the Cape, you've got to sit down and tell your mom and me everything that happened and how you felt about it."

"I promise, Dad."

Soon after our closet compromise ended, we reentered daylight and headed for dinner.

Some weeks later Mark went to the Cape with his friends. And when he returned on Sunday evening after the long weekend, he was exhausted. But keeping his promise, he sat and reflected upon his weekend experience with us.

Supervision had indeed been minimal. The kids had stayed up all night both nights. On one of the nights Mr. and Mrs. K—— had gone out and left them alone until the early morning hours. There had been dares and double-dares about doing silly things, such as drinking and other kinds of "fooling around," but nothing untoward really happened.

"It wasn't half the fun I thought it would be," Mark told us. "You were right. Mr. and Mrs. K—— didn't care what we did, and we could have gotten into trouble. I'm glad I went, but you wouldn't have been wrong if you had not let me go."

For the next six years until Mark left the home on Grant Street and went off to college, our relationship with our son took on a new level of intimacy. Somehow on that closet floor we had learned something important about each other. He had learned that a people-building parent, the kind I wanted to be, could admit that a decision might not always be the best one and that it was possible to change ones mind. And I had learned that Mark's judgments could be trusted and that he could handle himself responsibly in marginal situations. In that room, in the closet, we took at step toward a new respect and trust for one another. And it was never abused.

# TEN

## LIFE IN WHITE WATER

ಎಲ *There's no place like home if someone is looking ahead in order to avoid destructive surprises.*

MARK was in the bow of our eighteen-foot canoe; I was in the stern. Tied to the thwarts between us was the duffel: tent, sleeping bags, and lots of food. The river was boiling white— that is to say, it was running furiously, smashing around and over rocks, here and there reaching gunwale-high waves. We were both paddling downriver, frantically trying to keep afloat through each combination of rapids. Our "survival" depended upon being able to pick a route back and forth across the river that would avoid the ultimate disaster of tipping over and losing everything—especially our pride as great wilderness explorers.

Then it happened! A water-soaked tree lying just below the surface caught the shoekeel of our Grumman canoe providing the split second the river needed to spin us around. In an instant we were upside down in freezing water, the canoe filling with half the river. Our equipment could be seen floating downstream.

White water is relentless and unforgiving. There is only one possible way to beat it, and that is to keep an eye thirty-five to fifty yards downriver, anticipating what is ahead. Entering a series of rapids is not time to begin making decisions about where the canoe should be guided. With the practice of reasonable foresight, the paddler may manage to keep dry most of the time.

There is something about the instinct of a canoeist that reminds me of the way young people are to be developed in a home. The person in white water threading a canoe through eddies and standing waves demonstrates something a people-building parent must learn. Effective judgments and decisions that enhance growth are the result of looking "downstream" and anticipating actions at the critical turns—the obstacles and the opportunities—so that everyone stays dry and ready for the next part of the journey.

When Mark arrived home from school with his Cape Cod plan that day, we were all, to use the lingo of the canoeist, in danger of being swamped by his surprise. To be sure, I'd already established a principle: no commitments without permission. But it was clear that I'd not established it with the strength necessary to overcome the excitement a sixth-grade boy might develop when asked to become part of such an exciting venture. Ambushed, I acted impulsively. I probably came close to losing what turned out to be a great opportunity to develop rapport with him as he headed into the peer-oriented teen years.

That is why it is important to say that people-building mothers and fathers aim at being foresightful rather than impulsive. Because impulsive parents find themselves too often taken by surprise, they are forced to respond to family issues without time to think or to make sound judgments. This leads to overreaction—acting too strongly (as I did), or underreaction—acting too weakly. In the impulsive home, everything seems to be a crisis or nothing is a crisis. People get wet in circumstances like that.

If you've ever been in the bow of a canoe when the steering done at the other end was impulsive and ragged, you understand uneasiness and insecurity. You find yourself checking to see if your wristwatch is waterproofed and your life belt buckled. It's scary. But living in a home where those who are steering (a mother and father or a single parent) are not looking down-stream is no less scary. Children in such homes are not dumb. They become adept at family politics: playing one parent against another, using surprise, guilt, threats of rebellion, or rupture in a relationship to assert their wills. The result is a home out of control. Before long everyone gets wet.

A single parent of two children, Rita Vargas (not her real name), dumped in her "canoe" when her home was in white water on a Saturday midmorning. She had planned a spring cleanup of the family apartment, and she made it plain that everyone, mother and children, was going to help complete a list of tasks that had been postponed for too long. Floors were going to be scrubbed, walls and windows washed, drawers cleaned out, closets reorganized, and broken toys fixed or discarded.

It was Roger, her ten-year-old, who precipitated the "drenching" that Saturday morning by acknowledging his lack of enthusiasm for the program. He was irritable, sluggish, and resistant to every suggestion his mother made about the quality and quantity of work he was doing in his room.

When Roger aggravated her one too many times, Rita exploded. Having failed in her reasoning with him and having been unable to get him to respond to threats, she resorted to venting her anger and frustration: name-calling, threats of punishment, and—when nothing worked—banishing him to his room, without lunch, for the rest of the day. I think her final words were something like: "You like living in a pigpen? Then stay in the pigpen, and don't come out until I tell you to!"

Then Rita and her daughter set off to finish what they could for the rest of the day, doing it in bad humor and only out of sheer determination. Her great plan for a family project was a failure, and Rita spent the day telling herself that if their father had still been in the home, things would have been different.

Perhaps. But where did things really go wrong? Could it be that it turned sour the night before when she and her two children had been invited to the home of friends and had stayed past midnight? Roger, in the company of other children, had been up long after his normal bedtime. Exhilarated by the excitement, he was alert and stimulated when they returned to the apartment. He was full of promises for tomorrow's activities—promises his youthful emotions and limited physical strength could not keep the next morning.

Rita made a strategic mistake when she expected her son to perform at top level the next day. She hadn't thought ahead—"downriver"—when she kept her boy out so late the night before. The next morning her son's reluctance took her by surprise, and she showed it in her impulsive anger and vindictive punishment. *She measured her son by adult standards, and she didn't conceal her rage when Roger fell short.*

A foresightful parent would have anticipated these Saturday morning events based on the past evening's situation. Rita should have reasoned that a ten-year-old simply does not have the emotional and physical reserves to respond to an extraordinary challenge on the morning after a late night out.

What might have been the more foresightful judgments? Obviously, she could have brought her boy home earlier on Friday night. Or she could have permitted more time for sleep in the morning. Or perhaps, simply, she could have concluded that the early morning behavior patterns were probably not those of an uncooperative child, but of a tired, worn-out boy. That kind of foresight might have produced a different attitude and treatment. Roger and his mother would not have been estranged at noontime; they might have worked out the problem together.

Every parent has made Rita Vargas's errors over and over

again. We might be tempted to think that her lack of foresight is amazingly naive. It really isn't. It's typical in countless homes. It embarrasses me to think of how many times Rita's mistake has been mine.

Jesus was a foresightful people builder. One regularly sees examples of this in his relationships to his disciples. Take Peter, the enthusiastic fisherman with the quick-draw mouth. When he gave all sorts of assurances about the heroic things he was going to do in the future, Jesus responded from the perspective of anticipation and foresight. He knew Peter's capacities better than Peter did. He was aware that Peter simply could not fulfill all the promises he made. While the average person would have gotten tough with Peter and perhaps—in the long run—even cut him from the team, Jesus didn't. Why? Because he understood Peter completely. In that context of foresight, he could take Peter's promises for what they were: expressions of sincere desire and nothing else.

In the last hours before the arrest of Jesus in the garden, it was the foresightful Jesus who told the impulsive Peter that he would face some terrible moments of personal crisis. Instead of standing tall for the Master, he would fall flat on his face. But then Jesus tenderly capped it all off with a reminder that he was praying for the fisherman. He prayed that, after the crisis was all over, Peter could get back on his feet and move on with the business of spiritual and leadership development.

The entire formula for foresightful leadership is found in that conversation. Jesus knew Peter; he sensed the situation; he was ready to respond to it; he was already looking "downstream" to the good that would come out of it. Whether you choose the model of the expert canoeist in white water or the mentoring principles of Jesus, the procedure that surfaces is helpful. The pattern is one of foresight: the capacity to know one's children in terms of their limitations and capabilities. It is the awareness of what to expect from them in each situation and agreement about the ultimate objective of growing up in a family.

When Mark and I take our Grumman off the top of the car and slip it into the water, we're aware of the potential danger of accidents. We've tried, therefore, to learn the capabilities of our canoe—how it will perform in various situations of wind, speed, depth of water, and rate of current. Beyond that, we've studied and practiced the art of canoeing; we know the rules and the consequences of breaking them. Finally, we've worked together enough so that we know how to make a crucial decision when we're out on the water.

Those three principles—knowing the stress limits of our craft, establishing rules of conduct on the water, and creating a program for decision making in the clutch—are all part of foresightful living on the river and in our people-building home. That was something of what Mark and I had to reframe as we sat on the floor in his closet in the earth-toned bedroom.

# ELEVEN

## STAYING DRY

*&* *There's no place like home if someone acknowledges, respects, and takes great delight in each phase of young life.*

WHEN our family first got a canoe, we were warned never to venture out into any water that was white with rips or rapids until we had gained enough knowledge and experience together in water that was flat and still. White water is exciting but dangerous, we were told by the experts; you get wet very quickly if you are not prepared. Remaining safe and dry is the result of knowing the canoe, the peculiarities of the river, and the limits of your own skill.

The experts were right. We didn't know enough when we went out on white water, and that's why Mark and I will always remember that our first canoe trip in a fast-moving river turned out to be a wet one.

We set out to learn more about our canoe: what it took to be good enough to enjoy a trip and, at the same time, not get dumped out of it. And what about skills? We practiced various styles of paddling and how to coordinate our efforts so that the person in the bow and the person in the stern wouldn't work against each another. We found out how tolerant the canoe might be under certain conditions before it would swamp or tip over. And since the mother in our family is not a swimmer, we studied the safety procedures that would make her feel comfortable to be aboard.

People building in the home follows the same principle of preparation and training. If you want to help steer a child through the growth process to maturity, you must know that child, know something about the pressures that are real to him, and you must know what it takes for you to be an asset to that child's growth.

What would be the key issues of life our children would be likely to face? How could we help them maneuver through? Where would the pressures come from? The surprises? The intrusions? How could we provide the guidance that would help our children come through the white water reasonably dry and confident that they could handle increasingly more difficult challenges?

This kind of information does not come simply by comparing our children with ourselves as we were at their age. It comes from knowing and studying *them*, watching *them*, listening to *them*. How do they handle stress? Where are their weaknesses and fears? What will motivate them to grow?

As I look back across the years at the house on Grant Street, a list of themes begin to form in my mind. Not an exhaustive list, but a representative one. They are typical issues similar to the one Mark and I faced together on the floor of his bedroom closet. I doubt if there are many mothers, fathers, or single-parents who won't find each of these people-building issues in their family experience. The first comes very early in one's life.

THE RAPIDS OF INSECURITY

To some extent every human being is a "feeler," each of us seeking signals from the immediate world about us that will indicate whether we are safe, valued, and loved. If the signals are negative or confusing, we become anxious and defensive, and we try to compensate for our unprotected or vulnerable position. We begin to plan how never to get into that situation again.

But if the signals bring good news, then we feel a kind of pleasure and try to amplify or maximize the experience. We immediately begin planning how to repeat that situation as often as possible.

This capacity to sense things (whether we are always accurate or not) begins earlier in life than most of us could ever imagine. Recent advances in fetal research have taught us that the unborn are capable of feeling and reacting to all sorts of stimuli that are coming from within and beyond the womb. Furthermore, adverse or pleasant experiences in the womb can make a significant mark on the development of a person that will last all of life. That's a sobering thought for the mothers of the unborn.

The Bible includes a description of the reaction of John the Baptist, still in the womb of his mother, Elizabeth, when Mary, the mother of yet unborn Jesus, came to visit. "The baby leaped in my womb," Elizabeth said.

We are not told anything more than that, but the inference is that the unborn John felt great joy and security as he picked up the signals that the unborn Christ was present. What John picked up could be called positive signals.

But negative signals create the opposite sensation: sadness and insecurity. I'm convinced that dealing with feelings of insecurity is the first "white water" challenge most children face.

Insecurity arises as the result of unsure or unpredictable conditions. You can often detect insecurity on the face of a baby when a stranger tries to coax him from the more familiar arms of a parent. Only the most confident and outgoing of infants will easily accept such an invitation. The arms, the smells, the voice of a familiar parent are sure and predictable. Insecurity is in the thought of leaving that even for a moment.

Many samples of unsure conditions offer the potential of insecurity: a child left with a parade of babysitters or day-care workers, a high level of conflict in the home, a family relocation to another community, inconsistency in the way a child is related to, or—maybe the most unsettling events of all—separation, divorce, or a death in the immediate family.

Adults often underestimate the capacity of children of any age to sense and to react to these uneasy or unsettling situations. A child may not be able to identify the events in grown-up terminology or even understand their long term implications, but, he or she will invariably know something is wrong and that well-being, esteem, and love are in jeopardy.

Insecurity is that indescribable feeling a person has when he doesn't know what he can hang on to if something goes wrong. Watch a small child learning to ride his first two-wheeled bicycle. The one teaching him runs through the park with his hand on the back of the seat, giving encouragement and an added sensation of balance. When the hand on the seat is removed, the bike rider is on his own. Everything continues as before until the child becomes aware that the hand on the back is gone. The front wheel begins to wobble, and within a few yards the once-confident rider is usually on the ground. What has happened? A crash generated first by insecurity and then a resulting loss of balance! Insecurity appears the instant the rider becomes aware that he is on his own, that the steady hand (although invisible to the rider) is gone.

Children of every age need to know that there's a hand on (or near) them, providing balance, should anything upset their stability. Or, to return to our canoeing metaphor, they need to know that a competent paddler is at the stern, steering when the water is white. If they sense that the balancing hand is missing or that the paddler at the stern is absent, there will be some form of distress. The symptoms of insecurity are numerous: a stomachache, regressive behavior, unacceptable aggressiveness toward others, and any technique designed to gain unwarranted attention.

These indicators merely become more sophisticated as a child gets older. In teen years insecurity may show itself in the boy or girl who becomes romantically obsessed with someone of the opposite gender. An almost irrational tie to a peer group, or an unyielding need to dress in conformity with a certain style can be a signal of insecurity. In each case it is a reaching out to someone or something that provides a feeling of safety, belonging, and value.

I watch a child express anxiety and insecurity in an airport while a crowd of impatient adults wait to board a flight. There is an air of irritability because the plane is behind schedule. The adults handle their feelings of loss of control by complaining to the gate agent (who himself usually has no control over the situation), telling each other stories of past bad experiences, and pushing and shoving to get closer to the front in case the boarding line does begin to move.

The child in the crowd feels all of these negative signals, but his or her reaction may be through tears or erratic behavior. He senses his parents are upset, and he joins them in expressing it in his own way. Strangely enough, his parents do not read his expression of insecurity as anything but bad behavior. Since that behavior seems unacceptable to adults, the child is punished for expressing in his "language" the same insecurity the adults are expressing in theirs. The problem? No one was looking downriver far enough to see the "rapids" that are created in a crowded airport gate.

The positive signals that build security in a child are normally established by a reasonable amount of predictability in a home: consistency of schedule, stability of place, and normalcy of responsibilities and relationships. Frequent expressions of love, verbal and affectionate. Discipline which is fair and consistent. Even decor—simple or lavish—that is not constantly changed.

In a fast-paced, hard-changing world like ours, where personal schedules have become clogged with commitments and activities, where people are coming and going, where there is noise and constant interruption, it's easy for a child to feel unsafe, unvalued, unloved. He or she interprets all this as the absence of a strong hand to steady things if the bike wobbles or the canoe swamps.

Gail and I knew that we were inviting insecurity into our home if either of us traveled excessively when Mark and Kristy were young. We couldn't avoid noticing that even an overnight trip could make one or both children uneasy, sometimes about our personal safety (just as much as theirs) or simply because the family routines were disrupted. Knowing this, we learned to schedule blocks of special time just before and after a trip to compensate for the adjustment. I made sure that I had enough personal time with each of the children to explain the purpose of the trip. I learned to emphasize my return so that no doubt of that was permitted to enter their thinking processes. While I was away, I arranged for frequent telephone calls home so I could talk not only to Gail but also to the children if they were available.

If Gail or I (depending upon who was the traveler) were successful in our reassurances, the children had no reason to say a sad, wistful good-bye. They could join in an enthusiastic send-off with a feeling of support and anticipation for the purpose of the trip. The moment of return was an occasion for a special family time together to report the results. When the children were older, it became possible to enhance this experience by occasionally taking one of them with us.

Looking downriver in those earliest days on Grant Street meant working hard to create as steady and tranquil a home as we could manage even though we were busy people. It meant looking just far enough ahead to recognize the times of turbulence and give warning to the family that white water was just ahead. And it meant that while we were in the "zone of insecurity" we needed to work extra hard to give assurance to our son and daughter that they were loved, they were valuable, and they were safe.


## THE RAPIDS OF PUBERTY

As children mature, the onset of puberty brings a second group of stresses downriver, and more than a few mothers or fathers are simply not prepared for what it means. Puberty, the massive set of changes that introduce physical maturity, is certainly "white water." If we have not asked ourselves ahead of time about the nature of pubescent behavior, we are likely to be swamped in one way or another.

Puberty brings enormous changes in the dispositions and feelings of young boys and girls. Various glands move into operation to trigger later adult functions, and it may take several months or years for the new hormonal secretions to gain proper balance. In the meantime, crazy things can happen. The endocrinologist tells us that early adolescents can be overwhelmed by massive "overdoses" of one hormone or another, causing high moments of exhilaration or low moments of mild depression. There is a reasonable similarity between puberty and menopause: the former, the commencement of various hormonal activities, the latter being the cessation of some of those same functions. Both experiences—puberty and menopause—can cause mystifying attitudes and moods that are easily misunderstood by others. Parents who do not easily understand the pubescent child should remember that he is no doubt having as difficult a time figuring himself out.

At such times, some of us are tempted to demand that certain youthful moods be explained, that physical clumsiness be better controlled, or that long periods of time spent staring into space be better used.

About the time our oldest was about to enter this period of life, Dr. James Dobson's well-known book *Hide or Seek* was published. There was no doubt of the author's strong feelings about the "rapids" of puberty and that he thought that families had to give major attention to preparing themselves and their children for this universal experience of life change.

Gail and I had thought that we had prepared ourselves and instructed our children carefully on the subject of puberty. But since Dobson was so insistent that families be on top of the matter, I decided that I would reinforce what we'd done with one more conversation just to be sure that we'd passed the test and were ready for any eventuality downriver.

I invited Mark to go on a walk with me. After we had passed the conversational 'time of day' on a number of trivial items, I said, "Have you noticed any times lately when you seem to get suddenly sad for no reason at all?" His response was immediate and assertive: "Good grief, Dad; are we going to talk about puberty again?" It was clear that we'd done the job, and we were as ready as one can be for the white water when we got to it.

Puberty became such a fact of life in our home that it was the subject matter for more than one family joke. When someone responded to a problem in less than an acceptable way, another could be heard to comment, "He's (or she's) just going through puberty." Not only did it remind us regularly that the experience was real, it lightened the moment. Perhaps it went a bit too far when one morning everyone sensed irritability in me. When Gail asked, "What's bothering you this morning?" Kristy quickly answered for me: "It's OK, Mom. Dad's just going through puberty today."

### THE RAPIDS OF ACHIEVEMENT
Down the river lies not only the white water of insecurity and puberty (emotional and physiological realities) but the

challenge of achievement, competition, and pride (functional realities). These struggles appear to face almost every teenager as he or she tries to find a place and a role in society.

Whether we like it or not, a large part of a person's self-esteem is wrapped up in what he does, how well he does it, and whether or not it is recognized and valued by others. The good news is that we are motivated to work at excellence in the things we do. The bad news is that too many of us are enslaved to our achievements as the proof of manhood or womanhood.

This is a kind of white water, a section of life's rapids that very few young people are going to navigate very well if they do not have a parent or two helping to steer in the back of the "canoe," at least in the first phases of the challenge.

We find two extreme kinds of people in this white water: the overachiever who always has to win and the underachiever who becomes apathetic and indifferent to events in life. These symptoms can be equally dangerous.

Parents who are looking with foresight down the river seek to spot the roots of these patterns long before they become a form of concrete behavior. This competitive instinct will probably appear first in the way children play games. Do they have to win every time? Do they lose composure when there is a loss?

When Mark was playing baseball, in the days of Little League, I became fascinated one day with a catcher on another team who went to pieces during the middle innings of a ball game as his club gave up a series of runs. A couple of errors by an outfielder and a second basemen brought him close to uncontrolled rage. When the umpire called a base runner safe at third when he slid under the tag of the infielder, the boy dissolved into tears. Then I watched him come to bat and swing for the fences and miss three times. He flung the bat back to the bench, slammed the safety helmet to the ground, and tried to claim that the pitcher was throwing illegal pitches.

What intensified my interest in this situation was that the

boy's father was the team coach. The win-at-all-costs instinct had been passed from father to son, and the fruit of that compulsion was in full bloom as the game progressed. Being a student of people, I gradually lost interest in the game and concentrated my attention on the Little League catcher and his father-coach. Rather than rebuking the boy for his unrestrained conduct, the father literally egged him on by his own anger and frustration. When in the later innings their team managed a rally to come from behind and win, I watched father-coach and son-catcher run and grab each other in a frenzy of excitement. They had achieved; they had a win.

I thought I saw a boy headed for trouble that day because he didn't have a parent looking downriver far enough to see in a nine-year-old boy some patterns of behavior that would betray him. Some day people would disagree with him, he might fail in a business venture, or he could come head-on with someone who was simply more skilled in some area than he was.

A parent thinking of what's ahead downriver is sensitive to the fact that teenage offspring are fiercely pride-oriented. Girls will worry about their appearance; boys about their size. In the drive to assert their identity and integrity, they will find it very hard to admit that they are misinformed, that they are ignorant of something, or that they made a mistake. In the mind of the adolescent, failure is a final disaster that is larger than life.

A daughter invests many hours of fantasy and flirtation in the hopes of attracting a boy for whom she has strong feelings. A son dreams of a starting position on an athletic team. A boy or a girl has a passionate desire to win a starting role in a play or musical. These are sample possibilities for white water. The girl may lose out in her quest for the relationship; the boy may not make the team; and the would-be performer may not get the part. The times call for a sensitive parent to be prepared to come along with either comfort and stabilizing affirmation or the kind of guidance that offers perspective on how to handle success and achievement.

While all of this may seem obvious when set out on paper, many parents have trouble making it work. Usually the reason for difficulty has to do with differing temperaments. A mother or father who is primarily guided by a logical or reasoning style of thinking will tend to overlook the sensitivities of a child who is more feelings oriented. We should hope that at least one parent in the home shares a similarity in temperament with the boy or girl in question, who will be able to interpret some of these nuances to the other.

## THE RAPIDS OF PEER LIFE

Downriver may lurk the white water of peer identification and pressure, the issue Mark and I were facing when we discussed his Cape Cod hopes on the closet floor.

This is one parent who saw the approaching rapids of peer life somewhere about the eleventh or twelfth year of our children's lives. It was clearly an urge to identify with a group of friends in the fellowship of tastes, life-style, opinions, and judgments.

In a sense, this was the first attempt at a "departure" from our home on Grant Street. It was a search beyond the family for another kind of security and bondedness. In its own way, this pursuit of peer relationships was a widening quest for love, for value, and even safety with the expectation that these things could be found in a set of relationships with friends one's own age.

The development of peer relationships is not a new phenomenon. Recent research on the subculture of North American teenagers shows that in the last few years the peer group now has the dominant position of influence in the lives of young people. What we're hearing is that the peer group has suddenly bested the influence of parents, institutions such as the church or school, and traditionally influential personalities such as teachers, coaches, and pastors or priests. The bleakest interpretation of the data proposes that young people begin to care more about the opinions and judgments of their friends than they care for those of family members.

This research is certainly not good news. While peer friendships are normal and healthy, that they might become more important for this age group than the influence of family life is a serious matter. Rarely do peer relationships stimulate disciplined growth and development. Rarely do they reinforce the values that supposedly were taught in the home.

So this is the fourth of the great white water challenges a parent faces: how to provide the kind of steering that will encourage the socialization so important to every child without letting it become so dominant that people-building efforts in the home are neutralized.

Peer orientation appears to parallel the moment when boys and girls first evidence an interest in the opposite sex. When Mark and I reminisce, I love to remind him that there was a time (before girls) when his friendships were exclusively male and his sole future ambition in life was to be an unmarried dolphin-trainer who owned a monkey, a boa constrictor, and a German shepherd as house pets. Assessing Mark's dream, his mother remarked that he could not have contrived a life-style that would more effectively preclude girls, wives, . . . and probably mothers.

Mark's "pre-peer" ambitions were hardly part of a "world-in-life" view that invited intimacy. And no wonder: he wasn't searching for more intimacy than he then enjoyed in his family experience. But that would change.

Mark's conversion in social values came in one seven-day period—the visible change, anyway. As if a curtain had been drawn shut on one life-style and opened dramatically on another, monkeys, boa constrictors, and German shepherds were traded for interest in a girl. Why *that* particular girl, no one knew. Both choice and timing were a mystery. All we knew was that the impossible had happened. Blame it on glands, on a growing need to expand a personal perimeter of intimacy, or even on an exceptionally cute little girl. But there was indeed a conversion.

Along with this new preoccupation came a new alignment in the nature of boyhood friendships. No longer were conversations restricted to discussions about soccer and baseball. Talk included a new and vast social dimension: which boy liked what girl, and which girl had glanced sideways at what boy. One heard quiet, sometimes giggling comments out on the basketball patio that clearly referred to the physical attributes of one girl or another—things Mark and his friends had never noticed or cared about before.

It became important to dress the way others dressed: styles, brand names, and colors. Boys did not lace their shoes; girls wore their clothes in layers. Using certain words in certain ways—words like *wicked* and *wow* and *bad*—were proof that one belonged. These were the codes, the secrets, the traditions of the new groups that suddenly sprang to life. And those that made it into the group gained new confidence in themselves. Those that did not often suffered.

All of this amounted to the pursuit of one value that was more important than anything else: to be considered cool. In a word, coolness is self-perpetuating: the group decides what "cool" is; the group decides who is "cool." Sometimes coolness is determined by the appearance or the behavioral traits of certain media and music personalities. Or coolness can be just about anything that effectively puts distance between an older and a younger generation.

The intensity of a teenager's need to be cool is usually a reflection of how secure that boy or girl feels in the love of the family. This takes us back to the earlier issue of security in this chapter. Almost all of us have to bond—to achieve acceptance and intimacy—with someone. If the family home has not been a place where one feels loved, valued, and competent, then a substitute experience has to be discovered. A second "family" has to be created. That is usually the peer group, and the price of admission is conformity to the rules of coolness.

Coolness is not evil in itself. To some extent, all of us try to be cool throughout our lives, or at least until we reach a point of such personal confidence and freedom that we care little about other's opinions (and that may be a danger of its own). Men usually wear neckties for no reason that makes sense to me except that it is cool. Women take note of prevailing hemline levels, wear or don't wear shoulder pads, and adopt certain colors for makeup and accessories. Why? To be cool, of course—only we use the word *stylish* for *cool*.

Coolness is at the root of social integration. It provides a language and a vehicle for us to engage one another, and a reasonable amount of conformity and adherence to "group think" in styles is not bad. A mother or father knows they're in white water, however, if a reasonable amount turns out to be an obsessive amount.

The challenge Mark and I faced on the floor of his closet was really a matter of coolness. It was only the first of many that we would work with as the teen years came.

One version of sixth-grade coolness meant that boys and girls should already be pairing off for a twelve-year-old version of a date. Coolness meant going for a first kiss, and, within a year or two, coolness meant sexual experimentation to whatever extent a partner would permit. This pressure to experiment was not only generated by boys, but increasingly initiated by girls. It was, as I said, a matter of coolness.

This is why Gail and I had looked downriver at this kind of social white water and determined that dating in our family would not begin until about the age of sixteen. The principle of foresight meant that we had to sit down with our son and our daughter when they reached their twelfth year and say something like this.

> *The day is soon coming when you're going to want to go on a date. Your mother (or father) and I need for you to know that group activities—well planned and properly chaperoned—are terrific. But single or double dates aren't going to happen until about four years from now. And we're not going to be open to overnight functions where there are both boys and girls. So don't put us under the pressure of caving in to a choice you've already made because we're not likely to change our perspective simply to save you from some sort of embarrassment because you didn't check with us first.*

What had brought Mark home with such joy that day had been the fact that he was considered cool enough to be invited to Cape Cod. He wasn't thinking *principle* as his mother and dad were; he was thinking *coolness*. What he heard when I impulsively refused permission was: my mother and father are standing in the way of my social integration and acceptance (although I doubt that he used those words) not to mention my fun.

I had to make a decision there on the closet floor. Was it possible that the principle could be better taught by compromising and letting him go, or should I bar the door and remain unwilling to negotiate? Would I win a battle in our relationship and lose a war?

This no-dating policy was difficult to hold to during the years of junior high school. What made it so was the fact that so many of our children's friends *were* permitted to date and *were* permitted to go on "overnighters" that involved both genders. The stories began to abound about experimentation and then steady use of alcohol (later drugs). Unfortunately, not a few of these friends came from religious families. We discovered that there was little solidarity among many parents because all of us wanted our children to be cool, too.

It took many, many repetitive conversations and occasional artful compromises to hold to this principle. What we learned as time went by was that more than a few other young people were dating and enjoying it less and less as time went on. Not ready to control emerging sexual drives or to resist group persuasion to drink and use drugs, and not yet fully prepared to live by internal convictions or values, they often found themselves in situations that turned out to be destructive.

Sixteen (or really about fifteen and a half) came quicker than anyone realized in our home on Grant Street. When the "dating season" and extended peer activity began, it went rather smoothly because the young man or woman who left our home for the evening to join someone else went with a confidence that they did not have to prove themselves to be liked or accepted.

Only a policy based on foresight, looking downriver, made this dimension of our family's life relatively smooth. Mistakes? Of course. Many. But moments of frantic worry, feelings that we had all lost control of our family destiny? Not many.

# TWELVE

## IN OUR FAMILY
## WE STICK TOGETHER

*There's no place like home if each family member understands the necessity of laws, convictions, and values.*

THAT DAY Mark came home from school with his great Cape Cod plan, Gail and I did not realize until it was too late that we were in white water with him. Looking back on that afternoon, I haven't the slightest idea how we could have known what was about to happen. He presented us with a surprise, but surprises come with regularity in any home where people (parents or children) have lots of energy and many dreams. It's just that we were . . . well, surprised.

Initially, I botched the Cape Cod surprise badly. I jumped to conclusions, didn't listen, wasn't monitoring Mark's feelings and hopes, and generally avoided the use of judgment: all the things that sometimes unwise parents do. I took refuge in rules. Mark didn't ask permission before he committed, I concluded, and besides, we didn't approve of mixed groups of that age going away for a weekend. So it was simple: he couldn't go.

As I said, you can't live a surprise-free life in a family where people are being encouraged to think, to make choices, to explore, and to engage both the opportunities and people in their worlds. That means that a people-building parent needs to develop an increasingly effective "surprise strategy" as his or her children grow older.

Handle surprises with calmness and wisdom, and everyone becomes more confident, more at ease, and less afraid of the problem-solving process the next time. The result? People do a bit more growing. But if we react to surprises in panic or with rigidity, as I did at first, the probability increases that everyone will just stop asking. They will instead choose more deceitful ways to pursue their goals or just stop attempting new things. I do not like these alternatives.

There in the closet, I am in the dark, sitting on the floor next to Mark. We have yet to speak. I think about how to better manage a white water experience that I've mismanaged so far. Better judgment demands equal time. I have yet to consider the possibility of a reasonable exception to the rules. I've not yet asked whether this is a time to suspend rules in favor of a learning experience.

What is Mark thinking as he sits beside me?—this sixth-grader son of ours, who wants a shot at being part of a group, at having the weekend of a lifetime (so far), and at being trusted by his parents? Does he think that I am arbitrary? That I enjoy short-circuiting fun? That fathers (or mothers) exist only to make life miserable? Probably, he thinks all of the above.

Mark deserves to be treated with dignity and respect, I remind myself. He needs to know that he's at least going to get a hearing when he wants to do something unprecedented. While I may have to say an occasional parental no, I must make sure that our relationship is strong enough to handle the stress of resulting disagreement and conflict. I do want him to believe there are occasions when I can say a risky yes, and there are times when he must be prepared to accept a safety-driven no.

What this means is that in each white water experience I have to know whether I am dealing with a *rule* or a *value*. *Rules* are nonnegotiable; they cannot be broken. *Values* are operational principles, open to interpretation and testing. There should only be a few rules. But there can be many values.

If the Cape Cod weekend comes under a blanket rule (and that was my initial instinct), then it's simple. Mark can't go anywhere overnight with a mixed group, no matter what the situation. Or, if I say that he can never go anywhere unless it's with a church group, then I had better make sure that the quality of the experience with the church group is decidedly superior to another group. I'm not sure that's always adequate criteria.

When we began to learn canoeing, the first thing we determined was what the rules would be. Can a canoe turn over in the middle of a quiet, lazy river just three feet deep? Absolutely!—if someone stands up and waves to a friend on the shore. Canoeing-rule number one, we learned the wet way, is that one *never* stands up when out on the water.

Obviously, families need rules for living together—rules that are probably few in number but inviolable in observance. The parent who does not believe that encourages an atmosphere of constant uncertainty and reaps a grim result. He or she should expect an unstable home life in which there is little order and constant strife. Good behavior and long-term growth cannot be built on parental forcefulness or impromptu procedures made up as we go along. That is common sense.

When I look back on the rules that governed our family, I discover that they fell into two categories: laws and convictions.

*Laws* are those matters of behavior that were not open to interpretation. We did not dream them up. They are given to us in the Scriptures by God himself. Laws are the inviolable forms of behavior that everyone has to learn or face serious consequences. The ten laws God gave Israel on Mount Sinai are applicable for any family, and they formed a foundation for behavior in our home. If we broke any of those biblical laws, and there were some sad occasions in which one or more of them were broken, there was usually a very painful consequence.

*Convictions*, on the other hand, were those standards of conduct that the family decided to maintain because we believed them to be right for us. Certain convictions or standards may differ from person to person, or family to family, and we can't afford to look on in judgment of other homes. We're responsible to formulate those principles that will provide the environment for maximum growth in our home.

Some laws? Let me mention a few. Take the regard for truthfulness, for example. Respect for truth is something that should be established at the very beginning of childhood. It was an issue that God said was important when he first confronted Israel with his plan for righteous living.

My youth was marked by the emphasis that my father placed upon truth-telling. In my earliest childhood years, he made it plain that lying would be matched with the severest of punishments. Truthfulness, on the other hand, would be enthusiastically affirmed, and it would result in trust building in our family's relationships. I soon found out that my father meant what he said. It was better, I learned, to own up to bad behavior than to attempt a cover-up. The man had a way of finding things out, and improper behavior, compounded by lying, was the ultimate family crime in our home. If such an occasion arose, "the book" was thrown at me.

I'm glad my father pressed the issue of truth. I came to realize later in life that I had a propensity for not being transparent about my true feelings, my real motives, or my actual opinions. More than once when I have been tempted to deceive myself or others, I have heard the firm voice of my father in childhood, admonishing me to be truthful. With few exceptions, I have heeded the rule, and when I didn't, there were grave results.

By the age of five or six I had no doubt that truth telling was a rule of paramount importance. Trust developed between my father and myself, and that became a valuable asset.

I think, for example, of the day someone set fire to the underbrush in an empty lot near our home. Firemen with their water hoses soon arrived to extinguish the fire, and right behind them came the police with lots of questions. Someone pointed the finger of suspicion at me saying that I'd been seen earlier in the day with matches in my hand. It didn't take long for the policemen to try to pin the blame on me, and for a six- or seven-year-old, that can be a harrowing moment.

I remember—I vividly remember—my father taking me aside and saying, "I'm just going to ask this question once; think carefully before you answer: did you have anything to do with starting that fire?"

My no was all that he needed. He never asked a follow-up question. He didn't demand proof. My word was sufficient. He informed the police that I was not guilty, and they resumed their investigation. Later in the day, another boy confessed to the arson, and I learned the inestimable value of establishing credibility and building trust.

I think my father was a foresightful man when he set the rule of truth-telling in motion. You could say that he was looking downriver with a set of rapids in mind—like the day of the fire—when he knew that the power of a person's word would be enough to solve the problem.

We "codified" some other basic laws for family relationships. One of them was respect for those in authority—one's elders and those who fill special offices beyond the home. There are people to whom all of us must learn to submit: teachers, law enforcement agents, spiritual leaders, and people with special knowledge.

Don't confuse respect for authority with a suppressive environment. We tried never to squelch responsible disagreement. In fact, we encouraged it. We did move quickly to suppress the use of sarcasm, ridicule, or what we came to call "back-talking." We wanted our children to learn that after an issue has been defined and opinions heard, a judgment has to be made. And it would be made by whomever is in authority at that moment.

Respect for authority can be one of the most thorny situations in family relationships where there is a divorce and children are making periodic (even weekly) visits to the home of the other parent. If one of the parents, often motivated by a desire to gain affection and intimacy with a child, permits great laxity here, everyone will suffer. The parent attempting to develop an orderly life suffers. The child, who later must learn the hard way that authority is a part of reality, suffers. Finally, the permissive parent loses, as he or she ends up losing the respect that was so badly wanted in the first place.

Even in the sadness of a divorce situation, separated parents must define and mutually pursue a set of laws—including this one—that are taught consistently and enforced, no matter where the child is at any moment.

Foresightful mothers and fathers—who find themselves sitting in the stern of this metaphorical canoe we've been talking about—establish this law early in family life. If there is both a mother and father in the home, each demonstrates to children that disrespect for the other parent is intolerable. One might hope that each relationship and conversation is carried on in an attitude of respect. Parents respect each other and model it by the way they speak to and treat one another. Should it be added that children deserve respect from their parents also? This precluded, nothing will have been learned by all the other actions.

In our Grant Street home, obedience was a third law, which grew out of the first two: truth-telling and respect for authority. We put obedience high on the list in our home because we knew that there might be potential moments when automatic obedience might be the thing that would save a life. We believed that in the earliest years, a child should be taught to obey his parents as a reflex. The Bible makes that plain.

While we always believed that parental directives ought to be rational and reasonably explained, we didn't believe that obedience should ever be tied to the question, Why? It seemed obvious that as a child grew older, we parents would have to engage in greater explanation of decisions. But, in the earliest days, it was important that a child learn to obey, not because there was a reason, but because a mother or a father had made a judgment.

Some parents reject this notion. To require blind obedience, they suggest, is to hinder a person's ability to make a good decision on his own. But obedience is based on the concept that the one in authority is in control for the child's good. If we are not first taught to obey our parents, we will never learn how to obey God or other necessary authorities in our lives where we work or live.

To all of this we added a corollary: delayed obedience is really disobedience. It was a response to a human tendency that our children inherited from us, I'm afraid: Never respond to "authority" until you are really sure that it means what it says. We found ourselves saying things twice and three times or more. More than once we ended up counting: "I'm going to count to five, and if you are not . . ."

A bad habit formed in the house on Grant Street. Certain people learned that until a matter was mentioned three times, there was latitude to do whatever one wanted. And until the count reached four and a half, one could relax.

"I need to tell you guys something," I said one night at the table in the kitchen. "Mom and I have come to understand that delayed obedience is the same thing as disobedience. So from this point forward, when we need for either of you to do something or stop doing something we're only going to say it once. And if we are confident that you've heard what we said, we're going to assume disobedience. We're not going to wait; we're not going to repeat; and we're no longer going to count. Does everybody hear me?" Everybody did, and so I asked them to repeat the principle: delayed obedience is disobedience.

There was a test of wills on this principle for a short while afterward. But we made the principle work, and the quality of life in the house on Grant Street took a great leap forward.

If obedience has been given a high priority in the earliest years, it becomes less and less necessary for a parent to restrict his children through sheer command in the later years. They will have been provided a basic order of life upon which they can build independently as they mature.

There are other basic laws of family life that are inviolable, but these three seem most significant. If basic laws—and there are not too many—are established, the foresightful parent will have defused about 85 percent of the classic bad family experiences.

### VALUES OR CONVICTIONS

Another set of positive controls parents use in the family experience can be called *operating values* or (an older term) *convictions*. These are principles that guide choices and decisions.

Among the values that we adopted in our home on Grant Street was the principle of loyalty: loyalty to God and the people of God and loyalty to our family. That affected, for example, our normal schedule for Sundays. With few exceptions (and the Cape Cod plan was an exception) none of us would make any plans for a Sunday morning that would take us away from worshiping with our congregation. And on Sunday afternoon, we felt strongly that time should be spent on quieter matters, preferably at home. Our conviction was that there was something called Sabbath, which meant rest and reordering of life. While we would not turn it into legalism, we pursued the

Sabbath as a principle borne out of loyalty to the Lord and the people who loved him.

The value of loyalty has other applications to the family. We believed that God had brought us together and that we owed a certain faithfulness to each other, no matter what the situation. We might disagree energetically with one another over issues when we were together. But when one of us was in trouble, we would stick together. Our children found out the importance of this value in a multitude of ways. When they faced an emergency, a crisis, a pressurized situation, I think they came to know that one of us in the family would do our very best to come to their support. One such example comes quickly to mind.

On the big day that Mark was to take his automobile driver's test, I had left the house early for a breakfast, promising to return in time so that Mark and his mother could take the car out to the testing station.

But somehow, I became confused about the time they were to leave the house. I arrived back home more than thirty minutes after they were to have left for the appointment.

The house was empty, and when I checked the garage, it was obvious that they had felt compelled to go on without me and had driven off in our battered red pickup truck. The motor vehicle station where Mark was to take his test was more than thirty minutes away. I drove the distance as fast as I could.

As I arrived, I saw a sight I will never forget. Our pickup was just exiting the parking lot of the station. Mark was at the wheel; the state inspector was at his side. That much was normal. What was abnormal was what was in back, in the open bed of the truck. There was Gail, tight-lipped and white-faced, very well dressed, and hanging on as tightly as she could.

Mark stopped as soon as he saw me. Soon we had switched vehicles and the driver's test proceeded in more respectable transportation.

"What in the world was going on back there?" I asked Gail when we had a chance to talk.

"It's very simple," she said. "Massachusetts law says that a third party has to be in the vehicle along with the person being tested and the inspector."

*But*, she explained, the third person cannot sit in the front seat. And the pickup has no back seat. So the inspector took one look at the truck and said to Mark, "I'm sorry, but according to law your mother cannot ride in the front seat so you'll have to come back in another month when we can get you on the calendar again."

"Wait," Gail had said, "can I ride in the back of the truck. Is that legal?"

"I can't see anything wrong with it, ma'am," he replied, "but you're rather well dressed," he went on, noting Gail's dress and high-heeled shoes. "Are you sure you want to ride around town in the back of a pickup looking like that?"

"Sir," Gail replied, "in our family we stick together. And if that's what it takes for our son to get his driver's test today, then I'll be happy to ride in the back. All you have to do is help me get up there."

And that's when I arrived with the car that Mark should have had in the first place. Gail had been prepared to ride all about the town while Mark made all the required turns, backups, and parking maneuvers.

"In our family, we stick together." It had been a lesson in loyalty, and Mark never forgot it. (Gail never let me forget it, either!)

One school year Mark was preparing a project that required him to rise extremely early each morning for a week. It was an opportunity to share a hardship. He learned a lesson about loyalty and support by the way his mother or father arranged to get up with him and keep him company as he worked through the dark hours of a winter morning. Such responses as this that flowed from the conviction that our family would stick together established a pattern that has borne fruit in later years. In a time when Gail and I felt enormous stress and pressure in our lives, it was Mark and Kristy who, operating out of loyalty and love, became our strongest supporters.

We tried to engender the conviction that, as a family, we would work together in coming to the aid of people who were in trouble as well as those who simply needed to receive hospitality. When guests came to us, it was assumed that each of us would take on added responsibilities to provide the warm welcome we believed God wanted us to give. If someone in the community needed our generosity, Gail was good at figuring out ways the children could have the joy of participating in whatever our family decided to do.

We thought it important to establish some convictions concerning standards of personal living. Financially, we decided to live beneath our income level and to resist the temptation of indebtedness for purchases other than a home. We believed in tithing, or proportionate giving, and we taught the children that a certain percentage of anything they earned should be set aside for the purpose of generosity. We "high-profiled" Gail's purchasing system (coupon collecting, sale monitoring, fad resisting) for the children whenever possible. Today—many years later—it's pleasing to see our adult children and their spouses perpetuating many of these fiscal values in the development of their homes.

We believed in values that pertained to the handling of alcohol and tobacco, the wasteful use of food, and the pursuit of good health. It seemed important to teach the virtue of personal orderliness and neatness, even if we were not always successful.

Wise parents occasionally inventory their convictions and values. They sit down and ask themselves, What are the central convictions about living that we are trying to transfer to our children in this phase of their lives? How are we doing in the process of that transference? Is there a need for an evaluation session (like the one about delayed obedience)? Are our sons and daughters seeing those values in their parents' individual and mutual life-styles, or are there conflicts between what we say and what we do? Should we consider any new family values? Are we able to discern ways in which our children are picking up these beliefs and absorbing them into their ways of living?

Is going to Cape Cod a matter of a rule, or are there values to be applied here? Mark has broken a rule: permission before commitment. But I also have a conviction. A person can only grow if there is an element of risk; a person can only learn his limits by testing them; a person can only discover the full value of his own belief system when it is pressed into action in difficult circumstances.

The great Cape Cod plan that Mark brought home that day could have been easily squelched. I had him by a rule. But there were values that were also important, important enough that I was willing to suspend the rule.

Yes, we were in white water that day as we sat in the dark on the floor of Mark's closet. Looking back, I know it was a key moment. When I opened my mouth to speak to our son, I could only trust God that the judgment I was about to make would pay off handsomely in an escalation of our mutual trust and his development. I'm thankful that God smiled on the decision.

# THIRTEEN

# THE BRADDOCK AVENUE PROCEDURE

*There's no place like home if the people in charge believe in a learning process that challenges children to mature in their ability to make responsible choices.*

GAIL and I turn to leave the earth-toned bedroom that had been "headquarters" to our son for twelve years. I take one more look around at the distinguishing marks: the scratches on the door from the basketball games, the hairline crack in the wall, the discolored carpet in the corner. It hurts me to close the door to this room where our firstborn lived most of the years of his young life. But I know that life is dynamic; it must move on; good-byes are part of the routine. Thus, we are always leaving special places behind, while we carry with us the memories of the experiences and, if we are wise, the lessons learned.

If there was one lesson played out in that room that the Cape Cod story had taught us, it was that people-building parents, charged with the responsibility of keeping the family dry in white water, have to be foresightful people. They always have to be looking downriver, identifying the approaching rapids and the routes through them. Foresightful parents do that; impulsive parents wait until the pressure is on and then do the best they can. But it is often not good enough. It concerns the application of rules or laws that are carefully thought out and communicated. It centers on the teaching of convictions and values and how they affect our choices and relationships. People building in a home means that this practice is always going on. How does it work?

Years ago, my mother looked downriver in my life when she practiced what I sometimes like to call the Braddock Avenue Procedure. The procedure was people building at its best: a parent making a rule, later modifying it into a principle, and then teaching it so that another person could apply it for himself.

When I was a small boy, my family lived in a home on Braddock Avenue in Queens, New York. It was a street of high density traffic, and mother made it clear that I was not only prohibited from crossing that street, I couldn't even go near the curb. You can call that a rule. She made it sound like a law.

I could only cross Braddock Avenue when she held my hand and we walked together. But the time came when Mother began to modify the rule. It began the day she took my hand and told me to look both ways and tell her when there was a good time to cross. When she saw, after a few experiments, that I could make a good choice, she began to allow me to make the decision as to when we both could cross.

Another phase in the Braddock Avenue Procedure came the day she stood at the curb and told me when I could cross alone. We advanced further when she stood close by and simply monitored my decision to cross the street. We were really moving ahead when she stood on the porch of our home (we called it a stoop) and simply observed from a distance. The day came when the Braddock Avenue Procedure was altered by permitting me to cross any time I'd requested permission ahead of time. The rule was abolished some time later, as I became older and more responsible. I was then free to cross the busy avenue any time I wished.

This is people building: a foresightful parent using rules

when they make sense, shifting to principles in the wake of growth, then offering freedom of choice when there is maturity. Then the teaching process has been completed. Almost every phase of growth in a family should follow the outline of the Braddock Avenue Procedure.

In the house on Grant Street, Gail and I launched a lot of Braddock Avenue-type procedures. There were procedures about the use of matches and the lighting of fires when our children were very young. Later, there were procedures concerning the telephone, the television, the spending of money, going out with friends, and (much later) using the family vehicles. In each case the procedure began with tight rules and ended with maximum freedom of choice. Lest I convey a wrong impression, I don't think any of us thought of our home life as an endless, bureaucratic list of rules and procedures. These were natural teaching processes in the relationships of parents and children. They demanded our consistency and our mutual determination as a father and mother to see them through.

For single parents, or married parents who gets little or no cooperation from a spouse, what Gail and I pursued together may seem like a great advantage, and it was. Theirs is a difficult, a very difficult, situation as they face children with hard decisions and unpopular procedures, which sometimes create turbulent moments. Difficult as it may be, single mothers or fathers cannot delay the process of foresightful thinking and choice-making. If they do, they risk the possibility of losing control of the people-building process.

As we thought through these procedures that led to growth and development, there were several things we had to keep in mind at all times. I'm not sure that we had them figured out in the same way that they are listed in this chapter. Somehow we were always aware that there were certain things we had to master: things to know and do if people building was going to happen.

## MASTERING THE CONTEXT

In our home *context* meant carefully considering the personal history, temperament, and present situation of our children as individuals when we had to set limits or ask for a certain kind of behavior. This was a primary principle when a child asked for permission for something, when he or she deserved punishment for an offense, or when he or she presented any kind of problem needing a family solution.

I remember watching a man employ this principle of context one year at a family camp. While we were visiting together, his wife came to tell him that she strongly suspected that their six-year-old had taken fifty cents out of her billfold. When she thought back through the morning's activities, it dawned on her that he must have carefully plotted the theft. On the way to the dining hall he had asked her to wait for him on the path while he returned to their room for something he said he'd forgotten. He apparently used that moment to rifle through his mother's wallet. When she asked, he denied any knowledge of the missing coins. It now appeared that the seriousness of stealing was compounded by lying.

An impulsive parent probably would have searched for the child, badgered him into a confession, and doled out punishment. Or, worse yet, an impulsive parent might have reasoned that fifty cents is a ridiculously small amount of money to be excited about. How many people would notice, much less care, that it was even missing? In this case, the matter would have ended as nothing more than an annoying memory.

But my friend was not an impulsive parent, and I listened as he and his wife talked the matter through before they acted.

First, they decided that they had something about which to be greatly concerned. What their son had done could not be overlooked or excused. They were dealing with a law. Stealing and deliberate lying are significant matters and must be named and confronted. Then, they tried to discern the reason why a child who had never stolen before would do so on this occasion. Call that discussion an inquiry into context.

In any person's theology, stealing is a sin, but it is often important to know *why* the sin occurred. Were there conditions that *prompted* it? Conversely, were there conditions that could have *prevented* it? Christian teaching proposes that any of us can fall into almost any kind of sinful act if we do not avoid exposure to temptation. That suggests the importance of asking ourselves, before judging a child guilty, what were the conditions of temptation that led to an act of defiance or wrongdoing. Call that mastering the context.

That's what my friends did at family camp. As he and his wife discussed the background of the situation, they asked themselves why their boy would go to such lengths to obtain a small amount of money. Then it occurred to them that most of the children in the camp, with the exception of their son, had received allowances from their parents to spend at the camp store. Probably he had been hurt as he saw his camp friends purchase candy and other items at the store while he was unable to do so. When he had asked for money earlier, his mother and father remembered that they had refused, supposing that spending money was unnecessary at camp. In so doing, they had inadvertently created a condition in which stealing became a temptation. The offense was his—there was no excuse—but they contributed to the context of the offense by making a decision not to provide spending money as other parents had done.

My friend took all of that into account when he confronted his son with what he knew. He shared with him that he had become aware that other children had money and were spending it; that his parents had made a mistake in not allowing their son to have some spending money; and that he could understand why one might be tempted to take a few coins from Mother's wallet. Could this have been the case? he asked.

When the child saw that his father understood the situation even more clearly than he did, he confessed that he had stolen the fifty cents.

Punishment was administered because stealing is a serious matter, a behavior that needs to be named and rebuked at an early age. But the conversation that surrounded the situation was salted with the admission that the parents had also made a mistake. Later, after the sin had been dealt with, father and mother settled on an allowance and how it should be used for the duration of family camp. Life was then resumed in an atmosphere of forgiveness and restoration. A good procedure replaced a bad one.

We must master the context of the matter and the background of the person involved if we are going to put good procedures into place. As an individual, each child must be evaluated based on his particular needs and weaknesses. A foresightful parent does not formulate a procedure until he or she knows all of this.

## MASTERING THE GROWTH DIMENSION OF DECISION MAKING

You could say that the second criterion for foresightful procedures involves the future tense. Where will this procedure eventually lead? Or, what is the *long-term growth potential?* Just about every page of this book says one thing: the foresightful parent is not a baby-sitter. He or she is part of the process in which a human being is being sculpted to maturity. The chiseling process may at times be painful. It may even appear at times to be out of line with the intended finished product. But a sculptor knows what he is creating even if no one else does. He is patient and deliberate. His work is based on the future.

Gail and I found it necessary to have repeated conversations with our children, reminding them that certain procedures would not always appear to them to be reasonable. We didn't expect them to see the logic of everything that we asked of them. That was because in those days they thought only of the present. But we were looking downriver (way downriver), trying to think of the future when our children would be a husband and a father, a mother and a wife. We wanted to set procedures in motion based on the results we hoped to see twenty years later.

As a prep school student, I ran track and cross country for a remarkable coach. Marvin Goldberg was a follower of Christ and believed that all athletics were aimed at the development of character and integrity. Year after year, he turned out championship teams and individuals. More important, he turned out men and (later) women whose adult lives were shaped by many of the learning experiences he created for them on the track.

I often recall a decision I made to leave the cross-country team in my senior year so I could—as I wrote to Mr. Goldberg during the preceding summer—"enjoy a few months of fun before I graduated." Cross-country—ten and fifteen miles a day in training, five miles each weekend in competition—was painful, unpleasant, and too demanding, I told him.

When he responded to my letter, Goldberg never denied that what I said about the unpleasantness of training was true. What he went on to say became a learning milestone in my life. Using my own words, he informed me that as I grew older, many issues I would face as an adult would also be "painful, unpleasant, and too demanding." Sooner or later, I would develop a pattern of response to such situations. I could acquire the habit of quitting or I could learn to bear the pain and inconvenience, doing the hard things anyway for the good of those around me. He warned that dropping out of a team sport where I was needed might set in motion a pattern of quitting or escaping that would hold me captive for the rest of my life.

To return and to master something that I didn't want to do—and to do it for the good of the team—would be to exercise a more important and healthy pattern of discipline and determination.

Like my mother, Marvin Goldberg was taking me to something like the curbside of Braddock Avenue and teaching me the procedure all over again. This time: how to make choices and decisions in the relatively easy moments so that I could grow to make harder choices and decisions in the tough moments later in life.

I followed his advice, and more than three decades later, Goldberg's character lesson based on his desire for my long-term growth still sticks with me. Having returned that year to run with the cross-country team—painfully and unenjoyably, I must admit—I have since faced almost every inconvenient situation with a similar mental determination that began those days on the running course: "I did it then; I can do it again."

Mastering the growth dimension means that parents are taking the future into account when they act. Their choices relate to what a child is becoming. That's because thinking must be long range—downriver. Sometimes it's a lonely perspective.

### MASTERING THE RELATIONAL IMPLICATIONS

Establishing family procedures must include the relational implications of how other people are affected by who we are and what we do. People-building parents begin in the earliest years to point out to children—in the words of poet John Donne—that "no man is an island." Everything we say, do, or have affects someone else. Our decisions, our exercise of personal rights, the pursuit of our goals cannot be conducted in a relational vacuum. The negative issue, of course, is selfishness.

Gail and I now live in a large apartment building in New

York City. I am often reminded that more than a few people have never built this relational principle of consideration or sensitivity into their value system. I realize this when I am awakened at three in the morning by someone's stereo playing at top volume in another part of the building. They are oblivious to the effect of their selfishness upon other sleeping residents.

The apostle Paul was eloquent about this subject. He reminded young Christ-followers that they should be careful not to be "stumbling blocks" for one another. He was saying that some decisions are bad because they do not take into account the effect they have on others—even if they are good for the person making the decision.

Watch children at play in the neighborhood or on the sidewalk in a city. Some are cruel with their words, criticizing and bullying others into submission, ignorant of the effect on the victim's self-esteem.

The person who has grown up to dominate people, exploit them, or use them for his own purposes in business or community politics is often a product of a home where life was never evaluated based on what is good for all concerned. A lack of such training leads to a kind of "default ethic": win at all costs; get in the first punch; what's in it for me; and take no prisoners.

These default ethics often become the basis for adult behavior, playing itself out in places like Wall Street or Capitol Hill. Suddenly the playground behavior that only hurt one or two in an earlier day now affects whole companies, if not nations.

MASTERING THE EXCEPTIONS

Establishing procedures for growth must make occasional exceptions, such as the kind I negotiated with Mark on the closet floor. Question: are we flexible enough to let out the rope on occasion to test our children and see if they are able to make their own decisions? The foresightful parent believes in laws and convictions, but he or she is never needlessly rigid.

We faced this principle the day our children asked about going to see a movie that had an *R* rating. As usual, social pressure was on; everyone was going to see it. But the *R* rating was a violation of a family conviction, and the normal answer would have been to say, "No way!"

Gail and I talked about the decision for some time. We felt it might be time for an exception because the film—although carrying an alarming rating—had some redeeming qualities that might provide benefit. We finally agreed that this could be a learning experience, and proposed a solution.

We would go with our children and see the film together so that we could talk about it later. The kids agreed, and there was great excitement and anticipation at venturing into such "forbidden territory." A few days later we all went, and it turned out to be one of the better decisions Gail and I made.

The learning experience was a success, but our kids were also repelled by the film. The violence that had drawn the R rating was shocking, and both of our children had a difficult time getting to sleep later that evening. In the process, they had come to understand why our family normally drew a line—a conviction—about *R*-rated movies. From that time forward, as long as our children remained in the age frame where we asked to approve the choice of movies they went to see (an early phase of a procedure), there was no further argument over the rating issue.

We had a similar experience with the use of tobacco. Since a large (but thankfully dwindling) percentage of our population chooses to ignore the obvious facts that link smoking to cancer, few children can avoid being curious about the experience. Early in their childhood, we told Mark and Kristy that they were welcome to try smoking a cigarette anytime they wished to satisfy their curiosity—as long as they would do it in our presence.

That time came during a family camping trip. It was the moment for an exception. We went to a general store nearby, and I purchased the smelliest unfiltered cigarettes I could find. That evening around the campfire we opened the pack and allowed them each to light a cigarette. At first they laughed at the ease with which they could puff and blow out the smoke. The fun lasted until I suggested that they do things "right" and inhale the smoke. Once was enough. Even though the light about the campfire was dim, one could not miss the fact that we suddenly had two green-faced children for whom the romance of smoking had been extinguished. The rest of the package was never used, and our children apparently resolved the smoking question for the rest of their lives.

We had a similar experience later on with a small taste of beer with the same results. Drugs, of course, are another matter. To be sure, one does not solve all the problems of dangerous choices and actions through the controlled experimentation we conducted about the campfire. But perhaps the point is this: if we understand the art of the occasional exception, we increase the matter of trust (that Father and Mother may indeed know best on most occasions), and we build a fellowship with our children in the search for truth and value rather than an adversarial relationship, which all too often exists between the generations.

Exceptions cannot be made on every issue of conviction. Exceptions can never be made on the laws of God. My mother could not make exceptions in the Braddock Avenue Procedure until she was sure of my competence to handle matters responsibly. The consequences of a bad choice on that busy street were unthinkable.

There are times when a parent must be sensitive enough to

know that he or she must loosen the lines and give opportunity for experiment and experience. Perhaps it is wise for the canoe to be allowed to tip in quiet waters in order to learn the proportions of disaster if it were to capsize in white water.

There are foresightful parents, but there are also impulsive parents. Jacob, the biblical father of twelve sons, was an impulsive parent, and he paid a heavy price on several occasions. One dramatic encounter came on a long overland trip when his daughter, Dinah, was raped by Shechem, the son of a village chieftain in the area where Jacob was living temporarily. The Bible says that Jacob did nothing at first until his sons returned from tending the cattle. Apparently having no game plan of his own, he allowed his sons to take the situation into their own hands. They had no long-range or relational criteria by which to make the decision either. When they finally moved into motion, it was only for vengeance. In a violent confrontation, they killed every male and plundered everything of value in Shechem's village.

Only after it was all over did Jacob decide to offer a value judgment: "You have brought trouble upon me by making me odious to all the inhabitants of the land. . . . My numbers are few, and if they gather themselves against me and attack me, I shall be destroyed, both I and my household" (Genesis 34:30). Hardly a version of the Braddock Avenue Procedure!

Does one need to say that this is hardly people-building parenthood? That is hardly foresightful leadership. Is this not a parent acting by impulse, permitting things to get out of control? No thought in the early phases of this episode about laws, convictions, consequences. No foresightful decisions; no growth.

The door to Mark's bedroom is closed now. Today, many years later, I look upon the man who, once a boy, lived in that room. I love what I see. I'm thankful for the decisions I see him making as a husband, and it's clear to me that the company for which he works puts faith in his judgment also.

Where did these traits I so admire in him today get their beginning? In places like that earth-toned bedroom, of course. When? Well, on days like the one where he and I spent time in the dark on a closet floor. We each learned that the procedures we'd developed out on the water worked equally well in other parts of life. We'd learned the laws and developed the convictions; we'd looked downriver to see what was coming so there were few surprises; and we made some choices about the appropriate ways to do things. Now sometimes you do your best and still get wet. But it's likely that on most occasions, you remain dry and enjoy the voyage.

*It would be so easy, God,*
*To make the simple, decisions*
*That convenience, the desire*
*To be liked,*
*And momentary peace*
*Dictate.*

*But just as I withdraw the hand*
*That offers pain, adversity,*
*And exhaustion, You remind me*
*That one never learns, never grows,*
*Never blooms when things are easy.*

*Teach me, therefore, God*
*To think with eyes and ears,*
*To brood with a heart just like*
*Yours—*
*That sees things in the scope*
*Of Eternity's process: what makes*
*People become like your Son,*
*Christ.*

*The ecstasy of this one moment—*
*When simple decisions bring*
*Temporary tranquility—*
*Is not to be compared with the*
*Maturity of all the tomorrows*
*Through which we must live.*

# PART VI

## The Family Bathroom

# FOURTEEN

## THE BATHROOM

🙶 *There's no place like home if parents make effective use of the common routines of life to reveal themselves as models of healthy humanness to their children.*

THE HOUSE on Grant Street was built in a day when most American homes had one bathroom. Later, newer homes featured convenient bathrooms on each floor or in every section of the house. Of course, in large parts of the world even our one bathroom would still be considered a luxury.

This final tour of our Massachusetts home brought us to the doorway of that one bathroom, and for the last time we looked in upon its compact arrangement of a bathtub, a toilet, and a counter with two sinks and large mirror. "Is there something worth remembering about this room?" I asked Gail.

"Well, there's that pink and black tile that I could never quite get used to," she quipped. "On the other hand, I always enjoyed the huge mirror, and the lighting was great. What strikes you?"

At first, I thought it might be rather difficult to think of a bathroom as a place where one practiced people-building skills. Then, several things quickly came back to me.

Because we were a one-bathroom house, our family had been forced to make several things happen during the "rush hours," from the times of rising in the morning and of going to bed at night. Cooperation was one of those things. In the space of about fifty minutes on any given morning, four people had converged upon that little room to accomplish all the different tasks one does in a bathroom. Some of them one prefers to do alone. That meant that all four of us had to take turns, be considerate of others who were waiting, and know when some bathroom chores could be done in concert with others.

"Dad, come on: open the door and let me in. I've got to get moving," was a familiar plea from outside the bathroom door.

"Honey, are you reading the paper in there?" was another.

"Daddy, let me in; I won't look."

"Hello in there: did you fall in?"

It was in this room that we also communicated. While shaving I was apt to learn the details of last night's date from Kristy who stood at my side flossing her teeth. Or Gail might debrief Mark concerning his expectations of an encounter with a girlfriend later that day. Standing at those mirrors, Gail and I heard all sorts of stories. Like the kitchen, the bathroom was sometimes a public square of family activity. More than once the whole family (I mean all four of us plus the dog!) found itself in that bathroom while someone related an important story.

May I be frank? The bathroom was also a place of transparency and vulnerability. While we were careful to respect each other's desire for privacy (and this increased as our children grew older), there was also a degree of healthy familiarity. Conversations between two people who are in their night clothes or their underwear are quite likely to be unassuming and intimate. I mean: what's there to hide? We were real people with one another in that small bathroom, and that was one important key to the relationships we built.

There were certain rules that went along with shared bathroom activities. No one threw cold water on the person in the shower. The integrity of toothbrushes was respected. The toilet was flushed and the seat put down. Empty toilet paper rolls were replaced. During "rush hour" everyone had to be prudent in their use of the hot water.

We associate bathrooms and bedrooms with privacy and intimacy. They are also places where we learn about personal life from one another. People building in the home implies that there is a parent (or parents) who is committed to opening up his or her life at the right time so that the younger ones can understand what is normal and what is mature in life. I have this feeling that around the bathroom our family gained some of its most powerful insights about how human beings live with one another in peace and cooperation. None of us would have gotten off to the larger items of the day's schedule if we hadn't made harmonious trade-offs of bathroom time in the early morning hours.

That's why I now see the bathroom as symbolic of some important matters of people building. Lots of routine things between people happened there. We earned influence with one another; we lived our most private lives around that room. It was about that place that we were most likely to reveal our inconsistencies and hypocrisies. It was also a place where our incompatibilities showed. The bathroom was one of the key places where we earned our right to be heard and respected.

If we'd had more than one bathroom, the family would have spread out. Each of us would have practiced a more private portion of life in silence and solitude. Many of the finest conversations and the best memories would never have happened if the one bathroom in the house on Grant Street hadn't been our meeting place every morning.

People building demands this bulk time in which good things are likely to happen if people cooperate and consider one another. Later on, when you need to communicate on a very serious level, it is the time of openness with one another, built up on a daily basis (in places like the bathroom), that pays off.

Mordecai is one of the Bible's outstanding single parents.

And he reveals the fruit of a life lived in deep personal communion with Esther, his stepdaughter. Esther became queen of Babylon in a strange set of circumstances. Her story in the Old Testament book that bears her name is a remarkable account of how one person can provide the leveraged influence that literally saved the lives of thousands of people. While she was the agent of deliverance, it was her single-parent stepfather who deserves a large share of the credit. It was he who influenced her life, from beginning to end.

Every day Mordecai walked in front of the harem to learn how Esther was and how she fared (Esther 2:11). Esther had not made known her kindred or her people, as Mordecai had charged her; for Esther obeyed Mordecai just as when she was a child in his home (2:20).

The moment of truth came in Esther's life. She faced a decision as to whether or not she should enter the presence of her husband, the king, and confront him about certain political matters detrimental to the interests of her people. It was Mordecai who provided the motivation and the courage to make the right choice. After years and years of implanting valuable advice and counsel into her life, the payoff came for Mordecai at this moment. She knew her stepfather to be trustworthy, a man whose finger was on the truth. She listened—as always—when he said: "If you keep silence at such a time as this, relief and deliverance will rise for the Jews from another quarter, but you and your father's house will perish" (4:14).

These verses and the story that hangs between them focus on a man who sets a demanding pace for Esther's courageous performance. He got positive response from her in the crisis moment because he had taught her the force and value of his wisdom in her early years. It was instinctive for Esther to listen and trust Mordecai. In the same way, an instrumentalist pins the success of his solo part on the conductor by playing in careful response to the director's beat.

This influence undoubtedly came because the two had accumulated long hours of life together. Out of the bulk of time spent came the creation of trust that stood them both in such good stead in the later years.

What Mordecai effectively accomplished eluded another man, perhaps also a single parent, who faced similar opportunities. Unlike the first, this second experience of parenthood ended in disaster. In a time of national anarchy, Eli, the priest at the tabernacle of Shiloh, came as close as anyone to enforcing moral order among the people of Israel. Somehow he didn't plan ahead, and his two sons began to betray every ideal for which Eli stood.

At a time when most men should have been turning the family business over to the offspring, Eli received a disquieting visit from an angelic messenger. His sons, he was told, were simply unfit to fill his priestly sandals at the tabernacle. Their years of apprenticeship were filled with moral corruption, graft, and exploitation. Face it, Eli—because you've avoided it until now—your boys have blighted everything they've touched. The tabernacle leadership will have to go to other, cleaner hands. The country needs your two sons, but since they've chosen such a pattern of behavior, forget it!

Where did Eli go wrong?

> *Now Eli was very old, and he heard all that his sons were doing to all Israel, and how they lay with the women who served at the entrance to the tent of meeting. And he said to them, "Why do you do such things? For I hear of your evil dealings from all the people. No, my sons; it is no good report that I hear the people of the LORD spreading abroad. If a man sins against a man, God will mediate for him; but if a man sins against the LORD, who can intercede for him?" But they would not listen to the voice of their father* (1 Samuel 2:22ff).

That paragraph is depressing. The futility of Eli's relationship with his boys is even more remarkable when you set it in contrast with Mordecai and the responsiveness of his step-daughter, Esther. There are several things worth noticing in this tragic account.

First, note the word *heard*—used twice. The verb should have been *to know*, but it wasn't. Why did Eli have to hear about his sons' life-style from outside sources? Why didn't Eli know when the family tempo slowed up at Shiloh? To make things worse, he appears to have faced his sons with this rebuke only when he was an old man and they were adults. In other words, he'd let this thing escape his control for years. No wonder the paragraph ends telling that the boys wouldn't listen to the voice of their father. Why should they? They hadn't listened before. Apparently there hadn't even been a voice as far as they were concerned, and this was no time to start.

The next paragraph records a visit from a special person who confronted Eli with the mess he was in. Eli is given a bit of history. God appointed priests in the past and made sure that they would be well cared for, so they wouldn't have to worry about their own security. Then God asks through the messenger:

> *Why then look with greedy eye at my sacrifices and my offerings which I commanded, and honor your sons above me by fattening yourselves upon the choicest parts of every offering of my people of Israel?* (2:29)

Something leaks out of that statement: it appears that Eli did in fact do some teaching: the wrong kind. Apparently he winked at little overages in the past, small bits of embezzlement when he himself was hungry. Here was Eli in earlier days, saying by his actions, "A little extra for myself won't hurt from time to time." His sons picked up the idea and carried it to the logical extreme. Isn't it a bit ridiculous for Eli to stand before his sons when he is old and rebuke them for something he started through benign neglect of the rules in the first place?

The end of Eli's parenting is indicated in one further

statement from the messenger: "Tell [Eli] that I am about to punish his house for ever, for the iniquity which he knew, because his sons were blaspheming God, and he did not restrain them" (3:13).

God is really saying that Eli knew all the time—at least, in his innermost being—what was going on, and did nothing about it. As a people-building father, Eli was an unfortunate failure.

The bathroom in our home on Grant Street was a place of routine meeting and activity. It was a place where any of us was most likely to be our real selves: moods, levels of self-interest, real appearances. If we could be likable and relational to one another under conditions like that, we were indeed a healthy family, and we could grow as persons under each other's influence. It seems odd to think that maybe this was one of the most strategic places in our history of people building in the home. Perhaps the challenge could have been won *or* lost right here by how we lived together in the routine.

# FIFTEEN

# THE POWER OF WORDS

*There's no place like home if each person respects the power of words and thinks carefully about the impact they can have upon other members of the family.*

COMMUNICATING with one another: in spite of the natural obstacles of the generations, the genders, the temperaments, the momentary moods, and even the unattractive, dark side of ourselves that are prone to cover-up and deceit. There is hardly a greater challenge in family relationships than this: one person sending a message to another that will be heard exactly as the sender intended. Messages of affection and approval; messages of concern and rebuke; request and command messages that have to happen in any home.

When Mordecai sent a message (was it a request or a demand message?) to Esther, he gained an instant reaction. Why? Because the two shared a common language built upon earlier years of intimate give and take in their home. There was power in Mordecai's words, and Esther had learned by experience that when the man spoke, it was beneficial for her to listen.

Words have an awesome impact. They can build, or they can destroy. I've often heard people speak of memories of the sarcastic, cutting words of a mother that could reduce any child to tears. Or memories of the voice of a father who once dominated and demeaned: the same result.

If there is a parent in a home who is prone to an easy loss of temper and who pours out uncontrolled streams of belittling sentences, the result may be a child whose personhood is crushed for a lifetime. Words that explode at an impressionable moment can shape a personality, leaving an indelible mark that may never be erased.

Elsewhere I have written of a forty-year-old man, Tom, who in conversation once allowed me a look into the inner recesses of his life to see what made him what he is. Today he is a man who regularly works himself into exhaustion and who spends every dime he makes for the impressive luxury items that signal a modern view of success. He is volatile—his temper explodes at the slightest hint of disagreement or criticism. As we talked, I asked him to tell me about his childhood.

At one impressionable point in his boyhood, when my friend apparently displeased his father with his way of doing a task, he heard, "Tom, you're going to be a bum. You know that? You're not going to amount to a thing; you're a bum."

Tom told me that he heard variations of those words over and over again when he and his father clashed. The words burned their way into his spirit so deeply that, like shrapnel embedded in flesh, they were never far from consciousness.

Thirty years later, this man still suffers from his father's verbal malpractice. Those phrases he once heard relentlessly drive him to prove to his father that he was wrong. Even though the father died long ago, this bad memory presses Tom to try to prove to the dead man (and maybe even to himself) that he is not a bum.

No one seems to be able to convince him that this is a foolish waste of psychic energy and painful to his family. Let anyone criticize Tom, suggesting that he is deficient in some aspect of his life, and hostility, defensiveness, and furious energy are unleashed to guard against what he senses is a resurrection of the old accusations.

Not a few children are extremely sensitive to what they hear from their mother or father. What seems like an incidental remark from an adult can be a crippling blow to a child. An impulsive comment suggesting the possibility of something in the future can sound to certain boys and girls as outright promises, whose fulfillment will be expected with great anticipation.

There are some of us who can remember painful parental encounters that happened fifty years ago. Question the parent about such a memorable moment, and there is liable to be no recollection at all. But the child—now an adult—has never forgotten. Tom's story witnesses to that.

Because we respect the power of words, Gail and I learned to play a game to help us. The game is built upon the knowledge that what we say and how it is heard are often two different things—especially when it comes to communication with children. A parent, large in comparative size, looming over a child, with a booming voice, may have no idea how intimidating, how fearful he or she sounds to a small child.

Our "unnovel" game is based on a scale of one to ten. Gail will comment, "I think you said that at a *three*, but you were heard at an *eight*." That's her way of telling me that a small expression of irritation about something may have been perceived as the words of a very angry man.

This game, played now in our home for many years, has done much to help us learn how to shape our words so that they more accurately express what we want each other, our children, and others to hear from us.

*Clarity of speech between the generations and certainty of meaning were two very important principles of communication we pursued.* Perhaps we were sensitive to these issues because we believe that words are major tools in the people-building process. So being precise in what we said to one another and being sure we spoke in absolute sincerity and honesty were significant matters to us.

The importance of verbal clarity in family talking cannot be overemphasized. To me that means the choice of right words and right tone of voice and right facial and body language matters greatly.

Compare the subtle difference between these three statements when a parent attempts to initiate action:

"I want you to be in bed by nine o'clock."

"I think you should be in bed by nine o'clock."

"I'd appreciate it if you were in bed by nine o'clock."

Any of these three statements is valid if it is matched with the right listener. A younger child is probably going to need to hear the first of the three. The more mature the child, obviously, the softer the direction-giving. Eventually, the time comes when a habit pattern on an issue like this is established and no instruction at all is needed.

Clarity and precision of words are not always the hallmarks of parents in their verbal communications with children. Parents often fail by choosing concepts that are not clear to a child. We must ask ourselves if the child can do what we are asking him to do at his age.

A son or daughter is asked to clean up a bedroom. "Come on, get your room cleaned up; it's a mess." The child putters around and takes thirty minutes to do what appears to be nothing. The parent keeps repeating the same command, getting louder or more shrill each time.

But the child may have a rough time knowing what the standards of a clean room are. At what state of picking up will the room turn from the status of "a mess" to being "picked up"? That may be an easy conclusion for an adult, but it will certainly be a puzzle for a four-year-old until he has developed a series of adult-like standards for himself. How will a parent know if his direction to the child has been followed? Does the child have a clear picture of what a "picked-up room" is?

None of us, especially a child, ever warms to a task when the objectives are ill-defined and perhaps beyond our ability to perform.

I can hear a better conversation that goes like this:

"Bobby, the way you've left your room is unacceptable to me. I want every book and toy put away in its place. I want your bed made exactly the way you've been taught to make it. And I want your floor completely swept—even under the bed. Do you understand what I'm asking?"

A time limit is also important for young children, and it's part of the ground rules. Time, like words, means different things to different people. Time moves slowly for a child; it flies for an adult. Forgetting this, it is easy for a parent to expect a child to regard the value of time just as he or she might. The difference in perspective is enormous.

It was in the bathroom area of our Grant Street house that we first assigned daily chores to our children. Mark was to straighten towels, empty the wastebaskets, and vacuum the carpet just outside the bathroom door. Kristy was to clean the two sinks and empty the dishwasher down the hall. These were measurable chores, and in terms of time, they were to be done by breakfast.

Even that much specificity was inadequate, and at first there were many occasions when the children were slow, and breakfast came later and later while we lost our patience trying to get one another to finish what seemed to me to be simple little tasks.

The timer on the stove became the solution to the problem. We gathered the family for a talk. The children were informed that we were weary of raising our voices in order to scare them into action. Each morning, we said, we would set the timer for thirty minutes. When it reached the zero mark and the bell sounded, job time was over. During the half hour neither Gail nor I would speak about chores at all. At the zero mark we would all sit down to eat. The timer would be the judge, and if work was incomplete, there would be a consequence—possibly an earlier bedtime that evening.

We never had to interpret time and deadline again. The stove timer took care of everything. The clock was ruthless, and the kids discovered that they could not ask it to be lenient, to slow down to accommodate their moods or whims. Needlessly harsh? Probably not. Their parents have to live according to certain requirements of the community. The children also need to be structured into a kind of system. One day these children of ours would have to learn to respect the issues of responsibility. Almost everyone has to live with deadlines in work and quality standards of that work. We were just giving our children a start.

Clarity was an important principle in family talking. But so is another matter: certainty. When we talk to our children, do we mean what we say?

Small children become astute—outdone only by their older brothers and sisters—at making accurate assessments as to whether or not a parent really means what he says.

"John, I want you to go to bed," a father or mother says. John grunts a bit, but does not move. Four minutes later: "John, I told you to go to bed." The child's grunts now become English: "Oh, all right." This stalling tactic is worked to perfection after accumulated experience. John hardly breaks rhythm with what he is doing. He knows that the certain sound has yet to come. Everything so far is uncertain and inoperative.

"John!" (The parental voice is now raised several dozen decibels.) "I said get to bed." John is now motivated to move toward the bedroom. Why? Because he has heard noise levels that he has come to understand better than words. In John's home volume is the scale of seriousness. Words spoken with soft sounds are uncertain; words loudly spoken mean business. If John is bold enough, he might have the temerity to say as he leaves for the bedroom, "All right, you don't have to yell at me."

But he knows and acts in a way that proves that his father and mother do indeed have to yell. That is the system of communication they have developed. And it's not healthy.

John's sister, Karen, also has the communications system figured out. When she hears, "Karen, supper is ready; I'd appreciate it if you'd wash your hands," Karen gives a feminine version of her brother's grunt. A few minutes later, Karen's mother becomes aware that she did not respond. "Karen, I thought (apparently even she is not so sure now) I told you to get your hands washed." If the parental voice is angry enough, Karen may be on her way. But the odds are that she will not head for the wash basin yet. She has learned to wait for a special temperature of heat to be turned on. "Karen! (This is mother's third salvo.) I'm going to count to ten, and if you aren't in there . . ." The old counting method: it provides a child with ten seconds before a response is needed. Somewhere between six and eight the heat reaches a point high enough for Karen to move. It was not a question of knowing what mother wanted. It was a question of how seriously she wanted it.

All of us at times want to resist authority as long as possible. We often find ourselves seeking the loopholes, the excuses, that make it possible to avoid whatever leaders are asking us to do. Children are not an exception. Most of them instinctively drift from dead-center obedience as far as a lazy parent allows. Wise parents are constantly monitoring the time it takes to get a response from a clear-cut communication. When drift and delay set in—and they will in the best of situations—they have to be regarded as serious and in need of repair.

We found ourselves having occasional family meetings about this issue in the house on Grant Street. One of us would usually say:

> *We've become increasingly aware that you guys are putting us off when we speak to you about something and that you really don't give us your attention until we've shouted or*

179

*given several warnings. We can't accept that! Neither of us likes shouting, or repeating ourselves, and we're not going to count. I suspect that you don't care for it either. So because we all probably agree on that, I'm going to suggest that we push the reset button and return to the "first-time" system.*

*In case anyone doesn't remember, the rules for the first-time system are as follows: I'm going to say a thing once; if I'm sure you've heard and understood, I'll not repeat myself. If I see that there's no reaction to what's been said, there'll be a consequence. Now do you all understand the plan? Why don't each of you play back to me what you've just heard. And start with the problem that prompted this meeting.*

When the "first-time" system is implemented and a test-case arrives—as it will—there is promised performance. You can be sure that everyone will be watching to see if the mother or father who initiated the first-time system meant what was said.

This is a relentless process in the early childhood years. Recently, Gail and I were dinner guests of a couple who had two daughters, three and four years of age. When we came to their apartment at 7:30, the girls had already been fed and dressed in their pajamas. They were told that they could stay up until we arrived. That implied a specific, measurable point in time when bedtime would start.

Company can be exciting, and the girls quickly began to compete with one another for our attention. We could all see that, with their emotions rising, they would have a hard time settling down to bed in the wake of their excitement.

I watched the father take control of the situation. "Girls, we've said hello to Pastor and Mrs. Mac. Now it's bedtime. We're going to read our story, say prayers, and go to sleep."

The girls protested. They tried the old trick of wanting another round of kisses and hugs, even from us; then crying; then the old need-a-drink-of-water routine; then the but-I'm-not-sleepy protest. On more than one occasion in the past I've seen fathers or mothers simply give in to this subtle manipulation, not wanting to be embarrassed in front of company (don't we all want to seem the perfect parents?). Not this time.

Minutes later the girls were quiet. As the mother worked in the kitchen doing the last-minute preparations for our dinner, one of us said, "Your husband certainly knows how to cut through resistance and get the girls headed for bed. Does he do it often?"

"Not really. But when he takes over like that, the girls hear a fresh voice, and they're more responsive. When you have to do it night after night like I usually have to, you get tired of pushing and tend to give in more and more to their little schemes to stay up just a little bit longer."

I thought of the single mother who lacks a "fresh voice." Seven nights a week without a break! She should not be surprised at those times when she is tired of fighting the same battles over and over again. Yet she must keep telling herself that the clarity and certainty of words, leaving no room for her children to take advantage of her weariness, will pay off years later in the larger issues of the teen years.

The childish resistance to authority and to direction that we saw that evening is a part of the human condition. It seeks to wear down the best efforts of any parent.

If mothers or fathers do not take the issues of clarity and certainty of words seriously, they risk a different kind of parenting pattern emerging that hurts everyone in the home.

Take, for example, *the dishonest parent*—not purposefully dishonest, of course. Dishonesty happens when children begin to interpret our words as wishes rather than directives. A child is asked to play more quietly, to eat in a more orderly way, to wash hands, or—as we've already seen—prepare for bed. There is no follow-up to make sure that what has been asked was done. The result? A child who soon learns that parents don't really mean what they say. "I can do what I want, when I want to do it." A parent may not agree that this is dishonest.

But to appear to be asking for behavior we don't care enough to check up on later is dishonesty.

Is there any of us that hasn't at one time or another seen a parent who has lost control of an unruly child? He or she keeps telling the child to quiet down, but they never reinforce the action. These are the same parents who wonder in years to come why their children, now teenagers, tend to ignore them.

There is a character type I call *the threatening parent.* This is a mother or father who thinks that he or she is giving directions but unwittingly gives choices instead. Words are usually prefaced with the word *if,* as in: "If you don't turn off the TV and get to your homework, I'll take the TV away for the next two days." They don't know it, but they have confronted a son or daughter with a decision. Experience, the youthful mind reasons, may suggest that there is a fifty-fifty chance that the threat and its consequence will be forgotten by tomorrow because Mom and Dad are busy people and tend to live only in the present. "I'll risk it," a child may decide, and he continues watching TV and avoiding homework.

The parent never thought of the directive about TV and homework as a choice, but the child did. Threats can be bluffs, and the shrewd child reads them as a pro quarterback reads defenses. To put it another way, children can calculate the odds of the threatened consequence as well as the most experienced gambler.

There will be times when a son or daughter will accept the consequences of the threat in order to get what he or she wanted in the first place. This becomes particularly true in the teen years. A typical threat: "If you're not home by 11:30 P.M., you'll be grounded for two weeks," may be translated into a choice at 11:15 P.M. when a teenager decides that what he or she is doing is so attractive and exciting that the promise of a two-week suspension is worth the gamble. When the child comes home at 12:15, a parent is faced with implementing a consequence that he may never have wanted to hand down at all, especially if the next two weeks include some activities the parent actually wanted his son or daughter to experience.

The *exploding parent* doesn't understand the ground rules of response either. He just blows up, spewing words in every direction. He has been inconvenienced, embarrassed, or he simply feels defeated because, to use the words of a famous comedian, "I don't get no respect." I overheard two boys talking in the church hallway one day. One asked the other, "What's your old man going to say when Mr. Amsden tells him that you cut Sunday school class." The second responded, "Oh, he'll get mad and tell me off, but he'll get over it pretty quick. I'm not too worried about him."

But some children are worried. They reflect their concern with statements like, "My folks are going to kill me when they hear about this." But the attention is wrongly centered on the explosion, not the building process.

It is sad to hear these exchanges between young people and realize that what they're saying is that their parents are having temper tantrums—little else. They are saying that if they can devise a way to weather the parental storm, they can get almost anything they really want. The exploding parent isn't building a person through clear, certain directives. He is simply causing a mild inconvenience for the child. The child then grows up learning how to do exactly what he wants to do. A mother or father tells the child that he or she doesn't like what the child is doing, but if he can stand the heat, he can go ahead and do it.

The saddest of all uncertain sounds coming from parents is the sound of silence. It comes from parents who are ineffective in communicating with their children. *The silent parent* just says nothing. If we could bring some mothers and fathers into court under charges of malfeasance in people building, silent parents might face some of the sternest charges.

A woman talks with me about her husband, an athletic coach. On the playing field he is superhuman, running back and forth, urging his players with a booming voice, forcefully correcting their tiniest imperfections. He can affirm them with enthusiasm.

His wife tearfully describes his homecoming each evening: an exhausted, almost depressed man makes his way through the door, flops on the couch with the evening newspaper, and is asleep within minutes. He rises only for supper, returning to the couch for an evening of television and beer-drinking. His personality takes on color only if friends who know something about sports come by for a "skull" session on the next week's game. In the meantime, three children are growing up, and he takes little interest in them. He is a sensational coach, but a silent parent.

"Don't bug me. I don't care. Do what you want to do." They are the more familiar verbal sweeps of his fatherly baton. He avoids decision, laughs if the children make wisecracks at their mother during dinner, and turns aside with a groan any comment about their moral and spiritual development. He seems to have come to the point in his life where anything not associated with football is meaningless.

When I get a chance to visit with the coach, I learn that he has never been interested in anything but sports. His father affirmed him and made him feel accepted only when he was engaged in some form of athletics. Therefore, he has developed the habit of thinking that nothing in life is worthwhile unless it has something to do with playing on a team or coaching one. He thinks his wife is a strong woman. She wanted kids, he says; let her work with them until they're teenagers. He can cope with them then . . . *if*, I think to myself, *they can throw a good forward pass.*

My friend, the silent father, may understand the ground rules on the athletic field, but he doesn't know the ground rules for being a communicative parent. He wouldn't be impressed at all if I warned him that he was laying a foundation for his children to hate sports, hate rules, hate men, and even hate him.

*The dishonest parent, the threatening parent, the exploding parent, and the silent parent: what a quartet!* I wonder which one Eli was? You won't find Mordecai among them.

The writer of the Proverbs says, "The lips of the righteous feed many" (10:21). And, "The mouth of the righteous is a fountain of life" (10:11). We can apply the principle of those proverbs to the responsibility of the talking parent as he or she launches words to bring the family to maturity of mind-set and life-style. Let that parent's words always be a fountain of life— not a pit of destruction.

# SIXTEEN

## NO BUSY SIGNALS HERE

🙚 *There's no place like home if parents communicate a spirit of approachability to their children and are cautious to avoid any manner that might be misread as disinterest or scorn.*

HE WAS a tiny tot in a cartoon, and everywhere he turned to find attention from someone in the family, he got the brush-off. Mother was too busy; Dad was preoccupied. In frustration he finally gave up. Looking straight out at the reader, he analyzed his experience this way: "The story of my life is a busy signal."

Busy signals on the telephone rank near the top of my list of everyday irritants. That pulsating tone filling my ear seems to be an insult. Although I try hard not to, I sometimes take it personally that someone is not eagerly awaiting my call—and my call alone.

Of course the technology has provided an alternative to the busy signal in the answering machine. And some businesses, knowing that busy signals drive callers to competitors, provide computerized answering services: "We're sorry for the delay. Please do not hang up; your call will be handled by the next available agent." Then, music and occasional reminders to hang on while you wait.

Many children hear busy signals in the modern home. Sometimes they are handled like the sophisticated answering machines at the office: "I'm sorry for the delay. All parents in this home are tied up right now with other priorities. Why don't you play video games until your interests can be handled by the next available mother or father."

Typical busy signals can be heard in every home or apartment. Some begin with the words, "Not now; later," or "Wait until your dad finishes the . . . " or "Can't you find something else to do?" or "Ask your mother," or "I'm awfully tired right now."

I didn't have to do research in a hundred other homes to find these. They were phrases I used more than once.

More often than not, the first conversations of the day in the house on Grant Street happened near the door of that one bathroom we all shared. Standing side by side at the mirror, brushing hair, shaving, tying a tie, or putting makeup on a zit, we talked. These were the conversations that might continue on and off throughout the day when we intersected on other occasions: at the table in the kitchen for evening dinner or in the bedroom when we were saying good-night. How important it was to keep on talking without busy signals!

Now that we have left Grant Street, I look back on those routine morning encounters and mourn their passing with a deep nostalgia. I wish I could have "bottled" the best of those times so that I could uncork it today and retaste the simple joys of a parent talking with his or her son or daughter about the everyday incidentals of living.

Looking back, I see clearly that we all brought differing agendas to those chance meetings. Our children were looking for answers to questions, assurance that things were OK between us, reports about good or bad things that had happened or that they were anticipating, affection and physical tenderness, attention to hurt or insecure feelings, and companionship.

Gail and I were looking for evidences of struggle, for insight into what they were learning, for some sense of where they were in their spiritual lives, for our own assurance that they loved us and felt secure in our affection for them. We were also checking for storm signals—hints that something was amiss or that they were facing issues too large to control alone.

It would have been easy to avoid those conversations, to squelch the openness that often happened at the bathroom mirror. Pontification, overreaction, sarcasm, disinterest, or simply early morning fatigue: these would have been effective busy signals for our children at any age.

Parenting as a people-developing activity is a time-intensive task. One has to be listening all the time. The image of a radio scanner that is sweeping through all the frequencies in search of signals comes to mind. That is no easy task, especially when children are young.

The key word—at least in this chapter—is *approachability:* that quality better sensed than defined. There is no busy signal. What I have to say will be heard and the needs I have will be treated tenderly, and met, if possible. The question the people-building parent might start with each day is this: Am I approachable today? I fear that there were more than a few times when I wasn't. Why?

A child's needs often appear to be so impulsive—so unplanned in contrast to an adult's more ordered way of living (I make an assumption). I look forward to a quiet evening with a book, and the anticipation of that time has sustained me all day. The children have a different vision. Their wish is to play a new game. I've been planning to spend the evening finishing off the income tax forms, but one of the kids needs assistance on a science project.

Perhaps I've been turning my back on insignificant things all day: advertisements, meaningless conversations, hassles that do not concern me. The screening mechanism of my mind grows more efficient as the day passes, and I turn deaf ears to all but the most important matters. In the evening the children try to break through that screen with things that they find significant but that I do not. They find me dull of hearing and then turn away. "Dad is unapproachable today," they conclude. They hear busy signals turned up to full volume. They hear curtness. They take note of exasperated sighing. They sense a short temper. They conclude that it's wise to stay away from Dad tonight.

The Bible is not very helpful if you are looking for examples of the approachable parent. The only biblical "parent" that has ever impressed me is the heavenly model of parental approachability. I'm talking about God who reveals himself in a fathering role.

When David, the second king of Israel, wished to discourse on the nature of God, he often chose the expressions of a child and his father. When he wanted to express himself on the themes of security, protection, stability and dependability, he found himself talking about God. God was an approachable father to David.

During David's boyhood, it appears he had a less than satisfactory family experience. There are hints that his father, Jesse, favored others of his sons and had little regard for David's potential. One gets the feeling that David felt devalued and alienated, and that he had to fend for himself. The nurture he found in a parental relationship, he found in God.

As an adult, as king of Israel, the issues of life became much larger. David was surrounded by a hostile environment and enemies who sought his destruction. Many people would have loved to see David humiliated, defeated, dethroned, and David felt he could trust very few people. It was in that destabilized condition that David tested the approachability of his heavenly Parent.

When David called upon his heavenly Father, there was no busy signal; God was there. He reminds us, throughout his psalms, that God could be reached and communicated with at a moment's notice. That was David's greatest source of comfort. His God was approachable. What qualities does David find in his approachable heavenly Father? They may be worth a parent's meditation.

Perhaps at the top of David's list was the fact that his heavenly Parent had an open and discriminating ear. David was aware that God had provided a "hotline" between him and the heavenly throne. You sense David's feeling of awe about this in Psalm 8 when he ponders man's relationship to the expansiveness of the universe. Being a leader himself, he could reflect upon the demands that management of the universe would make. As a king, he was aware that he couldn't attend to the intricate and intimate matters of every individual subject in his small kingdom. Yet God did this in his larger kingdom. In spite of the enormity of it all, God is a listener to each of his children. "What is man," David asks, "that thou art mindful of him? (Psalm 8:4)"

"The LORD has set apart the godly for himself," David writes, "the LORD hears when I call" (Psalm 4:3). In other words, God is a listener, and that is the first criterion for approachable parents.

Many of us are not good listeners; we would rather speak. Or we struggle to listen because the filtering mechanisms of our minds become attuned to only those things that seem of importance to an adult. Some of us are not good listeners because we just don't know how it's done. We lack sensitivity to the multilayered methods of communication that most people use, of words, gestures, facial expressions, body posture, timing, context, even carefully chosen silences in addition to a host of other things.

A young father, trying very hard to be honest about the problems he was having with his wife and small children, said, "Look, I'm not a sensitive man. I am discovering that my family tries to tell me things about themselves and their needs, but I am not hearing them. I completely miss what they are trying to say. What am I doing wrong?"

Later, as I talked to him and his wife, it was not hard to see how far apart they were in their communication. When she spoke, he attacked her words as a scholar might evaluate a Greek phrase. In the few minutes I was with them, I was able to note how she communicated in tones of voice, pauses, facial configurations, and gestures of hands or arms. He seemed to miss all of that. I found myself sitting like an interpreter, telling a husband what his wife was saying to him. He is right: he is not sensitive. No one has ever taught him how to listen. If he cannot even understand his wife, his misunderstanding of his children must be immense.

Good listening takes training and discipline. In Tom Clancy's thrilling novel *The Hunt for Red October,* one of the key characters is a submarine sailor trained to listen to sounds deep in the ocean. His ability to locate and identify certain noises becomes one of the dominant themes in the book as submarines chase one another hundreds of feet beneath the surface of the sea. As I read the book and later saw the movie, I thought of him as a picture of the sensitive and approachable listener who is not passive in listening but aggressive: reaching out to seize every signal and concentrate on what it has to say.

Listening takes time, work, and prayer. It does not come by instinct. The best of us will make our share of miscalculations.

I recall a night when I failed to listen to Mark. I was preparing to take a house guest to the airport for his return home. Before we left, I suggested to Mark that he go along with me. He immediately accepted. But as we were getting our coats on, I issued the same invitation to Kristy, which she accepted. Out of the corner of my eye, I noticed a cloud come over Mark's face. I didn't read the signals correctly. I assumed the look was one of pure selfishness, and I was sure I was right when, throughout the ride to and from the airport, Mark remained absolutely silent, almost physically turning away whenever his sister spoke either to him or to me.

When we returned home I asked Kristy to go into the house. When Mark and I were alone I began a lecture on attitude, selfishness, and pouting. And I blew the moment completely.

I quickly learned that Mark's silent message to me had been one of great personal disappointment. What he should have been able to put into words, he could only speak through the symbols of silence and irritation. I found out that he had originally seized the chance to drive with me as an opportunity to talk about some things that were bothering him. He had thought that a conversation between the two of us would be helpful. I'd not appreciated this and inadvertently sent him a busy signal by including his sister in the ride.

It would be hard to do an instant replay of that whole affair and find out how I could have done things differently. Why couldn't Mark have simply said, "Dad, I need to talk with you alone." Why couldn't I have noted his original reaction and given him the "charitable assumption" that what I was seeing was not selfishness or "anti-sister" behavior but rather the only way he knew to express disappointment? Maybe it was an unavoidable problem between two fallible human beings. But it illustrates how we so easily fail one another because our listening skills are limited.

I learned that evening that there are times when any of us are not content to be simply part of a group, even a family group. There are times when we want and deserve prime time with another person, when talking and listening can be private, frank, and nourishing. David seems to be thinking of these sensitive and private times when he wrote of his heavenly Parent: "The LORD is near to the brokenhearted and saves the crushed in Spirit" (Psalm 34:18). And "Even before a word is on my tongue, lo, O LORD, thou knowest it altogether" (Psalm 139:4).

Approachable parents listen for *questions*, the answers to which will shape a child's mind and spirit. It is rush hour and the traffic is snarled beyond description. A voice comes from the backseat, "Mom, what does God look like?" Your approachability quotient hangs on how you handle that one. Is it the kind of question you've been looking for? Then traffic jams aren't going to stop you from conversation one bit.

You're listening to an important football game, and a voice interrupts the concentration. "Dad, how come that guy got thrown out of the game and he's a Christian?" With a question like that, there's no time for busy signals—even if the game is deadlocked with only two minutes to go.

We also listen for the hunger of *affection and tenderness*. A child turns moody and seemingly disrespectful at the dinner table. A parent's impulse might be to reprimand the child strongly and even punish her. But sensing the behavior is a bit out of character, a mother or father suggests that the two go into the child's bedroom for a few minutes. "Your behavior at the table was unacceptable. Now if you're just testing me to see how far I'll go, I'm ready to do something about it . . . now! But if you're telling me that something is really bothering you that I don't know about, I'd like you to share it with me."

The child dissolves into tears, and, piece by piece, feelings emerge. During the past few days it seems as if every judgment call in the house has gone against her. She feels alone. The parent realizes in a moment that it may seem like that. He draws the child close to himself and holds her quietly and lovingly for ten minutes while the youngster sobs out pent-up feelings of frustration and futility. In the hugging and touching is reaffirmation. This was not a time for discipline, and the approachable, listening parent caught the real message—perhaps just in time.

We listen for feelings of *inadequacy*. The child who constantly pesters his parents throughout an evening may be saying, "I have to keep on testing you to know if you really think I'm worthwhile and important." A child insists that he has no desire to read. He claims that he doesn't enjoy it and gets nothing out of it. What he may really be saying is that he's not sure that he's a very good student. An hour spent with a mother or dad reading together just may turn the tide in another direction.

Approachable parents listen for the need of *companionship*. "Mom, would you go to the store with me?" "Dad, would you drive for the Cub Scouts field trip next week?" "Mom, would you sit here for a few minutes while I go to sleep?" These are no times for busy signals.

If we know *what* to listen for, do we know *when* to listen? Again, approachability can frequently be jeopardized by a poor sense of timing. Those of us who have never thought about listening skills may not realize that there are certain times or occasions when valuable things are more likely to be heard.

Bedtimes for small children (and some older ones too) are occasions when guards are down and young people are willing to talk endlessly. To be sure, sometimes the willingness to talk is really a desire not to be left alone or have the lights turned off. Here is where questions are asked, fears unmasked, and deep introspective discussions are held. Children talk about dreams, desires, regrets, and resistances.

Other special times for listening may come when children are sick, exhilarated by some sort of triumph, repentant over something done, or when a parent has one child all to himself for a long unbroken period of time. As children grow older, it becomes possible to plan for times for talking. When Mark and Kristy were teenagers, I found they were delighted to talk about anything I wanted to discuss if we were in the car and *they* were driving.

In the light of this principle of approachability, I have come to appreciate the words of David: "I cried unto the LORD, and he heard my voice."

Our family did a lot of talking. It was important that we

believe in the principle of *unconditional acceptance*. Children and teenagers are far more prone to talk with a parent who accepts them as persons, placing no conditions upon the relationship.

We raised Mark and Kristy in an era when long hair was an issue in many homes. Today it may be earrings, or loud music. Who knows what another young generation will choose as its distinctives.

Some years ago, baseball manager Sparky Anderson told reporters about regrets he had in his relationship with his son. "It was about two years ago," he told them. "I told my boy, Lee, to get his hair cut. It was long and tied in a pony tail. I'd told him to get his hair cut before I came home again. I came home, and it wasn't cut. He was out in the garage, on his knees, fixing his motorbike. So I told him to get it cut, and he said no.

"There was no way I could win. I saw that if I wanted him to cut his hair, I was going to have to get down and whip him with my bare hands. I didn't want to do that. So I just walked away. I cut him off from me. I had no communication with my boy for a year. He talked to his mother, but not to me. I lost my boy."

What Sparky Anderson was saying is that he failed to see the difference between the person and external symbols. He placed the condition of their relationship on a relatively shallow base. What he was really saying to his son by words and action was, fit *my* values; be exactly like me, and *then* I'll accept you.

I'm sure that behind Anderson's thinking was the feeling of embarrassment. He saw a hairstyle as a mark of rebellion, perhaps unmasculine. The long hair, therefore, became a symbol of failure as a parent, or so Sparky Anderson thought.

When the baseball manager reflected upon this sad chapter in his broken relationship with his son, he said to fathers everywhere, "Don't protect your image. That's what I was doing. There was Lee with his long hair, and there I was with my image of short hair. When we argued out in the garage, I told him, 'Someday you'll respect me as your father,' and he said, 'I already respect you.' I didn't understand how he could say that and still have long hair. I was ashamed of myself. I was being the child, and Lee was being the man. I wasn't man enough to father my son."

When Isaac, son of Abraham, grew to be a man, he and his wife, Rebecca, raised two boys. In a day when it was culturally permissible, however unwise, the parents played favorites. Isaac was drawn to Esau while Rebecca favored Jacob. Doubtless, Isaac's prejudice had something to do with Esau's image as a hunter. Rebecca, for unknown reasons, felt much closer to Jacob and was inclined to defend his interests in family matters.

When Isaac, blinded and near death, determined that it was time to pass on the inheritance of family possession and leadership to his favorite son, Esau, Rebecca and the less appreciated Jacob plotted to fool the old man. Jacob was disguised in all of the externals that drew Isaac to Esau: a special menu of hunter's food, an arm dressed with sheepskin to remind Isaac of his older son's masculine physique, and all the right words. Because these disguises were just about the extent of Isaac's evaluation of his children, he was taken in by it.

Isaac's foolishness set in motion family struggles the consequences of which would go on for years—if not for centuries. He made it possible for Jacob to pursue advantage through deceit and deception. Long after Jacob would leave home, the dishonest streak that showed itself first in younger years became a basic pattern of life.

There is a very obvious moral to the story. When a parent judges children by external values and accepts them on that basis, the way is paved for relational dysfunctions, that may last a lifetime. Sparky Anderson figured that out. Isaac died before he could.

Among the many things that parents wish from their children is emulation, respect, and agreement. It may bother some of us when our children begin to prefer things that don't accord with our tastes. Perhaps we are confused when they reject our standards of music for another. As the years pass, we make the painful discovery that their understanding of success may be different from ours. Each of these and many others set off uneasy vibrations within us. We may mistake independent thought for rejection and rebellion. Thus, if we are not careful, we begin to get irritated at our sons and daughters. Conversations tend to concentrate on surface issues, and we begin to make it plain that we are disappointed, even embarrassed over their style and evaluation of life.

Little by little, we wall off large areas of conversational territory that cannot be touched. Before long, like Jacob, our children are lying to us—telling us what we want to hear only to get us off their backs. Or worse yet, they begin to tell us nothing. Communication on deep things is lost because the conditions stayed on the surface.

No book on people building in the home could ever hope to present a formula for knowing how much independence a child should have from the value system of his parents. Perhaps the answer lies not in formula, but rather in prayerful wisdom.

Wisdom—a gift from God—helps us discern real issues, and with it, parents remain open and approachable. They accept their children on the correct basis.

The mother and father whose ears are open and whose wisdom makes them able to accept their children as they are add a final quality to the issue of approachability. Call it *flexible response*. To use another telephone analogy, children are not "put on hold."

It was the middle of the night when Kristy, then a child, called her mother's name. Gail heard her first. "Mommy!" Immediately Gail sprang out of bed and down the hall to Kristy's room. She was in distress. There had been a bad dream, and she was having a rough time sorting out what was real and what was part of the dream.

Why had she called her mother? Because her instinct somehow told her that when equilibrium is in jeopardy, a mother or father can help restore the balance. Her young mind had set up a pattern of response to uneasy situations: call for Mom or Dad; they know how to make upside down things turn right side up again. In obedience to pattern she calls, and, on this occasion, it is a mother's privilege to come. On another occasion, it might be mine.

Suppose that Gail had chosen to belittle the "dumb dream." Suppose Gail had yelled down the hall, "What do you want?" When the report comes back that Kristy was agitated over a dream, suppose that Gail had responded with, "Don't worry about it! Everything will be all right. Go back to sleep."

What would Gail have been saying? "Don't dump your problems on me. Work them out for yourself. Your feelings are immature and stupid; make them dissolve. By all means, leave me alone so that I can get some sleep."

It means a lot to me today that Gail didn't do that. Because we learned over the years in the house on Grant Street that our children's security depended on how we responded to them in their moments of critical concern. I go back to David and his sense of security and read his words, "I keep the LORD before me; because he is at my right hand, I shall not be moved."

I have often wondered if David had some terrifying moments out in the fields while it was his responsibility to care for his father's sheep. When the lion or the bear came, did he cry out for an earthly father's help that was not available? Is that where he first learned about the approachability and the responsiveness of his heavenly Father?

It is in our response to our children that we often set in concrete exactly what they will become. We are the most important people in the world to them for many years. Our opinions are the ones that count the most. Our responses to their first experimental thrusts of independent personhood will shape a major part of their life perspectives.

A young teenage boy dares to share a short story he has written with his parents. Gingerly he brings it to the living room where they sit. The imagery in the story is crude, the words misspelled, and the thought expressed is so naive that to an adult it is really amusing. In sharing his thoughts, the child has laid his or her soul out on the carpet. Here is a crisis of response. The child is making a first tentative attempt to reach out of himself and gain affirmative reaction.

The proper people-building response must be praise. Even if the story is a literary disaster, the very act of creativity is in itself worthy of enthusiastic applause. But some mothers or fathers might dismiss the story with laughter, and if the laughter is cutting and derisive enough, the child may not take up the pen again.

Creativity is a delicate matter, fragile at birth and nurtured by affirmation. Are we approachable by a young person's expression of original and artistic ideas and capacities? We need not be insincere, praising quality where there is no quality. But in the very beginning, high marks can be given for even making the attempt.

Approachability demands flexible response, not only in creative moments, but when things sour also. "Here my cry, O God, listen to my prayer; from the ends of the earth, I call to thee when my heart is faint" (Psalm 61:1-2). David's approach to God, his heavenly Father, was uncowering because he knew God's responses to his struggles were fair and reasonable. Whether he had miserably failed or impressively triumphed, God was approachable.

One day Gail and I heard the crash of breaking glass come from the living room. Running in the direction of the noise, we found Kristy behind a table where she was trying to retrieve a ball. Her foot had caught a cord, and a lamp—one both her mother and I prized—had fallen over. The globe of the lamp was in several pieces. Down deep within me was an impulse of immediate anger. I was ready to give vent to the anger because Kristy had been playing ball in an area of the house where ball playing was out of bounds. She deserved—I thought—what my instincts prompted me to deliver.

But on the other hand, one look at her face told me that it was obvious that she knew she had been wrong. There she knelt, frozen, awaiting our response. I think we both sensed that she was on the razor's edge between trusting us with honest repentance or hardening into a defensive posture of excuses and passing the buck. My anger would provoke her to excuses; my understanding would give rise to her honest acknowledgment of guilt.

Why is it hard to grant to children the same forgiveness we adults so desperately desire when we make mistakes? Must there be punishment for something that is done unintentionally—even if the initial act was actual disobedience? The anger dissolved, and Gail took her in her arms and hugged her. The tears flowed freely, and she expressed her sorrow. She now understood why we didn't play games of that sort in the living room. She came to comprehend something more significant—that her mother and father were approachable when she had made a bad mistake. In the future when the mistakes are even more dramatic, I wanted her to remember our response to the broken lamp. We wanted her to cry out our names instinctively whether it was a bad dream or a bad mistake, knowing that we were approachable and likely to respond flexibly in a mature way.

There is an ironic twist to approachability. The more approachable we are, the more we hasten the day when our children will need to approach us no longer. For as a mother or father listens, accepts, and responds affirmatively, the quality of inner stability and maturity is enhanced. When a child "dials" the number of parents like that, they know there will be no busy signals. They know that caring people are just a call away. It frees them to take greater risks in self-development and acceptance. They grow faster and more wholesomely. And as they mature, they need to call less and less. They work out their own bad dreams; they develop their own ability at self-criticism in creativity. They become independent. But they do so because they know there is a parent out there who never responds with a busy signal.

Unapproachable parents retard growth for a while. Their children seek attention, and due to various conflicting inputs, they do not get it. They search for correction, for affirmation, for stability, and it isn't there. They seek evaluation of their world views, but it isn't available. Children under these conditions mature slowly and often not healthfully. Psychologically and emotionally, they remain children far into biological adulthood. Ultimately, having experienced so many busy signals, they begin to dial other numbers. There is no turning back.

More than a few fathers and mothers have been startled by the piercing indictment of Harry Chapin's song, *Cat's in the Cradle:*

> *My child arrived just the other day.*
> *He came to the world in the usual way.*
> *But there were planes to catch and bills to pay.*
> *He learned to walk while I was away.*
> *And he was talkin' 'fore I knew it and as he grew*
> *He'd say, "I'm gonna be like you, Dad,*
> *You know I'm gonna be like you."*
>
> *And the cat's in the cradle and the silver spoon.*
> *Little boy blue and the man on the moon.*
> *"When you comin' home, Dad?"*
> *"I don't know when, but we'll get together then.*
> *You know we'll have a good time then."*
>
> *My son turned ten just the other day.*
> *He said, "Thanks for the ball, Dad, come on, let's play,*
> *Can you teach me to throw?" I said, "Not today*
> *I got a lot to do." He said, "That's OK."*
> *And he walked away, but his smile never dimmed.*

*And said "I'm gonna be like him, yeah,*
*You know I'm gonna be like him."*

*And the cat's in the cradle and the silver spoon.*
*Little boy blue and the man on the moon.*
*"When you comin' home, Dad?"*
*"I don't know when, but we'll get together then.*
*You know we'll have a good time then."*

*Well he came home from college just the other day*
*So much like a man I just had to say*
*"Son, I'm proud of you; can't you sit for a while?"*
*He shook his head and said with a smile,*
*"What I'd really like, Dad, is to borrow the car keys.*
*See you later. Can I have them please?"*

*And the cat's in the cradle and the silver spoon.*
*Little boy blue and the man on the moon.*
*"When you comin' home, Dad?"*
*"I don't know when, but we'll get together then.*
*You know we'll have a good time then."*

*I've long since retired. My son's moved away.*
*I called him up just the other day.*
*I said, "I'd like to see you if you don't mind."*
*He said, "I'd love to, Dad, if I can find the time.*
*You see my new job's a hassle and the kids have the flu.*
*But it's sure nice talking to you, Dad.*
*It's been sure nice talking to you."*
*And as I hung up the phone it occurred to me—*
*He'd grown up just like me.*
*My boy was just like me.*

Sandy Chapin and Harry Chapin ©1974 Story Songs Ltd. (ASCAP). Used by permission. All rights reserved.

For David, king of Israel, approachability meant intimacy with a heavenly Parent who knew how to talk and listen. David wrote of his special relationship:

*Answer me when I call, O God of my right!*
*Thou hast given me room when I was in distress.*
*Be gracious to me and hear my prayer.*
*O men, how long shall my honor suffer shame?*
*How long will you love vain words, and seek after lies?*
*But know that the LORD has set apart the godly for himself;*
*The LORD hears when I call to him.* (Psalm 4:1-3)

There are no busy signals when the children of God "dial" heaven.

We tried our very best to make sure there were a limited number of them in the house on Grant Street. But I know there were some, and I grieve for those.

# PART VII

## The Garage

# SEVENTEEN

## THE GARAGE—
## EACH DAY IS FISHING DAY

*%* *There's no place like home if parents realize that every moment and every experience—even those that seem trivial or unim-
portant to an adult—provide chances to shape the minds and
character of children.*

I OPENED the door of our one-car garage attached to the house
on Grant Street for one last look. It was an all-purpose area,
serving as a storage place for snow shovels, bicycles, tools,
sports and camping equipment. The little space left over was
usually occupied by that red Chevrolet pickup truck that had
played a key role on the day Mark went to get his driver's
license. I loved that truck, but I lost control of it the day that
Mark passed the examination.

It was in this garage two weeks after he had passed his test
that Mark ambushed me with one of the great landmark questions in modern family life. I must confess that I was not totally
prepared for it.

Mark approached the question by reminding me that he had
plans to take a lovely young lady to the annual "Junior Extrav-
aganza." The class had planned a spectacular evening, he said,
beginning with the six o'clock boarding of a charter boat for a
tour of Boston Harbor. He knew we were delighted with his
choice of companionship for the evening, and he knew that

we'd said we'd help out in any way possible. That was the windup. The next words were the delivery.

"Dad, what do you think about my driving J—— and me in the pickup?"

I was shocked! I'm not sure any parent is ready for that first use of the family car.

After a nervous laugh, I said, "For a minute there, I actually thought I heard you say that you'd like to drive *my* pickup on *your* date next week."

"Yeah, I did."

I paused for effect. Then, "It's too bad that you can't, son." I said it very thoughtfully as if I perceived his idea a thing of beauty but unworkable because of a wonderful Massachusetts law. "But you can't drive without an adult for another six months. That's the law, you know."

I was sure I'd dodged a bullet. I loved my red pickup truck, and of course, I loved my son more. The thought of Mark and my truck and his date (in no particular priority order) negotiating their way through Boston rush-hour traffic on a Friday evening unraveled me. A New York City rush hour? Maybe. But Boston? Never! So there was a certain pleasurable sense of relief when I reminded Mark that his notion was a legal impossibility.

"You're right about the law, Dad. But maybe you didn't know that J—— just turned eighteen last week. She's an adult now. So I'd be legally driving if she's in the truck."

I should have known that Mark would not have raised this subject if he had not been sure that he'd covered all his bases. The bullet I'd dodged had swung back and was aimed at me a second time.

"Bud, I've got to think about this one. Will you give me a day to give you an answer?"

"Sure," he replied, "no problem." He could afford to be generous with patience. At least I'd not said no.

I wasn't too excited about Mark driving into Boston, but I was hard pressed to come up with a good explanation for my feelings. He'd had the standard driver's training course, and he'd passed it with flying colors. Yet, I wasn't prepared to release him to the challenges of Boston driving, and I couldn't say why.

Seeking an easy way out, I picked up the phone that evening and called J——'s father, a family friend. "Don, I have a decision to make, and I thought you'd like to help me make it."

"Sure, Gordon, how can I help?"

"Well, Mark and J—— have plans to go into Boston next week for the junior party. Mark would like to drive our pickup for the evening, and because J——'s eighteen, it makes it legal for him to do the driving, even though he's only sixteen.

"Now, Don, it occurs to me that you might be a bit uneasy having J—— in a car with a newly licensed driver, and before I make up my mind about what I'm going to tell Mark, I'd like to know how you feel about this."

Didn't I secretly hope that my friend, Don, would say something like, "Gordon, forgive my caution, but my wife and I would feel much more at ease if the kids went with someone else." That would make my decision a simple one. "Son," I would say, "I've thought about this matter of the pickup next week, and I don't think J——'s parents would feel good about your driving into Boston so soon after you have gotten your permit. So we'll have to make other transportation plans for the evening." That's what I thought I'd be able to say.

But it didn't work out that way. Instead, J——'s father said, "Gordon, we've known Mark for several years now, and we trust him completely. If you think he's ready to drive into the city next week, I'm sure the kids will have a great time."

These are the times that test the souls of those who want to be good parents. No one was going to make my decision easy. Not the law of the state of Massachusetts, not the young lady who was planning to go with Mark, and not her father who just happened to think a lot of our son.

So the decision reverted to me where it should have been all the time.

The next day Mark and I sat at breakfast. "I've made my decision about the junior party next week," I said.

"I can drive?"

"Yeah, but there's one condition to the deal."

"What's that?"

"The night before the party, you and I will drive the entire route of the upcoming evening, and you'll have to prove to me that you can handle any emergency."

"No sweat. Thanks, Dad."

The days passed, and soon we came to the evening before the party, the evening of our dry run to Boston. I picked an hour that would coincide with the time Mark and J—— would drive to Boston Harbor the following evening.

As we got into the truck, I said, "Now, I want you to remember that our agreement was that you would prove that you can handle any eventuality. So during our drive, I reserve the right to create any emergency I want, and you have to respond to it. OK?"

"OK." Mark started the pickup and we headed down Grant Street toward route I-95.

I-95 is a six-lane freeway known for its serious traffic during rush hour. It was certainly serious that evening. We were driving along the middle lane when I suddenly said, "Oh, oh: you've got a flat tire on the right front."

"No, I don't," Mark said. "Everything feels fine."

"You didn't hear me, Son. On this ride, I create the emergencies, and you respond. If I say you've got a flat tire, you've got a very flat tire. May even be a blowout."

"What do you want me to do?" Mark asked.

"What does anyone do when a tire is flat?" I shot back.

"You pull over and change it."

"What's stopping you?" I asked.

"Are you serious?"

"I've never been more serious in my life."

We pulled over into the breakdown lane, and Mark and I got out. I sat on the guard rail while Mark crawled under the truck to find the spare tire and jack. He was there for several minutes while I sat hoping that no policeman would stop and inquire as to what our trouble was. Things were quickly complicated by a light rain that began to fall.

"Dad," a voice came from under the truck. "Where is the jack?"

"Hey, son," I replied, "I'm not here. This is J—— sitting here, and she doesn't know where the jack is either."

Now it was a frustrated and somewhat embarrassed Mark that crawled out from under the truck. He checked the cab: behind the seat, under the seat, behind it again. No jack. I was enjoying myself . . . as long as the police stayed away.

Finally, Mark looked under the truck hood and found the jack mounted on the side wall. "Do you want me to take it out and jack the truck up?" he asked.

"If that's what it takes to change the tire, I'd favor doing that," I responded.

Only when Mark had proved that he could use the jack and the truck tire was six inches off the ground, did I suggest that we terminate this exercise and get on down the road.

When we reached the off ramp where Mark was supposed to exit the freeway for the harbor, I mentioned that it was a shame that ramp was closed for repairs and that he'd have to find an alternate way to reach his destination, no simple task in Boston.

"The ramp's not closed, Dad."

"I just closed it, Son."

Fifteen minutes later we had successfully detoured to the parking garage, entered and found a parking spot, and headed back out much to the consternation of the attendant who couldn't understand why there was less than two minutes on our ticket.

On the way home, I announced that the alternator had fizzled out, and we sat by the side of the road discussing whether or not a young man and his date should sit in the truck and wait for help or leave the truck and seek it themselves. After that and a few other "emergencies" we finally made it back home. Mark was clearly not entertained by the process, but I was feeling much more confident that our son knew how to handle himself under any conditions that might arise when he assumed responsibility the next evening for his date, my truck, and himself.

This is a story about people development. We build people by permitting them increasing amounts of responsibility and giving them a chance to prove themselves. We allow them to enter situations that are often just an inch beyond what we think they are ready for. Then we let them perform.

In a couple of years, Gail and I would be sending Mark off to college more than a thousand miles away. By then we would have confidence in his ability to handle any situation. He had slowly proven himself to our satisfaction, and we could not have been more delighted.

During those years I came to see that a home can be a school as much as anything. A school of character, of personal manners, of relationships, of theology, and of vocation. It is a school that has no vacations or closings. In one way or another every home offers an education—a good education or a bad one. Mothers and fathers take the place of faculty.

The story is attributed to the biographies of several great men, and that probably makes it, more or less, apocryphal. True or not, it makes a valuable point. It is said that a certain man frequently alluded to a day in his childhood when his father had taken him fishing. The day became fixed in his mind because of the things he learned about his father and about life in general as the two talked together. He never hesitated in saying that this trip had turned out to be the most important day of his life.

But how had his father felt about that day? The son never knew until many years later when he came across the old man's journal and read underneath the date only one sentence: "Gone fishing today with my son: a day wasted."

I have been a son, and now I have been a father. I continually marvel at the contrasting memories of my own father and my children. All three generations often differ as to what things in the past are most memorable and most significant to us today. That's scary! How can I know that what I do or say in the presence of my children will not go down as one of the all-time impressions—for them, a life-changer of a moment—while for me it is forgotten, dissolved in insignificance.

Sometimes I will say to my father, "Dad, do you remember the day I did . . . and you were so angry that you . . ."

"No, nothing like that ever happened," he'll reply. "You've been dreaming."

Or one of our children will be talking and say, "I'll never forget the time we were . . . and Mom and Dad came home and . . ."

And Gail will say, "You've got to be kidding. I can't remember that at all. I would never have . . ."

Every moment in family life has to be treated as having potentially long-lasting implications in the shaping of values, convictions, and quality of personhood. What is incidental to me may have a lifelong impact on our son or daughter.

Family life on Grant Street was an existential classroom, and school was in session for about eighteen years. The children in that classroom were like lumps of clay. The longer they lived, the harder the work to keep them from becoming hard and unpliable. The longer they lived, the more opportunity Gail and I had to stamp into their lives words, convictions, attitudes, habits, and responses that—if they were meritorious—might become a part of their instincts. But, looking backward, the frightening thing is that even if what we had to teach had not been meritorious, a lot of it would have become ingrained in their instincts anyway. Whether we like it or not, each day is a "fishing day." Each day we are teaching in these homes of ours, whether we like it or not.

Teaching, conscious or unconscious, will make an indelible impression upon a child's personality and become part of a composite of future character. The weaknesses and flaws of the parent will be passed on to the children in either case. The questions confront us: do we teach to build or teach to cripple?

Let me distinguish between *attitudes* and *values* and *abilities* and *performance*. The first pair are more often taught by life-style, something we will look at later on. The second—abilities and performance—are more deliberately taught through positive planning of family experience. How does a child discover his or her abilities, gifts and capacities and then put them to work?

One answer might be to think about how many opportunities a father has to ask his children to assist him in family responsibilities. A bicycle needs to be repaired. There are at least three ways to approach the need: The *lazy* father postpones any action. The *busy* one typically grabs a few minutes, quickly runs the bike into the garage, turns a few screws, and delivers it to his child with the job done. The *wise* father adds a few minutes to his schedule and shows his child how to make the repair by sharing the work. He may have his patience tested, but the decision will pay off.

The wise father is perceptive. He knows that several things can be learned in the simple exercise of repairing a bicycle. Diagnosing the problem is something that can be learned, and so is the exercise of selecting the proper tools to use. A standard of excellence can be demonstrated as the repair job goes along—teaching the child how to do more than a halfway job, bringing it to completion. Proper maintenance of both machine and tools can be taught when it comes time to cleaning up. For some fathers, repairing a bicycle can be an hour wasted; not so for the effective father.

One day I watched an aircraft mechanic putting an engine together. We were not in the hangar of a major airline; we were in the Amazon jungle where Christian aviators fly across many miles of treacherous jungle to off-load missionaries and equipment at remote landing strips where they live among and serve Indians. As he torque-wrenched down the cylinder head, I asked him where he had developed enough interest in engines to come out to the jungle and service missionary planes.

"My father loved to tinker with engines," he started. "Every time I turned around he had me out in the garage, fooling around with something he was trying to put together. I think he gave me a monkey-wrench instead of a rattle when I was born." Each day when missionary pilots put their bush planes into the air, they do so with confidence. They have a good mechanic, and he is the product of an effective father who was wise enough to turn his garage into a classroom.

Don't leave this idea of working with tools as an illustration without realizing that a parent shouldn't restrict teaching about home and engine maintenance to sons. This is a place for daughters also. In the house on Grant Street, Gail and I decided that there was no such thing as "women's work" and "men's work." We wanted our son to feel comfortable in doing the domestic chores as life in a home demands. And we wished our daughter to be conversant with the fixing of faulty electric switches, seating a new faucet washer, and changing an automobile tire.

The teaching process is enhanced through the delegation of responsibilities. Children are assigned tasks that reasonably can be carried through to completion. It is wise occasionally to give children projects that are just a bit beyond their normal grasp, something that will require mind-exercising problem solving. Frustration of a creative sort can be a mind-bender; a child needs it. Perceptive parents may drop a hint now and then, but for the most part, there are times when we should leave our children on their own to surmount obstacles and develop the satisfaction of completing a task without assistance.

There aren't many mothers and fathers who can master all skills and arts. That is why we want to expose our children to as many other people and their skills as possible. Tours of factories, art studios, business offices, and construction sites have tremendous value. They provide time together, learning experiences, and wholesome recreation. Looking across the spectrum of activity, children begin to sense their own interests. As they respond with enthusiasm, the discerning parent makes a note to provide extra amounts of opportunity in that direction.

Sharing with children *how* things are done is not enough. Relationships in the context of work are important also. For example, teaching children about the meaning of lines of authority is a significant exercise.

Our children, once twelve and nine, decided to go out on the pond for a canoe ride. As I pushed them off, I reminded both of them that the older one was the captain of the ship; what he said went. I made sure that both of them understood this important rule of the high seas. Canoeing has certain dangers. Therefore, it was important, I said, that Mark recognized that he was in charge. If he said it was time to come in, that was the decision. Kristy faced an experience in which she had to accept her brother's authority and appeal to him if she had a certain desire. In the guise of summer fun, a lesson was taught: how to use authority and how to submit to it for the good of the "ship" and its passengers.

I have watched these two reverse the order of that authority in an occasion where Kristy's knowledge of a subject made her the obvious choice to offer leadership. I was gratified to see that Mark was more than glad to submit to her judgment just as she had once done to his.

We are teachers: we fathers and mothers. When we are driving or traveling on a bus or subway with our children, we engage our children in conversations with simple *why* questions. "Why do you think they have put all those signs up?" "Why do you think the builder made the bridge like that?" "How would you go about making that situation get better?"

*What* questions are also valuable. "What makes that painting appealing?" "What does that cloud make you think about?" Add to your bag the *how* questions. "How do you think people will react when they see that load of wrecked cars in the open field?" "How do you think we could help that lady who looks sad?"

When children have been exposed to various capacities and methods, when they have responsibly carried out tasks delegated to them, when they have shown greater and greater ability to participate in family decision making, the wise parent insures that the challenge will never be relaxed. As children grow older they become more of an integral part of the family's "survival."

On long-distance trips, children can read the map and enjoy the satisfaction of giving directions. If mistakes are made, a few detours will point up the seriousness of shallow thinking and irresponsibility. Entertaining guests can be a chance to let children plan the menu, create innovative table decorations, and assist in serving.

Years ago, I determined that when our children reached sixteen, I would take them on a long journey with the intention of establishing a life-long memory of an intensive experience of intimacy. In both cases I named the destination but challenged Mark and Kristy to be responsible for as much of the planning of each day as possible. We had come full circle: from the days in which their mother and I plotted most of their external worlds for them to the day when they were plotting ours.

Camping provided many opportunities to divide significant family responsibilities in four ways. When the four of us tumbled out of the canoe after a long run downriver, each person knew what he must do first if the family was to have a decent meal, a dry sleeping location, and a private outdoor bathroom.

We came to appreciate in all of this process the nature of the *teachable moment*. Teachable moments are rarely created. They are sensed and seized. The intellect of a child has a door like the entryway of a building. A teaching moment happens when that door has, through some circumstance, been thrown open. A mother or father learns that the signals of the teachable moment vary with each child. For some, the signal is a wistful look on the face. For others, it begins with certain kinds of questions. Don't overlook the "captive-audience" moments at the table, in the car, and in the moments just before bedtime.

When the door to a child's mind is open, he is probably ready for any kind of experience of learning that his parents want him to have. When the door is closed, teaching a child will be like trying to jam things through the crack at the bottom.

No one can ever predict the instant of a teachable moment. He can only train himself to take advantage of it when it comes. The mother or father who makes it a point to put his or her children to bed and to pray with them will often find that those last moments are alive with potential conversation. A child is tired, not too anxious to be left alone, feeling especially tender and affectionate.

Teachable moments also come at times of need. Sickness, injury, pressure to finish some project for school, all provide extra special opportunities for closeness. When the door is open, the wise parent rushes to the entrance with the things a child, later a teenager, needs to hear.

Mark says to me: "I want to have the pickup so I can drive J—— to the party." I am startled by this question even though it was inevitable. When I come to my senses, I see that our encounter there in the garage has opened the door to a teachable moment. We learned a lot together out on I-95 as we changed a tired that wasn't flat, avoided an exit ramp that wasn't closed, and repaired an alternator that wasn't broken.

No day is ever wasted when parents become teachers. Every home is a classroom, and every event is a learning experience. The teachable moments are more abundant than any of us realize. But they don't last forever. If we will not do the teaching, there are others who will. We may not like their curriculum.

Gail and I close the garage door. Today the garage and the red pickup truck are just a memory. But the patterns of responsibility that Mark demonstrated that night live on into his manhood.

# EIGHTEEN

## TAMING THE BARBARIAN

🐦 *There's no place like home if loving but firm rebukes that warn, correct, and build are wisely spoken so that wrongdoing and punishment can be avoided.*

IT HAPPENED one day at the beach. Even though the day was hot, I shivered at the implications of what I saw. An eight-year-old was getting a bit too enthusiastic with a group of five-year-olds in the water. He didn't know his own strength, and what started out as fun was now getting out of control. Moments passed and some of the protective parents up on the sand were getting uneasy. They kept staring intermittently at the parents of the bigger child. Didn't they see what was going on? Couldn't they do something about it before someone got hurt? They had to see what was happening, but they were ignoring it. That is, until things became intolerable. Only then did one of the parents spring into action.

Shrill voice from the mother: "Robert, get out of the water this instant! D—— it, Robert, I'm sick and tired of the way you're acting. Look at what you've been doing down there. Can't you keep your hands off those children?"

The child—nervously glancing sideways to see how many others were taking in this tirade—offered a whimpering response, "But . . . "

"Don't talk back to me," the mother responded, more loudly

than before. "Don't you argue with me; I saw what you were doing, and I'm disgusted with you. Now you sit down on the sand here for the next half hour and see if it puts some sense in your head."

The humiliated child slumped to the hot beach, his fingers beginning to trace lines in the sand, and his eyes lowered so that they wouldn't meet those of the curious children back in the water. The mother turned, picked up her beer, and resumed her conversation with those around her as if nothing had happened. But something had happened: a person's spirit was being crushed.

The key words were "I saw what you were doing. . . . " How long had the mother and father seen what their son was doing? Why hadn't they done something when they first saw the problem arising? At the earlier stage one of them could have made a gentle correction; no one would have been hurt. Why had they waited until the matter had reached crisis proportions? Now, instead of the fun continuing, everyone felt embarrassed or vengeful. The parents' immaturity matched that of their son.

"Fathers [and mothers, may I add]," the apostle Paul wrote, "do not provoke your children to anger [like the parents at the beach], but bring them up in the discipline and instructions of the Lord" (Ephesians 6:4). Too bad the parents on the beach were unacquainted with Paul. Discipline and instruction means that sometimes a parent has to take corrective action with children. But it also means that the correction be done in such a way that it builds or redirects. It does not devastate. It is "of the Lord."

The Bible calls corrective confrontation a *rebuke*, which stands between an ungodly act and its painful consequence. It is the last warning sign given to a person who is headed in the wrong direction, toward the discard pile if he or she does not stop and turn around.

There are many examples of rebuke in the Bible. One of the first and most dramatic was a rebuke given by God himself. Cain, the firstborn son of Adam and Eve, had disobeyed God's instructions regarding the proper mode of sacrifice and worship. When Cain's disobedience was made more obvious by his brother's presentation of an offering that matched heavenly specifications, he began to seethe inside. The roots of murder were beginning to grow within him. The Bible says that "Cain was very angry, and his countenance fell" (Genesis 4:5). That is a way of saying that Cain pouted and plotted ways to vindicate his position.

God offered Cain one chance to defuse the act and the behind-the-scenes feeling. He rebuked him with a question and a statement.

"Why are you angry, and why has your countenance fallen? If you do well, will you not be accepted? And if you do not do well, sin is lying at the door; its desire is for you, but you must master it" (Genesis 4:6-7).

All the fine points of a healthy rebuke are here. The questions forced Cain to face the effects of his sin and willfulness. The statement pointed out the dangers of his trend of action and its consequences. Finally, God pointed out the alternative—the correct way. That is the rebuke of a people-building heavenly Father. Cain rejected the rebuke; the consequences set in; and Cain destroyed himself.

Rebukes uncover cover-ups, and that is what God did. He faced Cain down on his actions and feelings. He would not let actions remain unaccounted for, and he would not permit feelings to fester within the spirit.

Prophets were masters of rebuke, and some of the great scenes of the Old Testament involve prophets standing before kings, providing what one writer cleverly called a reality transplant. When Nathan rebuked David, things were already far down the line. But David got the point, and he melted. Some consequences, however, were already in motion. At least David repented. Ahab never did get Elijah's point; neither did Nebuchadnezzar when Daniel confronted him.

A people-building parent walks in the footsteps of the prophets; he is a "prophet-type" to his or her children, and as such, has a grasp on the proper standards of behavior that the Bible sets forth. Such parents are sensitized to violations, and they are prepared to deal with them before the more painful consequences set in.

A rebuke, properly done, is a difficult thing to administer. It is not always received by the person being rebuked with joy. Witness Cain. Imminent danger was ahead, and the warning had to be issued. A lighthouse says to the ship's captain there are rocks over here. An airline omni-station informs the pilot that the plane is a few degrees off course. An "idiot-light" on the automobile dashboard tells the driver that the emergency brake is on or that the engine is overheating.

But the operator of the lighthouse isn't trying to offend the ship's captain; the omni-station isn't trying to embarrass the pilot; and the idiot-light (despite its more popular name) isn't trying to anger the driver. In all three cases, the messages are for the principal good of the one who receives them. Normally, everyone—the captain, the pilot, and the driver—is actually glad to get the news. There would be disaster if they didn't get it.

Mothers and fathers sometimes get confused about rebukes. All too often, rebukes are launched out of vengeance and anger. A careful examination of my own rebukes tells me that many of them were not designed to build character in the lives of our children. Rather, they were designed to halt certain things that were momentarily inconvenient or annoying for me. Since I was bigger than they were (at one time; things are different now), I could assert myself. Then, I might speak sharply or in anger because I was irritable, or I was tired, or because I wanted some peace for myself. In fact, my rebukes were sometimes not rebukes at all; they were thinly disguised temper tantrums.

That was the kind of parental behavior I saw at the beach that day. The parental behavior was as bad as the child's. These parents were not builders; the child was not being built.

Rebukes build, correct, and warn. "A rebuke goes deeper into a man of understanding than a hundred blows into a fool," the writer of Proverbs said (17:10). If we are sending rebukes that go deep into our children's hearts, then we had better be extremely careful about the nature of those rebukes. Before the effort is made, the people-building parent will weigh the contents, circumstances, and consequences of what he or she is about to say. Can it wait for a more appropriate time? Is it launched off a platform of love, or is it merely a sign of vengeance or irritability? And finally, will it not only center on the bad behavior that is leading to disaster, but also on the proper behavior that should replace it?

Training our children to hear rebukes and act upon them is a major aspect of our parental relationship when our children are young. If we have convinced them that the rebuke doesn't threaten their standing before us, their dignity, and their right to make a new attempt at what they have in mind, they will learn the value of a constructive rebuke.

A ten-year-old boy dissects an old alarm clock in his father's shop. When Dad arrives home that night, he discovers his work bench littered with tools and alarm clock parts. Finding his son downstairs, he explodes, "Son, I'm sick and tired of finding my shop in such a mess when I come home at night. You're not responsible about these things; you're messy and you never finish anything. Don't you realize how expensive these tools are?" A series of outbursts like that may stifle the boy's curiosity, his desire to work in the shop, or his hunger to enter this aspect of his father's world at all.

It could have been a teachable moment, engendered through

gentle rebuke. "Son, I'm delighted that you have had time to take a clock apart today. I'm anxious to hear what you learned about the clock. But what would I do if I had to use these tools right away for another job? Now it makes me excited to see you getting into something like this, and you know that most of the tools are there for you to use. But part of the way we do things here in the shop is never to use something without putting it back. In fact, the job is never done until all the tools are put away. Why don't you share with me what you did with the clock while you clean things up? I'll stay here with you until the job is done."

Curiosity is affirmed; the father's pleasure in the boy's interest in tools is highlighted; and the necessary lesson is learned. That's a gentle rebuke, and it is sure to build in the boy's life.

OK, I'll admit it. There are some rebukes that will be exercised in anger. And rightly so! There are times of injustice and mistreatment of other people and their property, and it happens right in the family. It is hard to think of anger expressed apart from a louder-than-usual voice. But it's worth trying. The anger can be expressed in words, and it should be expressed at the action—not at the person.

Let's make sure that we distinguish between rebuke and punishment. They are two different things. A rebuke is something that takes place in time to help a person avoid drastically paying for his sins. There is still time to stop the trend before it's too late. A father expresses his anger in rebuke by saying, "I cannot accept what you are doing. It is wrong, and it must not happen in this family. It is not the way we are going to do things." No threats; no punishment. Just a signal that there are problems ahead . . . serious problems.

When David was an old man, he paid dearly for his failure to understand the necessity and nature of loving rebukes. When it became obvious that he was not going to live much longer, a power struggle began among his sons. Adonijah, second in line, got the jump on everyone and mounted a rebellion against his father. The writer of the Book of 1 Kings has a poignant comment about what made Adonijah the rebel that he was. The writer laid it right at the feet of his father. "His father had never at any time displeased him by asking, 'Why have you done thus and so?' " (1 Kings 1:6).

Compare the thinking of Paul on rebukes (Ephesians 6:1) with what David didn't do. There is an interesting tension in which a loving warning is given. Paul's view: don't do it in such a way that it makes your child angry and unappreciative of you. David's view: don't ever say anything that may upset or displease your son or daughter. David was dead wrong, of course. Rebukes may displease and disappoint a child for a moment, but he will be built up, and, in the long run, he will be thankful.

Rebukes should be given in private. Out in public the rebuke humiliates, as the one I witnessed at the beach. Also, a rebuke is to be aimed at the behavior of a child, not at the child. He does not have to be held up in front of his peer group as a loser. What he needs is a quiet experience with his mother or father in which he is informed of the destructive trends of his actions and the proper substitute.

Some years ago, Dr. Albert Siegel wrote of children in the *Stanford Observer:* "Respect, decency, honesty, customs, conventions, and manners. The barbarian must be tamed if civilization is to survive."

Call him a barbarian if you please, and in one sense you'll be right. But does that view mean that my rebukes must be stinging, sharp, and surgical as I try to tame the "barbarian" whose basic drive is a rebellious one? I must also remember that children are delicate human beings whom God has placed in our homes to receive training in the matrix of tender loving care. The label stamped upon packages that can easily break says, "Fragile, handle with care." The people-building parent sets out each day to administer correctives to the "barbarian."

But he or she keeps in mind all the time that the barbarian is also fragile: his spirit, his self-image, his personhood must be handled with Christlike care.

# PART VIII

## *The Basement*

# NINETEEN

## THE HOLE IN THE WALL

*There's no place like home if the attainment of wisdom is among the highest goals in the building of people.*

MOST New England homes have basements, and the house on Grant Street was no exception. But since this was a home built by a "do-it-yourself" family, our basement was a hodgepodge of bright building ideas envisioned by the former owners. There was a kitchenette for use when the family canned the vegetables they grew in the large garden out back. There was a paneled recreation room with a fireplace. An attached garden shed, a utility room, and a section of unfinished cellar for storage made up the rest.

The basement had extra-thick walls, and we got the impression that the unusual dimensions of thickness were the result of "deals" that the builders must have gotten on various kinds of odd-sized lumber and paneling. At any rate, this strangely designed and built basement was a fascinating place. Small children found all kinds of spots to play hide-and-seek on a rainy day.

When Gail and I took a final look at the basement, our first comments were about how relieved we were to have gotten it all cleaned out. Large basements accumulate junk. We discovered that fact during the days prior to the mover's arrival. Now the basement was empty, like all other parts of the house.

At first, neither of us could think of anything significant

about that basement except that it had been a place where we'd watched some television, played some Ping-Pong, and wiped up the residue of a few minor floods when the poorly plumbed drains had clogged. Nothing more than that.

As we walked toward the back door of the basement, I noticed a ten-inch hole in one of the extra-thick walls. I realized that I'd not seen the hole before because it had been concealed by a cabinet that had stood there for years. Suddenly, I was curious as to what I might find if I reached inside the hole.

Why I did that, I really don't know. Perhaps I was just concerned that we might not have removed everything that was ours from the house. But when I put my hand in the opening and poked around, I felt something smooth and pliable. I took a hold of it and pulled it out. Gail and I both gasped . . . and then began to laugh.

It was the "white thing"! That's what we had all called it: a small white paddle that had once hung in the hall closet during the years when the children were very small. It had been used sparingly to apply a modest pop on the rear end in early childhood days when intergenerational negotiations had been unsuccessful.

Somewhere along the line, the white thing had mysteriously disappeared, and no one had worried about it because there was little reason to need it. Now, years later, it had reappeared just as we were about to leave the house on Grant Street forever. Gail and I were fascinated. The mystery of the disappearing white thing had finally been solved (at least for us). It was clear that, years ago, one or both of the kids (then about six or seven years old) had decided that the best way to insure that the white thing would never again be used was to hide it. And it had been buried in this hole in the wall behind the cabinet for eight or ten years.

The white thing was more symbol than substance. As we stood there in the empty basement, it reminded us of that necessary people-building dimension in parenting when children have to be energetically trained so that their wills can be shaped to the highest purposes. We loved our children enough to want to forget that there were ever painful moments. But like us, our two were sinners, and the white thing was part of the memorabilia of how we dealt with that fact.

Solomon, writer of many of the Old Testament proverbs, was an enthusiastic proponent of people building. In particular he saw the importance of vigorous training in the search for wisdom and maturity.

"For he who finds me [wisdom] finds life and attains favor from the LORD. But he who misses me injures himself" (Proverbs 8:35-36).

What is this wisdom of which Solomon speaks? It is a capacity for judgment that grows in the spiritual depths of a person, permitting him to use his knowledge, his abilities, and his opportunities in a way designed by God to be fulfilling and satisfying. Give a child such a gift, and you have given a treasure that far surpasses the inheritances of the world's richest people.

If you analyze wisdom's message in Proverbs 8:35, you discover something else implicit in Solomon's view of things. Wisdom is not a natural or instinctive characteristic. We are not born with it. It is something that is first given, then exercised, and finally mastered. Wisdom becomes the operating system (to use a computer term) of one's life. But achieving wisdom is a process that involves experience. And it starts with people building in the home.

The wise person learns self-control. He makes decisions based on long-range perspective. He is sensitive to the real issues of human and heavenly relationships. He understands the purpose of his life and how to use the materials of creation to achieve that purpose. He's aware of his weaknesses and how they can be exploited by others, so he carefully avoids such possibilities. Finally, he knows how to serve people. He hungers to relate to the living God. Who of us would not like to raise children who fit that sort of description?

This then is the question upon which people-building parents must meditate: what does it mean to raise children to wisdom and Christlikeness? How is it done? And when do you know when you've succeeded? Obviously there comes a time when the final product depends upon the will of the child himself. But what must a parent do to increase the chances that a son or daughter will make the right choices and pursue a life of wisdom?

Listen to Solomon again:

> *Have two goals: wisdom—that is, knowing and doing right— and common sense. Don't let them slip away, for they will fill you with living energy, and bring you honor and respect. They keep you safe from defeat and disaster and from stumbling off the trail. With them on guard you can sleep without fear; you need not be afraid of disaster or the plots of wicked men, for the Lord is with you; he protects you. (Proverbs 3:21-26, TLB)*

After reading Solomon's thinking here and other places on the matter, I am convinced that he was telling us that a parent has three important things to give his or her children to provide conditions for the transplant of wisdom. Call them *Solomon's concerns.*

First, he was deeply concerned that we shape that part of a child that acts by custom, habit, and reflex. That is what we might call *training children.* Second, Solomon referred to the necessity of spiritual conditioning, the enlarging of one's capacity to function in a wise and Christlike way. That is what we call *discipline.* Third, Solomon saw the need for corrective action, a way of confronting the child with the consequences of living unwisely. And that we call *punishment.* Develop these functions of people building in a home and effectiveness in living will be dramatically increased.

## SOLOMON'S FIRST CONCERN:
## CUSTOMS, HABITS, AND REFLEXES

Solomon wrote, "Teach a child to choose the right path, and when he is older he will remain upon it" (Proverbs 22:6, TLB). Centuries later the finest minds on university faculties are vindicating Solomon's observation. They are telling us that the seeds of values and choices we hold in our thirties and forties are mainly planted in the first eight years of life and reinforced in the second eight years.

In one way or another, of course, this entire book speaks to this matter of training children in the home. In this never-ending exercise of people building we are creating a complex personality system of values, ambitions, and behavior.

Our friend the physical therapist understands something of the process of people building from a physical perspective when she works with the paralyzed limb of a patient in the hospital's PT section. She has helped patients rebuild useless limbs to activity by constant manipulation and exercise. It is impressive to watch her work with victims of stroke and terrible nerve and muscle damage. She does it in much the same way we train children: constant repetition of certain physical actions.

Something like that happens when we build customs (ways of doing things) in the lives of children. We do so by repeatedly exposing them to experiences like the manipulation program of the therapist. Little by little some things become internalized, automatic, and habitual.

Some examples? Among the first things we train children to do is to sleep at certain times, developing a regular bedtime hour. Then we teach them to recognize and respond to certain family members, helping them develop certain courtesies. And then, of course, we are concerned about the adherence to acceptable bathroom procedures, such as "potty training," when certain muscles are ready to be put to work.

There are many, many more customs we teach without even

realizing we're doing it. Not a few of these are simply taught by our own example. And that means that some customs we inadvertently teach will be bad ones. But good customs or bad ones, we use these tools: example, repetition, affirmation, and reinforcement.

Habits are daily activities that become so commonplace that we no longer have to think deliberately about doing them. They are there because we've done them repeatedly. Orderliness can be a habit if it is put in place within a child's mind early enough. The habit of rising early in the morning is another. Helping around the house, study habits, habits of dependability and consistency are habits we can press into the grain of our children's personalities early in their lives.

Reflexes are forms of automatic behavior that happen in response to situations around us. We help our children to become peacemakers rather than warriors when conflict arises; we train them to hold their tempers when others feel free to retaliate.

### SOLOMON'S SECOND CONCERN:
### VALUES AND AMBITIONS

We train children on an even deeper level when we teach values. By our own behavior and by consistent instruction, we teach our kids how to make wise choices. It is only in the first few years that we can totally control our children's moral environment. After that, we must depend upon the soundness of criteria by which they make decisions for themselves.

In the early schools years, Mark and Kristy were both fascinated by the life of a boy in the neighborhood whose parents wallowed in materialism. In awed tones they would describe the swimming pool in his backyard, the exotic sport cars his father drove, the video equipment spread throughout the house, and the vacation trips to Hawaii and Bermuda. At first I felt defensive because I couldn't provide all of these things that seemed to raise envy in our children's hearts.

But later at a school function I watched the boy whose family had "everything." I saw him stick his leg out to trip another boy who passed by. I saw him hit a girl on the arm. Gail and I took note of how he talked incessantly, tried to be the center of everything, getting attention in any possible way. Then I came to see that while he had everything material his family could provide, he was tragically far behind in the accumulation of wisdom, of habits, and even reflexes that would make him a desirable person in years to come.

In their immaturity, Mark and Kristy had once looked upon this boy and evaluated his life by the flow of material objects and pleasurable opportunities. Gail and I took a look and were dismayed. The kids had seen a form of "blessing" while we saw approaching disaster when the boy would have to fend for himself.

That sort of experience reminded us we had a long way to go in this business of people building in the home. We would know we'd made progress when our children could look at a boy in that sort of life-style and conclude that spiritual and people values were a much greater treasure.

We train children when we help them shape their ambitions, their senses of personal destiny. Training in this dimension is not primarily involved with what kind of careers childern are going to follow when they grow up. Rather, we should think about the sense of responsibility a mother and a father give to children. How can we help children perceive life as an act of contribution rather than an act of accumulation?

Encouraging children to reach out and give help to others may serve to stimulate their ultimate interest in being a physician, a pastor, or a counselor. Directing children's interest toward the fantastic opportunities of discovery in our world may provide direction toward science or engineering. Highlighting our children's creativity may lead them toward a life in the arts. But it all begins with our ability to high-profile their sense of self-esteem—their conviction that they are worth something and can make a contribution.

It becomes increasingly important for them to be aware that God wants to use their lives to make a significant impact upon society. How many children hear their parents pray for their future? Do we impress upon them the daily imperative of seeking the wisdom of God's Spirit to make sound decisions? It is not unwise to teach a healthy fear of making mistakes in planning for the future. Life is simply too precious to be wasted.

If we have implanted these habits and reflexes, these qualities of character, and this self-value deep enough, we can relax—assured that we have taken the first step in bringing our children toward a life grounded in wisdom. We have trained them, and set their feet on a way from which they will probably not depart when the going gets tough. At least that's the way Solomon, the Proverbs writer, saw it.


SOLOMON'S THIRD CONCERN:
PAIN MAKES THE PERSON

The white thing was hidden in the basement wall because it was a reminder of pain. I have yet to meet a person who likes pain; I have rarely met a person who wasn't prepared to sidestep it if he or she could. But Gail and I knew then, and we know now, that pain is one of life's greatest teachers. If we never introduced our children to certain forms of pain and adversity, they would be ill-equipped without their lessons. They would be ill-prepared for later days when pain was likely to come whether they sought it or not.

Two categories of pain in the family come to mind: *discipline* and *punishment.* They are often used as if they are synonymous. They are not.

*Discipline* is the deliberate stress we introduce into the lives of our sons and daughters to stretch their capacities for performance. *Punishment* is the painful consequence of misdeeds and violations of family standards and principles.

As I've mentioned in other places, Gail and I started the children working around the house at a very early age. We were impressed with what we had seen among families in which work was a part of life even among the smallest children.

In our home on Grant Street, work appeared to be less necessary. The kids did not really have to participate to keep the family machine going. That is why we constructed a list of jobs that they began to do at the age of four. We wanted them to experience fatigue, inconvenience, frustration, and puzzling problems. Face problems now, or you'll face them later, we said. But, in reality, we didn't give them a choice. They were going to face them now. That is a form of discipline.

Discipline helps children learn that feelings do not run their lives. Fluctuating moods, fatigue, ignorance, and even some types of pain will limit us to substandard performance if we allow them to do so. So a wise mother or father, keeping this in mind, attempts to help children understand that they can push through these barriers and increase their abilities and capacities.

I recall a long family bicycle ride in the country. We found ourselves pedaling up a much longer hill than we had anticipated. As we neared the top, Kristy cried out in fatigue, "I've got to stop and walk." Something told me that she could probably push on to the top if I encouraged her enthusiastically. "I'm positive you can make it," I called to her. "Keep pedaling, even if it hurts a little." A minute later: "We're almost there; only a few hundred more feet; you can do it."

She was exhausted, legs aching more thant they'd ever ached before. But she kept going, and she reached the top and enjoyed coasting down the other side of the hill. By pressing her to go beyond the threshold of pain, Gail and I added one more nail to the structure of her inner spirit, which says, "I can do many things my feelings tell me I can't do!" That is the development of people through discipline.

Discipline was the issue when children asked for a ride to school because the temperature had dropped a few degrees. Discipline was the point when they wanted to buy something that cost a dollar or two more than they had and they wanted to go into debt with Dad or Mom as the money-lender. Discipline was the subject when they kept procrastinating on projects that should have been done immediately. So we said, "Walk on the cold morning," "Wait for the time when you've earned all the money," and "Do it now instead of later."

Most of us instinctively fall into the trap of withholding the pain, making life relatively easy for our children. We would never have believed how subtle is the temptation to give our children money and freedoms rather than hurt or disappoint them. Like most other parents, we didn't want to see our children hurt, disappointed, or embarrassed because they couldn't do everything the other kids were doing. We didn't like to see them frustrated, facing problems difficult to solve without help. But then we reminded ourselves that God must not find it easy to watch us make our way through the stresses of life. He can remove pain in an instant. But he doesn't! In each experience, he is helping his children to become more of what he wants us to be like: his Son, Jesus.

All this because I stuck my hand through a hole in the wall!

# TWENTY

## FAMILY JUSTICE

*There's no place like home if punishment, when necessary, is generated out of a heart of love.*

IT WAS a rainy night in Los Angeles. I was at the airport along with thousands of others who were waiting for delayed airplanes to take off. Everyone was obviously tired and irritable. But in the midst of our mutual frustration an episode occurred that saddened a lot of us.

A young couple had been staring intently out of the observation windows looking for a plane that was—like all the others—late in arriving. So preoccupied were they that their three-year-old daughter wandered off unnoticed. When both mother and father finally turned to see where she was, they became hysterical. Rushing in all directions at once, they began to shout the girl's name. They were frantic, and everyone quickly caught their sense of panic.

It took a few minutes and several airline personnel to locate the child. We were all relieved. But when she was brought to her father, he immediately seized her and began to spank her angrily. At the same time he shouted humiliating and embarrassing threats concerning the consequences should she ever wander off again.

If the furious spanking had continued much longer, I think several of us would have intervened. What stopped us at first was our realization that a parent has a responsibility to punish a child, assuming, of course, that we're not talking about outright abuse or violence. But the question that was circulating in a lot of our minds as we looked on was whether what we witnessed was punishment. I suspect that we were seeing an uncontrolled man giving vent to his own rage at being exposed as an irresponsible parent. Ironically, the child was receiving the pain, but perhaps the father was actually punishing himself.

Mothers and fathers—and especially single parents, who experience enormous frustration at times—have to think about that sort of thing. When I deal harshly with my child, is it punishment? Or am I simply taking out my anxieties upon someone smaller than I—someone who won't fight back . . . at least for now? It could be that the punishment is really vengeance or just anger that I have been let down by my kids.

No subject in the area of child development is more controversial than that of punishment. Naturally, we have the extremes: those who claim that there is no place for punishment and those who see cause for punishment in every untoward act a child does.

We cannot avoid the startling amount of information that has emerged in more recent years of child neglect, child abuse, and child molestation. And there is no comforting evidence that religious homes are exempt from these problems.

The fact is that with the breakdown of families, the loss of structure in community and extended family life, and other causes too numerous to mention, there is an increasing number of immature and unstable parents resorting to violence. They often do it to exhaust their own frustration and to exert control over undisciplined children. The relative silence of good people on this matter within the church is shameful.

Christian people are in a quandary on this matter. They know that the Bible acknowledges the necessity of punishment as an act of justice and correction when there has been a revolt against family order. Yet, there is alarm over the incidents in which this parental responsibility has been horribly mishandled.

The scheme of biblical punishment seems to have several different objectives and patterns. *Corrective punishment* is meant to warn someone going in the wrong direction. *Judicial punishment,* on the other hand, symbolizes the satisfaction of justice when society has been wronged and the law of God offended. It is also employed to remove someone who proves to be a destructive element within a group of people.

Jonah is an example of the first kind: corrective punishment. God had called him to go to Nineveh. When Jonah decided to disobey, he boarded a ship going in the opposite direction. It wasn't long before God had Jonah overboard and in the belly of a great fish.

Jonah's description of the experience is quite vivid:

> *[God] threw me into the ocean depths; I sank down into the floods of waters and was covered by [his] wild and stormy waves. Then I said, "O LORD, you have rejected me and cast me away. . . ."*
>
> *I sank beneath the waves, and death was very near. The waters closed above me; the seaweed wrapped itself around my head. I went down to the bottoms of the mountains that rise from off the ocean floor. I was locked out of life and imprisoned in the land of death.* (Jonah 2:3-6, TLB)

Jonah's three days in the whale are a form of corrective punishment. It was designed by God to bring him to a point of submission, a realization of his responsibility. It appears to be a principle in God's dealings with people that he will permit (perhaps even cause?) pain in our lives in order to call our attention to mistakes we are making. He does it because he loves us and seeks our best. Jonah finally went to Nineveh, though kicking and screaming as he went. And God's purposes were carried out.

That's why the writer of Hebrews pictures God as a father who must sometimes punish his children:

> *My son, don't be angry when the Lord punishes you. Don't be discouraged when he has to show you where you are wrong. For when he punishes you, it proves that he loves you. When he whips you it proves you are really his child.* (Hebrews 12:5-6, TLB).

There are times when a parent—like the Lord—must inflict pain because he wants to high-profile the bad consequences that await a person who continues on the wrong path.

Judicial punishment emerges in the Bible when someone deliberately lives in violation of God's laws. That's what happened to Cain. He rejected God's warnings, and, unlike Jonah, he followed through with his own rebellious plans to eliminate his brother, Abel. Punishment was swift, and Cain was marked for life because he had rejected God's corrective warnings. The same thing happened to David, king of Israel. As a result of his sin of adultery with Bathsheba, he lost his newborn son in death. These were painful consequences to rebellious acts.

It appears that judicial punishment can be drastic. Sometimes a person appears to be so destructive an influence that he must be removed. You have the Old Testament story of Achan being executed because of his direct disobedience to God. There is the New Testament story of the death of Ananias and Sapphira in the early church for their attempt to "lie to the Holy Spirit." Both of these experiences seem to center on the problems created by people whose continued life in the community of God's people would have been a spiritually cancerous influence. There had to be surgery.

Perhaps the most impressive and unsettling passage on judicial punishment, however, is that found in Deuteronomy:

> *If a man has a stubborn, rebellious son who will not obey his father or mother, even though they punish him, then his*

*father and mother shall take him before the elders of the city and declare, "This son of ours is stubborn and rebellious and won't obey; he is a worthless drunkard." Then the men of the city shall stone him to death. In this way you shall put away this evil from among you, and all the young men of Israel will hear about what happened and be afraid.*(21:18-21, TLB)

This shocking directive deserves some deep thought. At the time it was written, the people of Israel were on the move toward the Promised Land. The rigors of that journey demanded the utmost discipline and orderliness from everyone. There was no time or opportunity for the nation to dissipate its energies coaxing and cajoling dissidents. The law provided that if a young man would not keep the law, he would have to be punished by execution.

Naturally we would recoil at the stoning of children today. But before we are tempted to discard this shocking piece of Scripture as irrelevant, let me suggest that there are some useful principles to be extracted from it.

The first and foremost lesson from these verses is that a family, then and now, cannot easily cope with rebellion. I have watched many parents try to keep their home running happily and efficiently while one child slashed away at the rules whenever they were an inconvenience to him. The home cannot survive under such conditions. This Deuteronomy passage recognizes that and arranges for the final removal of one who disrupts the family to an extreme.

A second important lesson in this verse is that God appears to recognize that sometimes children and parents have to part ways if the child decides to reject his parents' style of life. Jesus indicated this in the parable of the Prodigal Son. Here was a boy who had apparently received every opportunity his father could provide. I don't think I am making the parable say more than is there when I note that the father seemed to have been a good father. But he had a son who couldn't accept the family system. When the boy asked to leave, his father reluctantly let him go.

It apparently had to happen. The father could have chained the boy down, but he would never have captured his spirit. Better to surrender the boy to the consequences of his decision and hope that somewhere along the line the escalating forms of punishment would have an effect. The boy might find correction through consequences. But one thing was sure: as long as his rebellious attitude stayed, he had to go.

On a few occasions when an older teenager has flagrantly violated the family rules and brought heartbreak to his parents and negative influence to the younger children, I have used the Deuteronomy passage to demonstrate a parent's right to a drastic solution. The Old Testament verse forces a child to leave; the New Testament principle urges a parent to let him leave. By force or by voluntary act, a totally rebellious son or daughter may have to leave his or her home. If it comes to a question of the family's survival, the interest of the group must take precedence over the individual.

The agony of such a decision often leaves parents, who have invested a lifetime in a son or daughter, absolutely drained. They spend countless hours tracing their own failures; they try new approaches. They may have gone through countless times when it seemed as if there was hope, only to see it explode in pieces. The ultimate anguish comes when they recognize the need for "surgery." Perhaps in the leaving there will be consequences that will prompt repentance and renewal. Then they will be called upon—like the Prodigal's father—to open the door, forgive, and restore the relationship.

Solomon, convinced that there is an untamed tiger called rebellion in every young life, wrote much about punishment. He said, "Discipline your son in his early years while there is hope. If you don't you will ruin his life" (Proverbs 19:18, TLB).

Solomon seems to be contradicting the unconscious hope

many parents have that their children will grow out of their rebellious nature as they grow older. They are not likely to do so! If the punishment is not applied early in life, the rebellion will simply take on more and more sophisticated forms until one more family has been torn apart, each member broken and disheartened. The wise old king went on to say, "A youngster's heart is filled with rebellion, but punishment will drive it out of him" (Proverbs 22:15, TLB).

Corrective and judicial punishment in the Book of Proverbs take two forms. The first is artificial, and it is targeted at children. The second is natural, and it centers on the upper ages.

By artificial punishment, I am suggesting that a father or mother must devise consequences that help a child associate pain or hardship with his misdeed. That is all there is to a spanking. It is a very painful experience that dramatizes the seriousness of the wrong act that prompted it.

Natural punishment, which increases with age, is the obvious consequences that come as a result of wrong or rebellious acts. The consequences of loneliness, starvation, and bankruptcy in the life of the Prodigal Son were natural.

When I was a small child, my parents took me to a lovely new home to visit friends. While the "big folks" were talking, I quietly slipped into the bathroom and managed to pack the toilet with all kinds of objects that weren't meant to be in there. A flush or two jammed the plumbing and the toilet was out of use until it could be repaired.

It seems absurd to point it out, but for the sake of illustration, let me note that natural punishment would have forced me to pay for my vandalism, not only in terms of money, but also in the embarrassment and humiliation for doing such a dumb thing. But being a child, I had no appreciation for either of those natural consequences. I didn't have the money, and I wasn't particularly embarrassed about the matter because I couldn't appreciate the seriousness of what I'd done.

That means the punishment had to be fitted to suit my situation. While I couldn't understand dollar bills, I could comprehend pain. In fact God seemed to have provided a landing pad on the backside of my body that was easy to reach and had a reasonable number of nerve endings to transfer the message to the "inner me." My father was an impresario at artificial punishment, and I soon received the message—loud and clear. By that I mean he was clear, and I was loud!

Every family has its own forms of artificial punishment. The universal one appears to be spanking. If you have any respect for Solomon's wisdom, you won't be able to escape the fact that he believed strongly in the inducement of pain through spankings. "Scolding and spanking a child helps him to learn. Left to himself, he brings shame to his mother" (Proverbs 29:15, TLB). Much controversy has swirled about the use of corporal punishment in the family. Some have decried its "violent" quality; others have feared that it tends to express only a parent's momentary frustration and becomes a convenient way to take out rage on someone else. After all, a child can't fight back . . . until later.

Rather than go to either extreme, it might be better to ask ourselves what forms of corporal punishment are possible. My father used to say that, in the early years of his children's lives, he found it wise to use a simple flick of the finger on the backside when he sensed wrongful anger or rebellion in the cry of a child. Anyone who has had experience with infants knows that there are several different kinds of cries, and a perceptive parent quickly learns which is which. There are cries of pain, hunger, and anger. The first two are legitimate; the third needs to be checked. A disciplinary response in the earliest days is sometimes all a child needs to associate rebellion with painful consequences.

As a child grows, corporal punishment takes on an even more important role, probably until the age of eight or nine. By then a child's behavior should have been shaped to the point where this kind of enforcement is no longer necessary. With our children, Gail and I chose never to spank with our hands. That's why the white thing hung in the closet. While it was not used frequently, it could be easily removed from the closet and placed in a conspicuous location for anyone in the mood for testing authority to see. Simply taking it from the closet and laying it on the kitchen table—a kind of show of force—was all that was usually necessary in the house on Grant Street.

I am convinced that our readiness to use the white thing, and the effectiveness when it was occasionally used, contributed to the fact that it was rarely necessary to reach for it. Almost fifteen years ago, I wrote about the white thing and said at the time, "Somewhere in the age range of seven or eight the weapon disappeared, either by accident or design. But we never had need of it again anyway." Little did I know then that my suspicions were justified. The white thing had been secreted in the hole in the wall in the basement, found only on moving day many years later.

Except in very early childhood when pain is about the only enforcement process possible, I am convinced that spankings should never be impulsive. This is a form of punishment that should be reserved for only certain kinds of violations: disobedience, disrespect, lying, or injury to someone else. The conditions for its use should be well known to everyone.

When spanking is used as a form of punishment, it should be done by a parent who is in total control of himself. Any parent who has a tendency to lose his temper should be very careful to cool off before the act of punishment. A son or daughter should never be left with the impression of being punished by an angry parent.

Another form of artificial punishment is isolation. A day in one's bedroom may be an invitation to fun, since most children's bedrooms are equipped with a lot to do. We found that asking our children to stand with their faces in the corner of a room was an enforcement experience. Time passes slowly for a child. Thus thirty to sixty minutes in a corner with nothing to do but stand there looking at nothing gives considerable opportunity to look back on one's attitude and behavior with regret.

The loss of certain privileges or opportunities becomes meaningful in a few years. Toys left out in violation of cleanup laws can be impounded for a week or two. Denial of a favorite television show or video is a moderate response to certain kinds of unacceptable behavior.

When the children in the house on Grant Street began to learn how to write, Gail and I found that the old-time repetitive writing punishment ("I will not . . . again" —written seventy-five times) was quite helpful. I fashioned a sentence that described the wrongdoing and asked Mark or Kristy to record their repentance enough times to grind the meaning of it into their minds. It gives time to draw out remorse (and may even improve handwriting!).

As children grow, this exercise can be expanded by asking for essays that describe the offense and how it can be avoided the next time. All privileges are simply suspended until the essay is completed to the parent's satisfaction.

Punishment becomes more natural as children mature. Now a broken window—shattered out of carelessness—can be paid for out of one's allowance or through extra work to which a value is assigned. The familiar term used by all teenagers, "grounding," may be used as they become involved in the peer culture and schedule. "Grounding" implies the removal of privileges outside the home when a youngster has violated regulations concerning homecoming time or other forms of outside-the-home behavior. Grounding has to be associated with the concept that we remove privileges when a son or daughter has proved themselves unable to handle them responsibly.

Natural punishment becomes especially distressing when we

see our children penalized by people outside our home. Punishments applied by school authorities or even the local police ought not to be interfered with unless they are clearly unjustly administered. Unfortunate as it may be, it is probably advantageous for a young boy or girl to see firsthand what happens to someone who rebels against the rules of society. The parent who tries to weaken the effect of this by interceding may be making a big mistake. Surely, loving fathers and mothers should stand with their sons or daughters in times of trouble, but they make a serious error if they try to relieve their offspring of responsibility for their actions.

Whether punishment is corrective or judicial, it must happen if we are to bring our children to the wisdom way of life. But to make it effective, a parent must keep certain rules.

Obviously, a first rule of punishment would have to be this matter of anger. Compare the statements of two parents, one of whom says, "You make me so mad I could kill you," and another who says, "What you have done grieves me more than you could ever know; I'm upset about your actions."

The former statement implies wrath and anger from one person to another. It leaves unremovable scars upon the soul of a child and may even make him wonder if his mother or father will ever forgive him. But the latter is different. Note that it shows that the target of the anger is the actions of the person and not the person himself. Our children should know that we are capable of great disappointment and even anger over their actions—but never over them. This principle is entirely consistent with the biblical assertion that the wrath of God is directed at our sins. But God always loves the sinner. People-building parents can use that as a precedent.

A second principle of punishment is consistency. We inflict severe damage on children if our punishment of them is erratic and capricious. Here again, a parent is often motivated to punish children on the basis of one's level of irritability or inconvenience. One day a child does something of which a parent disapproves and little more than a sharp word is said. But the next day, the same offense is greeted with massive force. The child never knows how his mother or father is going to act. The uneven application of punishment is a mark of injustice, and it usually means that we destroy far more than we build in a young person's life.

A third significant principle to remember about punishment is that it must fit the person. Each child in a family will respond to different forms of punishment, and fathers and mothers have to know these differences. There can be great variations within a single family. One child is crushed over a simple statement of disappointment from a parent. But another will have to be severely reprimanded or spanked before the same message gets through. We have to search for those forms of correction that have the desired effect—no more, no less. Punishment sends a message, but if the message is not received, even though pain has been applied, the punishment has lost its point.

Not only must the punishment fit the person, it must fit the behavior. An undiscriminating mother blows her top at everything. Every violation—whether caused by mistake or rebellion—is met with furious shouting and retaliation. She doesn't measure the situation and prepare a controlled response which guides her little ones toward the development of wisdom. Little by little her children come to fear her, to see her as an obstacle or enemy. She has lost their respect.

We've all seen fathers who have grounded their teenage children for weeks at a time for apparently trivial reasons. They may have been revealing their own fear that the family situation was escaping their fatherly control. But in the long view of things, they may cause a far greater alienation than the immediate positive correction.

One day I learned two more principles about punishment as I watched a mother blow her top over something her small son and his friend were doing while they were shopping at a mall. She grabbed her child violently and proceeded to spank him. When she stopped—out of sheer exhaustion—the boy failed to respond: no tears, no apology, not even a recognition that there was a breakdown of relationship between him and his mother. The mother turned away in disgust, and then the child grinned and said to the friend who was with him, "It didn't really hurt a bit."

The mother's first mistake was punishing her son in public; that's a fourth principle. In the house on Grant Street, punishment was always done in private—never in front of anyone, including other members of the family. Punishment is not meant to humiliate; it is to retrain the destructive side of the will. It should be between only two people: a parent and the child. No one else should ever be present.

The mother's second mistake was a violation of my fifth principle: punish with reasonable thoroughness. In other words, make sure that the punishment delivers the appropriate message. That didn't happen at the shopping mall that day. A spanking, for example, which does not bring about a change of attitude and spirit (and this one certainly didn't), is probably worse than no spanking at all.

You can hardly ever go out in public these days without seeing some mother or father casually reaching out to swat a child. The child will often show no reaction; it's almost as if this is a routine exchange. In most cases, all the parent has done is alter the situation for a few minutes and get a load of rage off his own chest. But with a succession of such ineffective punishments comes an immunity to all punishment. The boy who says to his friend at the mall, "It didn't hurt a bit," is actually saying, "Hey, I can beat the system."

Ineffective punishment in childhood can develop an unhealthy attitude toward the natural punishments of later years. If there is no ultimate fear of any kind of punishment, there is no deterrent to rebellion. With no deterrent, you can expect the willful spirit to produce a chamber of horrors and heartbreaks.

I have a sixth principle of punishment, and like the seventh, it is distinctly Christian. Punishment must have a beginning and an ending. It begins when a child is informed as to why he is being punished. If both parent and child have not come to an understanding of what the violation has been, then the punishment has no meaning. That's why it is often important to wait until anger and frustration have subsided so that there is the possibility of full understanding of what happened and why it has to be addressed.

Doing that will insure that a child is not punished unjustly. A child must be given the chance to explain and tell how he feels about what he's done. He cannot always be allowed to apologize his way out of punishment because then he will learn that "I'm sorry" is a passport to freedom every time. Such apologies probably mean nothing.

Equally important is the fact that when the punishment is ended there is complete forgiveness and restoration. Among the traits I admired in my own father was his capacity to forgive. I never remember a time when he held past misbehavior against me or that he kept bringing them back up after they had been treated. I could be sure that when a matter had been concluded in private, it was ended forever.

That principle is distinctly Christian because it involves forgiveness. And forgiveness in the biblical context means that something is never again held against us. It may perhaps be a while before we are given a second chance, and it may be a while before total trust can be built up again. But in the broadest sense, a deed once punished must then be forgiven. Children must be taught in the context of punishment the necessity for repentance and the resulting forgiveness. Here in this crucible of pain, they may learn some of the greatest relational lessons of life.

The final principle of punishment that seems to encompass all of the others is this: punishment emanates from a heart of love, from a mission of people building—not vengeance. We bring pain to bear on a situation because we care deeply that aberrant behavior is a hindrance to mature, godly growth. It takes an adult mind to understand the wisdom of that. Or does it?

One day Kristy and Mark described to me a home in which they had recently visited. In commenting upon their experience, one of them said, "I don't think they love their children very much."

We were fascinated by that comment and asked, "What makes you say that?"

"Well, they never say no to their children, and they never get mad at them for anything. They just let them do anything they want."

We were hearing something special that day. It was an observation that called for further examination.

"But I thought that was the way you'd like to have parents act. Think of it: no one bossing you around; no one ever punishing you; no one ever stopping you from doing anything you want. I thought that's the way you wanted things to be."

"It may be the way we sometimes want things to be," came the reply, "but it's not what's best. Grown-ups know best what we need because they love us. Someday we'll know, too."

It was somewhere around that time that the white thing disappeared. Gail and I never worried about its disappearance because we didn't seem to need it any longer. We'd reached a period in our home when a clear word, a sharp rebuke, an occasional denial of some privilege was all that was needed to bring correction.

Looking back across the years we lived on Grant Street, I am now more convinced than ever that discipline and punishment carefully and prudently applied in the first eight years of a child's life will probably mean a minimum of discipline and punishment in the second eight years.

We made so many mistakes! I am embarrassed to recall the many times I was too angry to listen to the story a son or daughter had to tell me that was behind the "indiscretion." I wince when I think of times when I should have been more consistent, more open to negotiation, more caring. But we made it through. And as I hold the white thing in my hand and look at the dust that has caked its surface because of disuse, I have so many memories.

"What shall we do with it?" I ask Gail. "Shall we take it along?"

"No," she says. "It's connected with a past that needs to remain buried. That part of our lives has been over for a long time now."

So I put the white thing back into the hole in the wall in the basement. And I imagine that it's still there.

# PART IX

## The Patio

# TWENTY-ONE

## MOM PLAYED DIRTY

&❧ *There's no place like home when a family delights in playing together.*

THE HOUSE on Grant Street had a small but beautiful backyard. New England red maple trees marked the back property line. A crab apple tree stood at one end, and a dogwood at the other. In between, a stretch of grass grew from some of the richest soil that could be imagined. The good news was the health of the grass; the bad news was the number of times it had to be cut during the summer.

The centerpiece of the backyard was the patio, a concrete slab just below the kitchen window. Off to one side was a brick barbecue (the do-it-yourself family was at work again), which could sustain a sizable bed of coals and more than a few hamburgers.

Gail and I stood looking out at this patio from the back door. I wondered what she would pick as a single memory from this sight. Would it be the enormous number of hours she'd spent in the flower beds? That was an exercise which had always brought Gail joy, but not being a gardener, I found it difficult to understand. Would it be the picnic suppers? The quiet evenings when we sat out in the dark and looked at the stars? I didn't know; so I asked.

"Do you know what I'm remembering? The crazy basketball games. I'll never forget those."

The basketball games. Of course. I should have known Gail would pick those times.

"Dad," Mark had said to me one day years before, "what would you think if we put up a basketball backboard out on the patio?"

I thought it was a great idea. He and I headed off to the lumber yard to get the materials. There we got everything we needed. "You dig a hole thirty-six inches deep," the man said, "put some gravel in the bottom for drainage, drop the four-by-four in it, and pack it in with wet concrete. Let it set for a couple of days."

Mark and I did it all just as he said. And a few days later a white backboard hung from the wooden pole and an orange basketball rim and its net extended out at regulation height, just waiting for the first shot.

If Mark took the first shot, it went in. Even as a small boy, it was clear that he had the timing, the eye, the coordination, and everything else that it takes to be a good athlete. Soon we were all out on the patio shooting baskets, playing something called Horse or Twenty-one. We tried family basketball games, Kristy and me against Mark and Mom. Special rules: no one could guard Kristy; Mom got to play dirty. Dirty playing meant that she could push, grab, say silly things, and generally carry on distracting activities that usually had me convulsing in laughter so hard that I couldn't take my shots.

Three of us in the family played for fun. Mark played to win. And in the early days he had a difficult time disguising his feelings if any kind of competition on the patio didn't go his way. If he lost, he had to make an excuse. If he didn't play well, it was because someone else wasn't being fair. And we worried about this because we saw an emerging trait that, if carried into adulthood, would cause him many miserable experiences as he tried to cope with the real world.

Gail and I have pictures of Mark throwing and catching balls when he was three and four years old. I was sure, I told Gail in those days, that we had a superstar on our hands. She informed me that most fathers say that about their sons. I told her to just watch.

A year or two later Mark went off to his first practices in the community soccer league. On Saturday mornings he learned how to kick a miniature soccer ball, and before long he was part of a team playing a regular schedule. Eleven five- and six-year-old boys all bunched up with eleven others of the same age from the opposing team. They looked more like a Rugby scrum than soccer players. But each week brought improvement, and on one memorable Saturday Mark scored his first goal for his team.

I was hysterical with fatherly pride. Gail was not far behind me although she masked it with a mother's dignity. Little did we realize that that moment was just the first of many years of standing on the sidelines watching Mark play soccer and basketball. And when Kristy was old enough, she too became part of the organized community sports. We discovered that we had two athletes in our family.

The American way of life glorifies the sportsperson. Fathers and mothers can all too easily become so excited about their children's success on the playing field that they send a subtle message: your value is in winning. And if that message is sent and received, one is likely to build a child who will become remorseless in his need to conquer everything in his path. In my desire to see my son be the successful boy I never thought myself to be, I could have fallen into that trap. Gail was the balance that called that to my attention.

But I will admit that some of the most enjoyable moments of my life came on the sidelines as our children competed. In athletics, Mark was the more active of the two. I soon found myself penciling all of his soccer, basketball, and baseball games into my calendar months in advance. My work permitted enough flexibility for me to be there. And the result was that Gail and I rarely missed a contest in which either of our children were playing.

Because I was a pastor and because Mark had to enter my world regularly and see me as leading and speaking, I determined that sports would be *his* world. He would be the expert, and I would be the student. I would not be his coach; I would not take a leadership position in the town sports program. I would support the system with money, affirmation, behind-the-scenes activity. But Mark would never have to look out and see me in charge of one more part of his world.

So I stood on the sidelines and cheered. And when the games were over, I asked questions. "What were you all doing when you decided on that strategy? Why does the fullback . . . ? What was the coach wanting you to do when he said . . . ?"

Of course I could have found out the answers by myself. In fact I probably could have learned enough about the game in the early days so that I could have been Mark's coach or at least his instructor. Do all fathers think that? And there would have been a great temptation to do that, given my temperament. For I am the teacher, the man who likes to know something about everything. I like to be the informer, and it would have been instinctive for me to control Mark's life in this area.

But something (maybe it was Gail) told me that I shouldn't. That I should make sure that there were areas of my relationship with our son where he could teach me something.

Perhaps that is one of the reasons that many relationships between parents and children never gain the level of intimacy that mothers and fathers crave with their offspring. We have a hard time permitting the relationship to become reciprocal.

We value relationships where we can make a contribution to the other person's life. If this is true, then what do our children have to give us?

Standing on the sidelines of Mark's athletic world taught me that important insight. I would be *spectator* to his performance. I would be his cheerleader, his fan. And Gail and I loved doing it for seventeen years.

We watched the boy who shot baskets on the patio go from one successful athletic year to another. A state championship soccer final in high school. High scorer in his league for three years. A starter for a college team that won the NCAA soccer championship.

His bedroom began to become strewn with medals and trophies. In the high school days there were the calls and letters from college recruiters. It was exciting to stand on the sidelines of this boy's life and be a spectator. For I not only saw him grow in athletic ability, I saw him grow into manhood in terms of character and manly determination.

When the last game was played, I grieved. There had been something that had welded us so closely together in those years. We'd been there when he had been caked with mud and utterly defeated. We nursed him through his injuries. We'd prayed for him when he faced the big games and boiled over with pregame anxiety. So when the last game was played, and when the teams no longer went out on the field together, I was sad.

All of those sorts of memories came out of me as we stood looking at the now-quiet patio. We could hear the basketball as it used to thump on the concrete and send a vibration all the way through the house. We could recall the shouts of the boys playing pick-up games late in the evenings when someone made an unusual shot. We could almost see the silly moments when Gail would wrap her arms around Mark or me in a family game while we were trying to shoot the ball. Now it was over.

"What did we learn out there?" I asked out loud. "What was the meaning of all that?"

"We learned the importance there is of a family playing together. And we learned the importance of supporting each other in our moments of competition," Gail said. "Mark came to hear you preach every week; you went to see him play. It was a good trade-off, and he appreciated it."

Today as I think about those play days, I do so with a mixture of nostalgia and melancholy. Nostalgia, because they were some of the great high points of our lives. Melancholy, because, like all good things, they came to an end.

"Enjoy your kids," someone once said to us when they were very small. "Before you know it they'll be leaving you, and they'll only come back to visit."

We were busy people. It would have been so easy to skip the play. I could have filled the evenings with all the work people wanted me to do, and I would have missed the wonderful games on the patio. I could have filled my schedule with travel plans and missed all the games that Mark and Kristy played. It would not have been noticed by others if I had. As I often noted when at a game, there were very few parents who regularly attended games—even on Saturday. Too busy, I guess.

But we played. And we watched one another play. And it made all the difference. If praying together in the kitchen was important, playing together on the patio was not far behind.

I think the playing taught us at least four things while we lived on Grant Street.

First, we learned some amazing character lessons in competition. When boys and girls play on teams, stress mounts, and all of the classic relational problems are capable of arising.

There are the moments when a player begins to become frustrated and loses his temper. Mark learned the importance of keeping emotions under control out on the patio and on the playing field. He learned how to take orders from coaches and referees. He learned how to take a cheap shot (from his mother first?) from a competitor and not retaliate. He learned not to quit when the weather became adverse, the opposing team was superior, or injuries slowed him down. He discovered things on that playing field that stick with him as a man in the business world today.

Mark learned how to win and lose first on the patio and then on that field. There was the day on the basketball court as a junior-high player when he and his teammates were so intimidated that they failed to take a shot for the entire first half. Three successful free throws sent them into the locker room at halftime losing 37-3. The coach was understandably beside himself and told the team so at halftime.

When the second half offered little improvement, the coach took a major risk. He told the team as they showered that each of them would have to decide over the weekend whether or not they wished to continue playing. It would have to be a new team on Monday, he said. So each player would have to call the coach sometime in the next few days and discuss with him whether or not he really wanted to play basketball.

I watched Mark digest this rebuke and challenge for the next twenty-four hours. He was a thoroughly beaten player, embarrassed, and drained of self-confidence. I would pass his bedroom and see him staring out the window, and I was sure I knew what was on his mind.

"What are you going to do?" we finally asked.

"I'm going to call Mr. Hill and tell him that I want to play on Monday if he wants me, and then, if he does, I'll go out and do my best."

And he did. It wasn't a spectacular basketball season, but Mark and the others learned that there was life after defeat.

I stood on the sidelines the day he scored five goals in a high-school game. And I began to observe that Mark was little different ten minutes after a game in which he excelled or a game in which he had played poorly. He was learning an evenness that was not substantially affected by victory or defeat.

What made this possible? Perhaps it was because Mark was surrounded by Christian men and women in his school life, in his church life, and in his home. He was gaining a consistent message from all sources: life is a process of wins and losses, gains and losses, steps ahead and steps backward. The best lessons usually come from the losses; the greatest temptations come on the heels of the victories. He seemed to be able take these messages to heart and internalize them. Maybe one of the reasons was that his family was there to underscore the discoveries he was making.

On the patio and on the playing field, Mark learned the lesson of teamwork. "Talk to me," the man running with the soccer ball would cry out to his teammates. With that statement he was asking for several things, it seemed to me. He was asking where everyone else was so that he could pass off when he was ready. He was seeking information as to where opposing players might be coming up on his blind side. And maybe he was just asking for plain old encouragement.

I watched Mark and his fellow players slowly learn that an assist (helping another man score) was just as important as scoring the point themselves. And the day came when a player's assist record was as much a matter of pride for him as his record of scores. I came to appreciate the fact that Mark enjoyed making a successful pass as much as he did a shot on goal.

It was there on the field that he learned how to become a part of a crew of men working toward the same objective. There he learned how to rejoice in another person's success, how to celebrate another's unique talents and skills, how to give comfort or affirmation when another man was injured or highly successful.

And then I saw Mark learn the importance of self-discipline on the patio and out on the court. There were the nights when he shot the ball up toward the hoop endlessly, perfecting his jump shot or his lay-up. There were the long afternoons in the hot sun or frigid temperatures when he pushed his body into condition and timing for the competition ahead. Athletics demanded an ability to say no to impulses and laziness. It required a willingness to live with pain, not to be slowed down by superficial injuries. The world of the player—man or woman—required mental discipline that motivated a player to rise up from defeat and summon a new zeal for the next day's game.

We were thankful that God had given us bodies with which to play; for skills and health and opportunity to push ourselves that one extra bit to grow physically, mentally, and relationally.

I used to stand by the four-by-four pole in the backyard and feed the ball back to Mark so he could take his practice shots. Those days are over now. The times when we took down the soccer goal nets together will never be repeated. The hours Gail and I spent walking the sidelines or sitting in the stands are all history. It was a wonderful period of life, and Mark brought the two of us more joy than we ever deserved.

How proud we were to give him an embrace at the end of a game, to walk off the field and let others know that we belonged to him! How thankful we were that with that skilled body was a heart that was growing in a knowledge of God. And it all seemed to begin on the patio.

"We should have spent more time out here," I said to Gail as we got ready to go.

"I told you that, didn't I?"

"Yeah, you sure did. I'll listen better next time."

I'm grateful the house on Grant Street had a patio. We built people out there.

# PART X

# The
# Living Room

# TWENTY-TWO

## "WE CAN'T RUN HER LIFE FOREVER!"

 

❧ *There's no place like home if children are given permission to make choices that will prepare them to be responsible decision makers in the future.*

THE ORIGINAL builders must have placed a high priority on entertainment when they first drew lines on a piece of paper and allocated the space for their new Grant Street home. I say this because their design called for unusually large living and dining rooms. In the early years of our marriage when Gail and I had dreamed of a home of our own, we had never dared to imagine that spaces of these proportions would be our's one day.

When we first came to Lexington, Gail, with her usual resourcefulness, set about making the living room a warm and hospitable place. She hung wallpaper, made drapes, and spread around tasteful pictures and knickknacks. I built bookshelves and cabinets into one end.

A grand piano, a very special gift, stood at one end. Then there was a fireplace, which offered charm as well as heat on cold New England winter evenings. The room included several pieces of furniture: a collection of family hand-me-downs, restored and antiqued "derelicts" from people's garages, and bargains from country store sales and second-hand furniture outlets.

Now, with the movers gone, the cavernous room was empty:

no books, no piano, no furniture, no family pictures on the walls, and no crackling fire in a cleaned-out fireplace. Everything was so quiet, and it was easy to forget that we had regularly filled this place again and again with friends and visitors from all over the world. It hardly seemed possible that this room had been the site of many conversations with broken and distraught people who had come to seek guidance and hope in the midst of crushing problems. All of that was now history.

As we stood there staring into this blank space, it seemed to symbolize our exiting from Lexington more than any other place in the house. It was sinking in. We really were saying good-bye, and it was likely that we would never enter this room—or any of the others—again.

How does one say a good-bye to such a place and appreciate the finality of it all? A place where you have done the most important work you will ever do in a lifetime: raise your children and release them to a world that is sometimes friendly and sometimes harsh. A most important work: giving the next generation what you hope are a few good men and women who will be givers and not takers, making a positive difference in the human community. A very important work: helping a son and daughter figure out how to hear God's voice and then encouraging them to listen to it and obey.

Gail broke my reverie with the question we had asked ourselves in every other room. "What are you remembering?" she asked.

It was hard to focus on something specific. As if it were a slide show, I could recall quick pictures of one event after another. The day we entertained a U.S. Senator and leaders of the Massachusetts Republican Party (you could get all Massachusetts Republicans in one room in those days). The evening two delightful Austrian Christians, the late Walter Trobisch and his wife, Ingrid, had decided that Gail and I needed to learn how to waltz and set about to teach us. Playing games like

Group-Loop with friends Mark and Kristy had over for an evening and who did not mind "old folks" like us joining the party.

The occasions on which I had welcomed pastors and Christian leaders to talk about how we could participate in the renewal of the church in New England. The evening my first publisher, Victor Oliver, had come to convince my family and me that I had a gift in the area of writing, and asked if he and his company could see themselves as my first-string cheerleaders (which they became). Those pictures merely scratched the surface of my memories. So how could I answer Gail's question and do justice to one single event?

But then I remembered. There was one slide out of many which dropped into position, projected on the screen of my mind. One event, one encounter that stood out beyond all others. I immediately became teary. My most important memory? A simple conversation with Kristy in front of the picture window.

During the years we lived on Grant Street, no one in our family enjoyed the living room more than Kristy. When she grew into her teen years, she seemed to take the room over more and more as her personal living space. In the winter months, she might be found sitting in front of the fireplace staring thoughtfully into the flames; or you would walk in and see her entertaining friends from high school who were interested in talking about faith, or boys, or the future, or whatever else young people like to talk about. The living room became her study hall, and it was customary to see the floor strewn with papers as she plowed through her homework.

As I said, the living room had a large picture window, and it was not unusual to find Kristy leaning over the back of the couch looking out that window as she roamed throughout her inner life thinking the private thoughts of every young woman who looks toward the future and asks great questions about life.

The special moment I recalled came when Kristy was in her early teen years, and she came to a point where a serious decision about her education had to be made. Where would she attend junior high school in the eighth grade? Would it be the private Christian academy located nearby, or would it be Diamond Junior High in the town of Lexington?

This was no easy matter to decide. Both institutions offered fine educational programs and unusually high levels of teaching quality. I want to keep on saying with gratitude that we lived in a community where public education was at its best, and we would have been pleased for Kristy to go to either school.

The family was in the living room one evening when the subject of the school came up again. I was about to offer my opinion when Kristy posed a question. "Daddy, could I decide where to go to school this fall?"

I was about to say no to Kristy because Gail and I had always seen ourselves as the decision makers in matters of this magnitude. No, I would tell her; she could decide the small things, but her folks would handle this one. But just as I was about to say this, Gail shot me a look I couldn't ignore. The look said, "Wait!" And so I did, and I told Kristy that I'd let her know my answer to her question later.

"Why not let her make the decision?" Gail said when Kristy left the living room for a moment. "She's old enough to start thinking through questions like this. Let's see how she handles it."

"She's thirteen years old," I remonstrated.

"But it's time for her to start making more decisions and taking responsibility for them. We can't run her life forever. One day she's going to leave us, and she can't have her mother and dad following her around making her choices for her."

I reluctantly agreed, and when Kristy reentered the living room one of us told her the decision about school was hers to make. She was thankful and excited and bounded off to inform her friends that her mother and father had given her the chance to choose where she'd be going to school in the fall.

But what neither she nor Gail and I realized was that this would be no little exercise in decision making. Her excitement was short-lived, and before long we saw our enthusiastic thirteen-year-old look as if she were carrying the weight of the world.

The toughness of the decision lay in its social impact, in the effects it would have upon her friendships with people at both schools. To choose one school was to give the impression of rejecting friends in the other. A few days later Kristy began to realize that one group of her friends or another would take her decision personally. Probably not a problem for someone a few years older, but a major issue when one is thirteen.

Thus it happened that the choice was sidestepped more than once. Every few days, one of us would inquire of Kristy how her thinking was progressing. On one day she would inform us that she was leaning in the direction of this school; on another day she would admit that she was inclined in the direction of the other.

What became clear was that Kristy was the focus of a kind of pressure she'd not anticipated when she had asked us for the chance to handle this by herself. And when a couple of more weeks passed, Gail began to sense that the stress was becoming unhealthy, that it had a preoccupying effect that was leaving Kristy agitated and sad.

Everything seemed to reach a peak one Saturday afternoon, and when I came in the house, Gail met me in the kitchen. "Your daughter is in the living room looking out the window again. She's been there in silence for a couple of hours. You seem to be able to get her to talk in times like this. Why don't you see if you can help her out. I think this school decision has paralyzed her."

"But didn't we agree that this was her decision?" I asked.

"Yes, we did. But maybe I was wrong. Maybe I underestimated all the ramifications of this thing. I don't think any of us realized what sort of responses she'd get from friends. Yesterday A—— told her that if she didn't go to their school everyone would say that she was a snob and write her off."

"That's absurd," I said. "She's got to understand that . . . "

"You know that, and I know it. But a thirteen-year-old doesn't and probably won't for a few more years."

I headed toward the living room. Just as Gail said, Kristy was there at the window so deep in thought that she seemed unaware that I'd entered. Maybe she was wishing I'd stay away. I wasn't sure.

How deeply I loved her! We shared a similar temperament style, and I often thought I could read her heart better than anyone else. I could often predict her reactions to certain situations; I could decode her dreams; and I could feel her pain when the world turned dark for her. This moment was no exception.

One's instinct as a parent is to be overprotective or to want to siphon off as much anxiety about life as possible. Funny, we all look back across our lives and note that the most valuable lessons we ever learned were those learned in the midst of pain. But then we are tempted to try and provide our children with pain-free lives that teach almost nothing of enduring value.

As I sat there in the living room trying to frame a meaningful sentence or two, I thought about the process of decision making that Kristy had taken upon herself. What was she learning from it? Was it too much responsibility?

More than once I'd told both her and Mark: "If you're ever in a situation where you need an 'out' and you don't know how to tell others that you can't do something, just say that your folks won't let you do such and such. Complain, growl, gripe, put the blame on us: feel free to use us as an excuse when you feel uneasy about something. Because if *you're* uneasy about it, you can be sure *we're* going to be uneasy." The day was coming, however, when we could no longer be the scapegoats for choices. The kids would have to take their own stands: "I won't do this because I don't believe it's the correct thing to do." Or, "I've given this thing some thought, and I'm committed to going ahead even if I'm the only one on Grant Street that feels that way." Or they would have to accept responsibility for their own choices: "I'm sorry," I could hear Kristy saying, "you guys probably won't see it like I do, but my choice of schools has to be this one. . . . "

Was this the time for that much responsibility? I was no longer sure. Was this pressure good for Kristy? I wasn't sure about that, either.

*God, how can a man who's just turning forty* (I was forty . . . then) *figure out the mind of a thirteen-year-old? How can I be a people builder who provides only what a girl needs but avoids being so intrusive that she can't grow in the midst of this process? Lord, what are the words that could bring us together into a partnership of choice making where everyone wins?*

I chose to break the silence with a story. I like to think of myself as a storyteller. When I'm in doubt about how to invade someone's thoughts, I usually start with stories.

"Honey, I have a thought for you."

Kristy turned toward me and acknowledged my presence in the living room for the first time.

"There are times in life when every one of us is like an oak tree or a tulip."

"A what?"

"I said an oak tree or a tulip."

"What does that have to do with . . . ?"

"Let me tell you something about myself. There are lots of times in my life when I feel and act like an oak tree. Look at the one out there." She looked up at the familiar old tree.

"It's tall," I said; "it's got a very thick trunk. No one is going to mess with that tree. Even if a car drives into it, the car will probably suffer a lot more damage than the oak tree. No one needs to protect it when it's that strong. We just stand back and enjoy it."

Kristy stood there, still looking out the window, her eyes fixed on the oak tree. But I wasn't sure; so I went on, speaking to the back of her head of lovely blonde hair.

"There are also times in life when I feel like a tulip. The tulip can be just as mature and beautiful as the oak tree. But the problem is that the tulip is small and delicate. It usually needs protection. If it doesn't get it, the tulip might get stepped on by a person or an animal.

"The bottom line is that you walk around oak trees because you can't hurt them. But you build fences around tulips because you can hurt them. Tulips need protection; oak trees do not."

Was Kristy getting the point of my story? I wasn't sure yet. What I was trying to do was to gain access into her thinking process, to get her to feel some freedom to ask for help without feeling as if she were defeated in something she'd once thought she was so competent to handle alone.

I brought my story to its punch line. "Honey, I've been both an oak tree and a tulip. I know what both experiences feel like. On occasions, I've stood alone and taken care of myself. But on other occasions I've needed help, and I've had fences built around me by those who cared. And that's why I have this question for you.

"In this decision about school, are you an oak tree or a tulip? Because if you tell me you're an oak tree, I'll get out of your way and let you finish making this choice by yourself. But if you tell me you're a tulip this time around, I'll build a fence around you and help you in any way possible."

For a moment Kristy did not move. I sat still, worried that I might have overextended myself and that she would push me away out of teenage pride and a feeling that I wouldn't understand issues that were important to her.

But as I sat watching I noted that her shoulders began to shake just a bit. And then I saw her bow her head, and in the light coming through the window I spotted a large tear dropping from her cheek, soaking into the fabric of the couch. Finally she turned, and it was clear that there were also other tears.

Then in almost a whisper: "Daddy . . . I'm . . . a tulip."

Sometimes we need to help our children say "Help!" without having to literally say, "Help!" And that's what had happened in that moment.

I waited for a moment. Then: "Let's work this one through together, sweetheart," I said. And the two of us began one of our level-five conversations, which ultimately led to a choice. And when the process was all over, Kristy felt the confidence to say to her friends, "My folks and I have decided that I should . . . "

The living room in the house on Grant Street will always remind me of that very special exchange. For it was there that Kristy began that common practice, that great human drama, of trying to break away from her childhood and become a woman. It was the place where she (and I) discovered that it was not always a smooth process.

When our children were just infants, Gail and I managed almost everything in their external worlds. When they were older, we began that difficult process of permitting them increasing amounts of freedom. The Braddock Avenue Procedure became a way of family life: each day, a little more freedom; each day, a little more responsibility. And we'd remind ourselves that having been given roots, our children were now growing wings.

When Mark and Kristy began the teen years, we would say to them on various occasions: "The day is coming, you know, when you're going to want to leave us. We're not looking forward to it, but we know it's going to come. So we've all got to get ready for the day you break away." Did we really believe that day was coming? Judging by the amount of grief I went through when the breaking away finally came, I really wonder.

Daniel Levinson of Yale called the breaking-away procedure *BOOM:* Becoming One's Own Man (although he should have said *BOOP:* Becoming One's Own Person). BOOM is a perilous procedure because the younger person is always impatient to acquire more freedom than it may be wise to possess. But the older partner in the relationship (in this case a mother or father) is often anxious to maintain unreasonable control and tends to resist the momentum of breaking away. I experienced the pain of BOOM as a boy with my father, and now I knew the pain of BOOM as a father with our children.

In seeking freedom to make her own decision about schools, Kristy was doing something we had been training her to do. She wanted freedom to manage a significant matter in her life. But as she and her parents found out, breaking away does not always happen in a smooth, trouble-free fashion. Sometimes people have to admit that they underestimated their readiness for responsible performance.

In this case, Kristy had to acknowledge that she'd bitten off more than she could chew. And I had to find a face-saving way to reenter a matter Gail and I had relinquished. The oak tree/tulip exercise gave us a chance to buy back the matter and resolve it in a different way.

After that discussion in the living room, I began to watch both of our children from the perspective of the flower and the tree, and we used those words with frequency. In a sense, our two children had once been completely in the "tulip" category, and Gail and I had enjoyed the role of fences. But now, in their early teens, they were in that part of life when on one day they could be tulips and on another day be oak trees. We had to be flexible enough to accept both possibilities and respond in a proper fashion. And we had to be willing to face the possibility that we would occasionally make mistakes and one day treat an oak tree like a tulip or a tulip like an oak tree. The best solution was to use the code we'd discovered and laugh at its seeming triteness.

"Are you an oak tree or a tulip about preparing for this exam?" someone might ask. It was a way of asking: do you want me to push you on your study habits, or can you handle it by yourself?

When one of the kids was struggling with a romantic matter, it was easy to sneak into the thought process with a simple: "Am I talking to a tulip or an oak tree today?" If the answer came back "tulip," we knew that we were being invited into the thinking. If it was "oak tree," we knew we were being dis-invited, that it was time for parents to permit one or the other to become their own person. After all, they were breaking away.

When Kristy told me she was a tulip that day in the living room, there was a sense in which I knew the slow breaking away, which would come in the next few years, was going rather well. She was not afraid to acknowledge that she needed help, that she wasn't threatened by permitting me in on the partner-ship of an important decision. She was recognizing the need for independence, but she was facing the reality also of interde-pendence. I couldn't ask for more.

The day would come when the breaking away would be more painful. When Mark received his acceptance to a college that was located more than a thousand miles away, Gail and I began to brace for the eventual moment when he would leave the house on Grant Street and only return for occasional visits. Mark was now all oak tree.

We were proud of his achievements; we were proud that he was man enough to assume responsibilities away from home. Still we grieved for ourselves and nursed a bit of anxiety about whether or not he could handle all the exigencies of young adult life.

In the months just before he left our home, I began to notice that there were occasional turbulent moments between him and myself. Issues that had never before bothered either one of us suddenly got in the way of what had otherwise been a close relationship. I found myself critical of the way he drove the car; I judged him to be less sensitive than I thought he should have been to his mother. To be honest, there were times when he "bugged" me. And then I began to see that he was every bit as "bugged" with me.

What was happening? It occurred to me one day. We were going through the final phases of BOOM. He was sending signals about his independence. I was sending signals that I was in a state of resistance. He needed to go; I wanted him to stay. He was saying, "I'm not a tulip anymore"; I was saying, "But, son, I still want to be your fence."

But neither of us seemed to find it possible to say something like that; so our frustration occasionally erupted in overt irritability. Once Mark established himself at college, and his father accepted the reality that the break-away had indeed occurred, we resumed our intimacies. We were then two oak trees with occasional lapses into "tulip-ness."

Kristy had promised never to break away. At least I kept reminding her of the fact that she'd committed herself to be my tulip when she was five years old. "I'll never leave you, Daddy," she'd told me back then. I can still hear the tone in her voice, her great concern that I believe her. "I promise, Daddy; I'll never leave you; I'll always be here with you."

In those days, I would pretend to shed great tears, feign intense anxiety, dramatically shake my head in disbelief. "You say that now, but just you wait. Some handsome man will come into your life someday, and you'll be on your way. You'll forget about your old dad, and . . ."

"No," she would protest with unyielding force. "Even if that happens, Daddy, he and I will live right here and be with you. He won't mind."

But I knew better, and I waited for the day the handsome man would come. Gail and I even prayed for that unnamed man who would enter our daughter's life (just as we prayed for the woman who would someday come to our son). We prayed that he would love God, that he would appreciate the qualities that God had built into her life, that he would serve her just as we hoped we'd taught her to serve him.

The handsome man came. Sooner than I expected. And when he came, he came right to the living room. His name was Tom.

"Dad, Mom!" Kristy whispered as she burst into our bedroom late one night. "There was this gorgeous man at church tonight. His name is Tom. He's on the youth staff. He's out of college; he's fantastic!"

"But he's a lot older than you, honey. So don't get too interested because you'll get hurt." This was the know-it-all parent speaking. The fence-builder, worried about a special tulip that might get stepped on when she got disappointed.

But Kristy had become an oak tree, and we watched the handsome man, Tom, and this break-away child of ours become friends for the next three years.

The two of them would sit in that living room before the crackling fire and talk about a thousand things. I wanted to slip into the dining room and eavesdrop, but second thoughts prohibited me. In that room a friendship began to slowly grow into something deep and beautiful. And finally came the day when the young man asked to see Gail and me and suggested that he would like to help Kristy make the final break-away. He would like our daughter to be his wife.

This child, now a woman, who'd once sat on my lap in the kitchen pledging that she'd never leave was actually going to leave. This schoolgirl who'd sat at the desk in her bedroom and tried to convince me that her mind was not good enough to conquer a certain course in school. This teenager who was not afraid to admit she was sometimes a tulip and needed a fence. This young woman who was now ready to join in partnership with a man and start the cycle of people building all over again.

A year after we had left the house on Grant Street, Kristy and Tom were married. She had only finished her first year of college, and the two of them had promised Gail and me that she would go on to get her degree. (And in the week I write this chapter, Kristy graduates *magna cum laude*.)

On the day of her wedding the church sanctuary was full of invited guests. The organ had begun the wedding march, and the men and women in the bridal party had entered and taken their places at the altar. Tom stood at the head of the aisle waiting for his bride to appear.

Kristy and I stood together, alone, out in the church foyer, ready to walk down the aisle. Soon Tom would see her in a brilliant white wedding dress her mother had worn twenty-five years earlier. When we would reach the front of the sanctuary, the plans called for me to give her away on behalf of Gail and myself and then assume the role of the presiding minister and conduct the wedding ceremony.

I was shaking; I was emotional; I was scared that when we reached the front and I had to assume leadership of the wedding ceremony, I would lose my composure and be unable to speak. I had mental flashes of my making a fool of myself, of being an embarrassment to Kristy. I saw myself choking, or fainting, or weeping uncontrollably. I was sure I would ruin this moment.

But then I felt a tug. It was Kristy slipping her hand through my arm. "Come on, Dad," she said. "I know you're a tulip. But I'm an oak tree; I've got strength for both of us. I'll be your fence."

And we entered the sanctuary. There to the left toward the front was Gail standing, beaming, tears in her eyes. Our eyes connected. We didn't need words to know that we were thinking the same thing. This child we'd developed—now a woman—was one of our two trophies in life. Nothing we'd ever achieved in any other part of our lives came close to our sense of satisfaction in being a mother and a father.

I looked to the right, and there was Mark standing behind Tom as one of the groomsmen. Tall, steady as a rock, "oak tree" Mark, my son. I winked; he nodded. This was hard for him too because he'd often been Kristy's fence as the two of them had walked through adolescence together. We were comrades in this grief of breaking away.

"This is a place called home," I'd told Mark and Kristy when we first moved to Grant Street and they were in the middle of a destructive conflict. "Outside that front door people will find ways to stab you in the back. They'll call you names; sometimes they'll try to make you look bad, and occasionally they'll make you feel like dirt. But in this home we build one another. Do you hear that? We build one another. Now, say that to each other! What do you do in a home?"

"We build each other," a five-year-old and an eight-year-old had said obediently.

And that's what we'd tried to do in the house on Grant Street. There's no place like a home to do that.

# PART XI

## Our Bedroom: the Command Center

# TWENTY-THREE

## The Command Center

*&&* *There's no place like home if a mother and a father dearly love one another and, out of the strength of that love, furnish their children with security, judgment, and spiritual protection.*

THE FAREWELL tour of the house on Grant Street was almost over. The nostalgic exercise could not go on indefinitely, of course; outside, the car was fueled, filled, and pointing toward the open road, a new home, and a new adventure. In just a few minutes we would lock the side door and leave the key in the mail slot where the realtor would later pick it up and turn it over to the excited family that was planning to move in the next day. It was hard to comprehend that this place filled with so many of our unique moments would soon begin playing host to the building of another family's memories.

But one last room awaited our final visit: the bedroom Gail and I had shared for twelve years.

The long hallway that ran the length of the house on Grant Street was like an avenue that runs through the center of a city. Sometimes it seemed as if there were perpetual rush-hour traffic in that hallway as the family rushed to and fro, going from one room to another.

Anchoring one end of the hall was the kitchen, and at the other end, our bedroom. All other rooms were located in between.

Each night at bedtime, as the keeper of the door, I would

walk the length of the house, starting at the kitchen end, checking the doors to make sure they were secure. I would move up the hallway, peeking first into Mark's bedroom and then into Kristy's to make sure they were sleeping soundly and undisturbed. On a few occasions I'd find one of them still awake. "Good-night, Dad," or "Good-night, Daddy," a quiet voice might be heard in the dark when one of them was aware of my presence. And occasionally, I'd slip in for a quick word or two if he or she was still alert.

Then I'd check the bathroom to make sure all the water faucets were tightly closed. Somewhere in my early days I'd picked up this concern about wasting water (one of my better habits). And then, like a night watchman, I would conclude my tour at the other end of the hallway as I entered our bedroom and shut the door.

The master bedroom in our home was more than adequate in size. It's most outstanding architectural value was its room-length closet, which Gail loved.

In our first year in Lexington we'd received a phone call from a man who managed a chain of hotels in the Boston area. "We're doing some renovations," he'd told me, "and we have a load of old carpet that we're throwing away. Some of it might still be good enough for a few rooms at the church. Want to take a look at it?"

Yes, I'd told him, and when I'd seen the carpet, I not only wanted some for the church, but I had been presumptuous enough to ask if I could take a little for our home. That was fine with him, and before long our three bedrooms had floors of forest green carpet, certain stains and cigarette burns from the ravages of hotel life conveniently concealed under beds or pieces of furniture. Our then modest income precluded the luxury of bedroom carpeting, and so this man's gift made us most grateful. That carpeting stayed on the floors of those rooms until the day we said good-bye to Grant Street.

Responding to the green color of the carpet, Gail picked wallpaper and other accessories that gave our bedroom a "springy" atmosphere. Our bedroom furniture had been hers since the days when she was a child, and we painted it white. We thought we had a lovely room, and we often thanked God for it.

But now on moving day the bedroom was empty. The marks made on the carpet during the hotel days were again plain to see. The windows, once hung with delicate curtains were bare, and the closet looked strangely barren.

The children had always been aware that this room was the "command center" from which Gail and I had operated as we engaged in their parenting. Here was the place where we had talked through and made our most important decisions concerning them. This had been a very special and memorable room. And today as we moved through the house for the last time, the meaning of this room could hardly be reduced to one simple memory.

Over the years several principles had emerged that were keys to the ways we tried to do things in the house on Grant Street. These few come to mind as the most important.

This room was our private sanctuary. "Put a lock on your bedroom door," had been the strange advice of an older married couple when we were young parents. At first it had seemed a harsh piece of counsel. But we came to see the virtue of their perspective.

They were telling us that the bedroom of a mother and father is a sanctuary of sorts. While it is not off-limits to the children, it normally symbolizes the place where the marriage comes first.

*A marriage is fully a marriage with or without children.* The commitment was the first in the formation of a family, and it will be the first commitment long after the children have grown up and left the home. The lock on the door (the hardware store man called it a privacy lock) was more than protection from a child-intruder at an awkward moment. It was a message of sorts that there were times when a man and woman were *first* husband and wife and *then* mother and father.

Is this so obvious that it need not be said? No; in many homes it is not so obvious. For reasons best discussed in other literature, there is a temptation for one or both marriage partners to lose themselves in the raising and nurturing of children, to build their lives and their marriage on the children rather than on one another. The children become the "glue" of the marriage, the agenda of the marriage, the purpose of the marriage. Husband-wife relationships that fall into this trap may appear to be solid and even enviable *until* the children leave. Then an emptiness sets in and a couple sadly discover that without the children, their relationship is bankrupt. There is no longer an obvious reason to remain together.

Gail and I have never forgotten a conversation with a woman who had been married for thirty years. She approached us one day in a great state of anxiety. Her struggle? Her last child was leaving home in a matter of weeks, and her husband wished to take her on an extended round-the-world trip to celebrate this milestone in their lives.

But this was not good news for her. In fact, she dreaded the trip. Why? Because she hadn't the slightest idea of what they would talk about. Their married life had been built around the presence of children. The absence of children meant that the marriage no longer had a reason to be.

The lock on the door was the sign that there were times in the life of our family when the two of us, just Gordon and Gail, had to put their relationship first. And that meant two results. Strength there would insure that there was the possibility of strength in the larger family relationship. And strength there meant that our marriage would continue to have a reason to be, and that reason would endure long after Mark and Kristy had left to develop their own homes.

We loved one another in that room. The bedroom of a husband and wife who love one another is obviously a place of marital intimacy. In a practical sense the lock on the door insured that such intimacies could happen undisturbed.

As the children grew older and became acquainted with the loving ways of a man and woman in marriage, they were quite aware of what the closed, locked door might mean. Because our family life was quite transparent, there were even times when some good-natured kidding might go on back and forth at the breakfast table. They knew about these things, and it was good that they knew.

It was good that they knew because children are at their most secure when they have no doubt that their parents love one another. In the youngest years of a child's life there are those moments when he or she appears to be jealous of the physical affection a mother and father might share as they embrace in his presence. We have recollections of the times when Mark or Kristy tried to get in between us as we stood hugging before one of us left the house. It seemed as if the child were trying to break up the embrace, but in fact the child was merely trying to get inside the huddle to experience the strength of the intimacy.

I have always loved the words of an eleven-year-old boy quoted by Charlie Shedd in his book *Letters to Peter:*

> *My mother keeps a cookie jar in the kitchen and we can help ourselves except we can't if it is too close to meal time. Only my dad can anytime. When he comes home from the office, he helps himself no matter if it is just before we eat. He always slaps my mother on the behind and brags about how great she is and how good she can cook. Then she turns around and they hug. The way they do it you would think they just got married or something. It makes me feel good. This is what I like best about my home.*

I doubt if there can ever be too much healthy physical touching, embracing, or kissing in a home between family members. But it must begin with a husband and wife who share these things appropriately in private and then more openly in the other rooms of the house. They never said it, but I often got the feeling that Mark and Kristy firmly approved and quietly felt the more secure when they saw our bedroom door shut at night and knew that Mom and Dad were alone presumably enjoying the restorative moments of intimacy.

We talked things through in that bedroom. For the most part, all family decisions that a mother and father have to make were made there. Gail and I determined the kids would always see us in union about family issues. We did not mind their knowing that we sometimes disagreed about things. We didn't even mind them seeing us occasionally enter into conflict over something, for how could they learn to disagree respectfully and constructively if they did not see their parents challenge one another over an idea or over an error in judgment?

But when it came to the formation of laws, values, and convictions, or when it came to decisions about matters pertaining to the children's welfare, we wanted to touch base with one another *before* we engaged the children about these issues. That usually happened in the "command center" at the end of the hall.

As every parent soon learns (and as I've already observed), the best of children are quite political. They learn to exploit every fissure in the unity of a mother and father. They know who is the "softest" on what issue, and they are masterful at managing the political process in the direction of a decision advantageous to their cause. ("Mom, Dad said that I could . . . if you would . . . " or "Dad, I talked to Mom, and she sees nothing wrong with . . . as long as you . . . " )

The bedroom was our private caucus room. There we talked and talked. And when we came out from it, we were both committed to a direction. The talking minimized the number of family conflicts that could have given mixed messages and been otherwise destructive.

We tried to be available in that room if there were a sudden need. Since Gail and I have usually been people who are early to bed and early to rise, Mark and Kristy knew where to find us most nights after ten o'clock in the evening.

As teenagers, they knew that they were obliged to inform one of us concerning where they would be and the time they expected to be home. We usually let them pick the time but felt free to override their decision if we believed it was prudent for them to come home earlier. The corollary to this rule was that any time one of them was delayed for any reason, we expected an immediate phone call. ("But Mom, I knew you and Dad were asleep; I didn't want to disturb you." Answer: "We want to be disturbed.")

More than once a knock came on the bedroom door late at night. "Mom, Dad: Are you asleep? Can I come in?" Yes, we were asleep; but most certainly they were welcomed to come in. The door would be opened, and one of our two would enter into the "sanctuary."

I can see it even now. Half awake I would strain to see the dark silhouette of a teenaged son or daughter sitting on Gail's side of the bed, the only illumination coming from the light down the hallway.

"I don't know how to tell you this, but . . . I got a speeding ticket tonight." I came instantly awake.

"Remember how we prayed at supper that L—— would . . .? You won't believe what happened tonight."

"I had the most incredible time with T—— tonight. We were going to . . . but then we . . . and we saw . . . and then we . . . ."

"J—— and B—— and S—— are out in the living room. Do you mind if they sleep on the floor tonight?"

"D——'s really hurting. He says his folks are getting a divorce. Do you think you could come out and talk with him?"

"Mom, he's super . . . "

And so the bedside conversations went. One got the feeling that they were the extension of the conversations that happened at the table in the kitchen in the earlier hours of the evening. They happened because we were a talking, information-driven family. And they happened because we all desired to keep short accounts about how things were going. That has not changed, and even though Mark and Kristy and their spouses live hundreds of miles away, the information still flows. Both directions. Phone bills attest to that.

In that bedroom at the end of the hall we prayed together. We prayed more and more as the children got older. Perhaps someone might suggest that the praying could have been even more useful in our children's younger years. And there is correctness in that observation. But remember, I said that praying is hard for more than a few men. And in our younger years, I must confess that I did not invite my wife to join me in prayer as often as I should have. I say this to my regret. But I was self-conscious, afraid of revealing too much weakness, nervous about appearing to be overly sanctimonious and then not being able to live up to things said in that moment of spiritual vulnerability.

Whatever the reason, prayer in the bedroom came slowly. But as the children grew and the issues became more complex during the teen years, we both came to see the importance of prayerful intercession for our children. They were in a spiritual battle. There were persuasive messages coming through the door that even we, the doorkeepers, could not keep out. There were seductions, temptations, invitations, and coercive pressures outside the door that we could not control. How could we help our children identify negative influences and positive opportunities when they were away from us? Obviously we couldn't. We could only trust that our people-building efforts had prepared them to make their choices and that our prayer would witness to the heart of God that we trusted in heavenly protection.

Occasionally I see a small child walking with a parent through a shopping mall, a coiled, expandable wire tying the two together so that the child will not get separated from his mother or father. I am bothered by this sight. Perhaps it's because I have the feeling that the child is being treated something like a dog on a leash. But I must confess that there were times when I would have liked that arrangement in our family: not when the children were young but when they were older.

I saw them going out on dates, leaving home for overseas trips, heading out to jobs, departing for school, and I wanted to tie a coiled wire to their wrists so that I could make sure they'd not slip away into something dangerous to their intellectual, moral, or spiritual health. It was not that we didn't trust them; it was just the natural protective instincts of the parent who—rightly or wrongly—never wants to let go.

Prayer in the bedroom was the coiled wire. It was the invisible cable that went from the bedside to heaven and back to the child. How many times did Gail and I kneel by our bed and lift our children to the Father in heaven? How many times did we pray for their wisdom, their spiritual protection, their ability to serve people, their growth in Christlikeness? How many times did we pray that their choices would be insightful, that they would not be impulsive or overcome by a need to impress people? How often did we pray that they would keep themselves morally strong, that they would find strength in good friendships, that they would love their God?

Somehow we never feared booze and drugs; but we would today. We didn't really worry about promiscuous sexual behavior because it seemed to us that we'd talked enough about what it was all about and both kids had enough self-esteem not to have to seek tenuous relationships of that sort.

But we did worry that they would grow up too fast. Or that they would take the good things of life for granted and miss a spirit of thankfulness and gratitude. So we prayed about these and a lot of other things.

We prayed for their future choices of vocation, of mates, or faith. We asked the Lord to stimulate their minds to intellectual development; we prayed that he would make them peacemakers and team builders among their friends. And we prayed incessantly that they would grow up to be godly people.

The answer to that last prayer obviously lies now in their hands. But even to this day, long after the house on Grant Street is history, we still pray for their choices.

As we prayed in that bedroom, we often were confronted with our own sense of inadequacy. We did and said so many stupid things. We were aware that there were more than a few times when our children did not see the life of God in us. Others saw our public life which—like everyone else—we tried to keep as presentable as possible. But our children saw our private lives. And while we tried our very best to be as consistent inside the front door as we seemed outside the door, there were moments of failure. So our prayers in the bedroom were often prayers of confession, that the God of all grace would cover our faults with his kindness and protect the children from any kind of disillusionment with us, that we would be even more sensitive to the rebukes of the Spirit of God when heaven was trying to reveal to us how to be a better man and woman.

As I have written of our bedroom, I have been more than sensitive to the fact that there are men and women who may pick up this book who are single parents. One of my goals in writing this time was to include them as much as possible as I talked about life and people building on Grant Street.

I'm aware that on more than a few pages, I've advocated principles that are almost impossible for a single parent to carry out. And nowhere is that more evident than in a chapter like this, which describes a mother and father in intimate partnership. A people-building single parent does not have the luxury of retreating to a "sanctuary" with a caring spouse to strategize, to make decisions, to be mutually approachable, or to pray as a team. I really grieve for them. And I pray to God for their courage and their willingness to "bite the bullet" (as we say in North America when we know the way is tough) and see the process through.

It seems to me that if the Christ-following community seriously believes in what is sometimes called the discipling or the developing of young people, then the place to start is in helping our single parents. Why can't other singles or other families adopt a single-parent family and offer the kind of spiritual nourishment and support that is sometimes so sadly lacking? Why can't some of us make another's child a daily item on our prayer list? Why can't we invite the single parent and children into our home occasionally as well as visit theirs?

Just days ago a single mother approached Gail and me. The occasion was the college graduation of her son and our daughter. At first I could not remember her name because we had not seen her for more than five years. But quickly I began to recall her and her son, Stephan.

More than fifteen years ago she had come to our church, shattered, demoralized, and on the edge of bitterness over a broken marriage. It was clear that the raising of her son would be her responsibility and hers alone.

I recall the number of times that either Gail or I prayed with her, offered counsel in response to her questions, encouraged her to keep close to Stephan and believe in a future that was as bright as all of God's promises.

Somewhere along the line some single men in our congregation became interested in Stephan. They included him in sports activities, in camping trips, and in various church occasions. No one will ever be able to measure the impact of all of this. But the fact is that the boy is now a man, and he and his mother have made the long journey together. It's been twice as hard for her, but she has accomplished the task. Stephan is now a well-adjusted college graduate. And there was no place like a home for her to make it happen. Even if the home lacked a partner with whom to share the people-building endeavor.

This bedroom with its used green carpet, its oversized closet, its bright and cheery wallpaper, is now just a room. All of the furniture and the pictures that made it so personal are gone. But maybe in some strange way the memories of all the things which happened here in conversation, loving, prayer, and decision making are embedded in the walls. If only there were a way to tap those memories like sap from a maple tree, bottle them, and take them along. But we can't, of course. Maybe the only real evidence that these things really happened is what we see in the lives of our children—not children, but adults—today.

# PART XII

## The Empty House on Grant Street

# TWENTY-FOUR

## AGAIN! GOOD-BYE, GRANT STREET

*There's no place like a home, where you can look back upon treasured memories that were given as a gift by the kindness of God.*

WE LOCKED the door of the house on Grant Street and headed toward the car. Soon we would make our way toward the center of Lexington and beyond it to I-95 and the beginning of a long trip.

Mark was at college; Kristy had already moved to an apartment where she now lived with three other single women. A year later, she would marry Tom, and four years later Mark would marry Patty.

The great theme of our lives together on Grant Street had been people building. We had parented, mentored, discipled, built: say it however it suits you. Now it was time to release our two children—now adults—to their choices, and that had been the objective of the whole process from the very beginning.

Fortunately, a gracious God had covered our many mistakes along the way. The times when I could have been more firm and wasn't. The times when I could have been more kind and wasn't. The times when I could have tried harder to model the kind of man Mark and Kristy needed.

This has been a book that has highlighted a lot of warm memories. But all along the way, we knew that we were only

*303*

steps away from making fatal mistakes that could have set the stage for some terrible choices. We saw all too often from our vantage point the times when parents and single parents lost heart or lost their sense of mission in the home.

We saw the negative payoff when parents make materialism their goal; when the building of careers takes precedence over the building of people. We saw what happened when parents failed to live consistently inside the home as well as outside. We saw the results when parents withheld their affection, their feelings, their discipline. And we tried very, very hard to avoid those results. Without reservation we are grateful that we are able to enjoy what has resulted.

Both children decided to follow Jesus in the house on Grant Street. There they made their first attempts at personal spiritual disciplines. It was there that they made their first decisions to be builders of the Kingdom of God, that they would be obedient to God's purposes for them. Can you understand why that place has been so special?

It's a tough world in which to build children. Some have made the choice not to try. "Times are bad," they reason. "Why bring children into a world like this?" What they forget is that God sent his Son into a world easily as tough as this one. They misread history and do not understand that there probably have been very few good times to birth and build children.

You don't wait for the good times to become a parent. You pray for the faith to believe that you can build a child or two that will grow up to make a difference in a tough world.

When I look back on life on Grant Street, there are many occasions I remember where one or both of us said or did just the right thing and tended to surprise ourselves. Why was that possible? I have to believe that the Spirit of God was giving us wisdom and timing.

I believe he does that for any mother, father, or single parent who prayerfully seeks the mind of God in the pursuit of people building in the home. We made a decision early in the process: that Jesus would be Lord of our home. It was symbolized by a plaque just inside the front door, given to us years ago. It read: "As for me and my house, we will serve the Lord."

We tried hard to do that, and it worked.

I have this prayer for men and women who are in the midst of the people-building process in the home right now. I pray for their delight in what they do. For their resiliency when things go awry. For their grace when the youngsters fail. For positive outside influences and mentors where a mother lacks the partnership of a father. For daily awareness that they build their children in cooperation with and dependence on God. For good school teachers who will care. For churches who will make ministry to children and youth a priority. For opportunities to talk, to work together, to play, to kiss, to cheer one another on.

Mark and Kristy will always be our son and daughter. They are adults now: out of college, married, into careers. We still call them "the kids." Sometimes we even refer to them as the children. We can't seem to break the habit. But they are that and much more. They have become our friends.

There came a time in my life when I needed their friendship and love every bit as much as they had ever needed mine. There came a time when I needed their mercy and forgiveness when I had failed them. They were my friends; they gave it to me. Perhaps that did more to tell me that all the years spent building in the house on Grant Street were worth the effort.

We start the car, drive out the driveway. And now we take a final look behind at the locked-up empty house. Tomorrow we hope it will be filled once again by a family with the same agenda we'd had when we came there twelve years before.

We will dearly miss this modest ranch-style house. It's been a wonderful place to build people. There's no place like a home to do that. Good-bye, Grant Street . . . and thank you.